OPERATIONS
PLANNING
& CONTROL

OPERATIONS PLANNING & CONTROL

John L. Colley, Jr.
Robert D. Landel
Robert R. Fair

The Colgate Darden Graduate
School of Business Administration
University of Virginia,
Charlottesville, Virginia

HOLDEN-DAY, INC., *San Francisco*
Dusseldorf   Johannesburg   London
Panama   Singapore   Sydney   Mexico City

Copyright © 1978 by Holden-Day, Inc.
500 Sansome Street, San Francisco, California 94111
Philippines copyright 1978 by Holden-Day, Inc.

Library of Congress Catalog Card Number: 77-4804
ISBN: 0-8162-1736-1

Printed in the United States of America

234567890   09

Production supervision by Publishers' Service
Book design by Michael and Lorena Bass
Cover design by Lorena Laforest Bass

Preface

Several factors combine to make the successful management of the operations function crucial to any business. First, for U.S. manufacturing industries, 70% of the sales dollar is spent in the factory for labor, materials, or overhead (expense). Second, from one-half to three-fourths of the people to be managed in either manufacturing or service industries are in operations. Finally, the majority of the assets in a manufacturing business, such as plant and equipment and inventories, are under the control of the operations manager. Thus, most of the controllable costs and most of the assets in a business are managed by the operations function.

This text provides material for courses in operations or production in schools of business or industrial management. The level of the material presented is suitable for required or elective courses in graduate or MBA programs or a senior undergraduate course. No particular prerequisites are necessary, but the concepts covered in first courses in accounting and statistics would be helpful in understanding some of the material presented.

This book should also be of interest to managers, since it treats the requirements for operational performance which originate in the corporate planning process and those topics most essential to the understanding of the operations or production function in a functionally organized company or profit center.

The title *Operations Planning and Control* was chosen to reflect the emphasis on the operations function and the specific management tasks of planning and control. Business students are usually introduced to the planning and control tasks through the study of budgeting and variance analysis in accounting courses. In most organizations the task of detailed *financial* planning and control is delegated to the controller's department within the finance function. This book treats the management of the *physical flows* of man-hours, inventories, job orders, purchase orders, facilities, and so forth which are reflected in the financial statements. If the physical flows are properly planned and controlled, the accounting reports will reflect a well-planned and controlled operation.

Instructional problems have persisted in the area of operations or production for some time. These problems have emanated from the basic discrepancy between the teaching materials available and the needs of the business student who aspires to a career in either functional or general management. These problems have been compounded in recent years by fundamental changes in the functional area itself and by the rapid development of new methodologies.

The subjects traditionally covered in an operations course have included methods improvement, work measurement, production control, inventory control, and quality control. Many new mathematical techniques have been developed for, or have been found to be applicable to, the traditional operations subjects. These include quantitative developments which are generally referred to as management science, operations research, or systems analysis. The practical application of the new analytical methods and techniques has become feasible because of the reduced cost of large-scale computers. Finally, the range of operational functions has been broadened by the shift of the economy in recent years from a "production" orientation toward a new emphasis on "services."

The professor teaching an operations course has thus been faced with choices among several unpalatable and contradictory alternatives:

1) To teach the traditional subjects, which are quite detailed and lack a structural framework.
2) To add exposure to the new quantitative techniques and computer methods, at the expense of making his course even more detail-oriented.
3) To try to broaden his course to cover new and expanding problems in the service industries. This creates a problem for the student who is introduced to very detailed methodologies in some areas and almost no structure in others.

The disjointed nature of the text material from the three areas is confusing to the student, and lacks a structural emphasis on operating a business at a profit.

This text has been organized around the task of profit planning in a functionally organized profit center. Because of the instructional problems mentioned above, Chapter 1 is used to illustrate the setting within which the operations manager functions. This differentiates Chapter 1 from the other chapters in this book and provides a major difference between this book and other production or operations texts. The framework presented in Chapter 1 shows the student how the techniques and methodologies covered in the book relate to the general management problem of earning an adequate return on assets. This provides an understanding of the relevancy of the techniques covered and aids in overcoming the instructional problems inherent in teaching a collection of methodologies.

The planning process presented in Chapter 1 also provides a mechanism for choosing the topics to be included in the book from the large number available. We have thus omitted such topics as quality control, linear programming, and plant layout, which are usually found in operations texts. This was done with the feeling that the student is likely to be introduced to these techniques in specialized courses or in a quantitative methods course. Continuous reference to the profit-planning framework provides the best evidence that the techniques presented are those most relevant to the profitable operation of a business.

We endorse the rigor provided by instruction in basic techniques and feel that the additional material provided by this text will augment the students' capability with techniques by providing a better understanding of the framework within which they must be applied. We feel that this text should be useful as a second book for instructors using one of the customary technique-oriented texts in their operations courses. The profit-planning framework should assist the student in understanding the relationship of the numerous techniques to the problem of operating a business at a profit.

The sections of the book cover the planning problem, asset management, manpower planning and control, scheduling, and comprehensive problems. Although they are not covered with separate chapters, the importance of material costs and factory overhead cost is stressed in many of the chapters.

The authors wish to thank former Dean Charles C. Abbott, Dean C. Stewart Sheppard, and the members of the Faculty of The Colgate Darden Graduate School of Business Administration of the University of Virginia for their continued support of our efforts to develop a new and different approach to the teaching of the operations functional course. They encouraged our efforts to relate the various detailed techniques in work measurement, inventory control, and production scheduling to the general management problem of delivering an adequate return on assets.

The Center for Advanced Studies of the University of Virginia supported the project by naming John Colley a Sesquicentennial Associate of the Center for the academic year 1974-1975.

Professor Robert B. Fetter read the first two versions of the complete manuscript and made numerous valuable suggestions regarding the structure of the book. We especially acknowledge the contributions of Professor Brandt R. Allen, who wrote the Supplement on Investment Decisions, and Winston T. Shearon, who developed the Manpower Decision Framework approach to the master-scheduling problem which is described in Chapter 8. Bruce R. McGinnis of The Babcock and Wilcox Company contributed to the materials on planning models in Chapter 10.

We wish to thank Karen S. Corbett and Emily S. Moody for their contributions to the completion of this manuscript. They steadily tended to the numerous details of draft after draft of each piece of material and of major reorganizations of the text in a helpful and professional manner.

Finally, we appreciate the constructive comments of our MBA students at The Darden School who helped refine the material over several years of use in class.

John L. Colley, Jr.
Robert D. Landel
Robert R. Fair
Charlottesville, Virginia
December 1977

Biographical Sketches
of Authors

JOHN L. COLLEY, JR., *Professor of Business Administration, The Colgate Darden Graduate School of Business Administration, University of Virginia.*

Professor Colley was formerly Chief of Operations and Systems Analysis, Hughes Aircraft Company, and Group Leader, Research Triangle Institute. While he held these positions, he was a member of the faculties of the University of Southern California and North Carolina State University. His areas of special interest are operations management and production planning. He is President of Southeastern Consultants Group, a director of a commercial bank, and a consultant to a number of major corporations. B.S., North Carolina State University; M.I.A., Yale University; D.B.A., University of Southern California.

ROBERT D. LANDEL, *Professor of Business Administration, The Colgate Darden Graduate School of Business Administration, University of Virginia.*

Professor Landel worked with Westinghouse Electric Corporation as an industrial engineer and a buyer of raw materials. His special interests include managerial control systems in production and service-oriented organizations, and related approaches to operations management. He is a director of Southeastern Consultants Group and a director of Frigid Freeze Foods. B.M.E., M.S.I.M., Ph.D., Georgia Institute of Technology.

ROBERT R. FAIR, *Professor of Business Administration, The Colgate Darden Graduate School of Business Administration, University of Virginia.*

Professor Fair was formerly Executive Assistant to the Vice-President and General Manager, Transformer and Major Appliance Divisions, Westinghouse Electric Corporation. He is interested in the fields of operations management and management development and is Assistant Dean for Executive Programs at The Darden School. He is a past Chairman — Manufacturing Management Division of the Society of Manufacturing Engineers — B.M.E., University of Virginia; M.B.A., Harvard University.

Contents

PART IV   WORKFLOW PLANNING AND CONTROL   *223*

PART V   SUMMARY   *279*

I

PLANNING

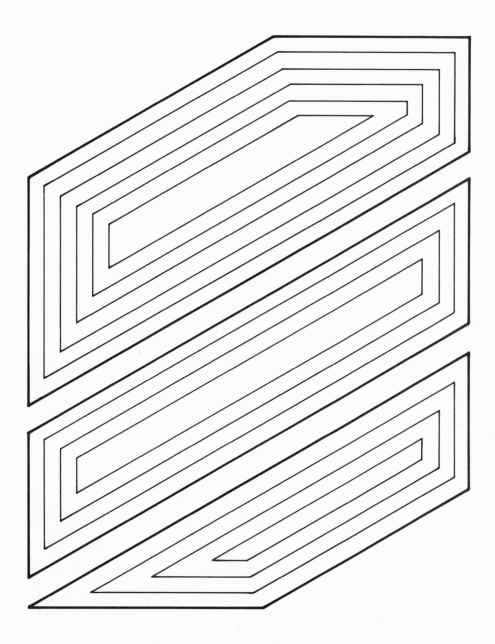

INTRODUCTION

Part I introduces the student to the planning problem faced by any profit-making organization. This brief introduction to the planning problem and a typical planning process is intended to provide two important advantages for the student. First, it provides a framework for the overall scheme within which the operations manager must perform. Second, the student sees the relevance to the general profit-planning process of the detailed methodologies he must master in regard to time standards, inventory control, facilities planning, aggregate planning, and scheduling. This prevents the student from wondering why he is studying a collection of unrelated and overly detailed techniques.

Figure I-1 shows the relationships between the various factors which must be managed to produce a desired return on stockholders' equity. Each block on the chart is the responsibility of one or more of the functional organizations. The topics which are treated in this book are circled. These are the factors which are usually the direct responsibility of the operations manager. Forecasts, time standards, and inventory projections are shown to be essential in order to derive estimates of revenues, costs, and the investment base for a one-year or five-year business plan.

While Figure I-1 shows the development of the return on stockholders' equity, the text hereafter concentrates on the return-on-assets portion of the chart, on the premise that the degree of financial leverage obtained in a firm is the responsibility of the finance function.

Chapter 1 describes the external pressures for performance, which lead to a goal-setting process requiring operating results appropriate to specific industry and general economic conditions. Chapter 1 also shows how a return-on-assets goal for an operating unit must be disaggregated to provide specific targets for such operating factors as man-hour levels, utilization and efficiency, inventories, and turnover rate. The planning and control of the numerous interrelated factors in order to produce a smooth, controlled pattern of results require a routine, formalized planning process. The general planning process used in many business organizations is presented.

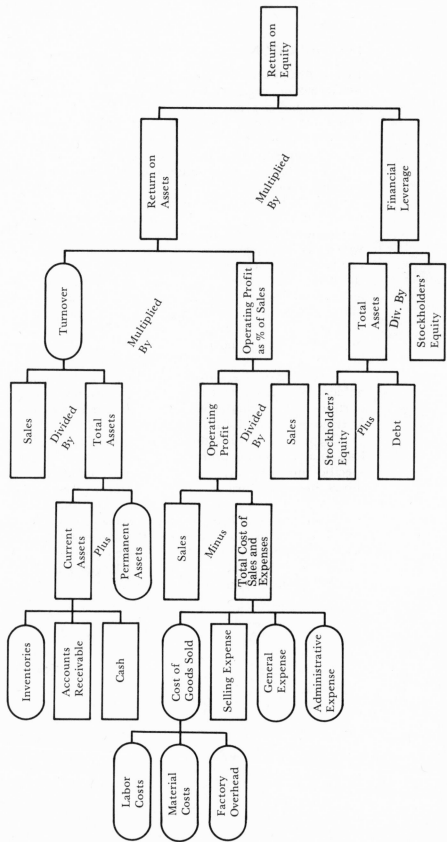

FIGURE I-1 Relationship of Factors Affecting Return-on-Assets

The Planning Problem

1.1 THE GROWTH OF FORMAL PLANNING

Most major business enterprises and many nonprofit organizations have established a planning function and some sort of formal planning system (e.g., forms, procedures, timetables) within the organization. Situational factors have led managers to realize that a planning function and some type of formal planning system are essential to the profitable operation of their businesses in the long run.

The fundamental impelling force which leads managers to plan is the eventual appraisal of their performance. Consider the questions of, "Who evaluates the performance of a company's management?" and "What criteria do they use?" Stockholders — or, more aptly, the owners — evaluate companies in terms of the profits earned, the dividends paid, the market price of the company's stock, and perhaps the public image of the company and its management. Customers continually appraise the performance of a business in terms of the prices charged for its products, their quality and reliability, and the ability of the organization to meet delivery dates. Vendors demand timely payment of obligations. Government agencies maintain a surveillance over such operational factors as market share and pricing policies (antitrust regulations), pollution control, and equal employment opportunities.

Perhaps the most crucial appraisers of company performance are professional financial analysts and bankers. Financial analysts are primarily interested in the long-term earnings pattern of the firm. Bankers evaluate companies in terms of debt payments, various financial ratios, cash position, and general financial strength. Why are the financial analysts and bankers so important to a firm? Analysts advise individual and institutional investors regarding potential company performance. Financial institutions employ analysts to guide their investments, which are now a significant factor in the market for corporate stocks. The market price of a company's stock is a major determinant of the firm's ability to raise capital by issuing stock. Financial analysts thus exert considerable influence over the sources of equity funding for a firm. The assessment by bankers of the risk inherent in a firm's operations directly affects the interest rate which the firm must pay for borrowed funds.

What, then, are the prime attributes which the professional evaluators prefer? First, stability in financial performance, as measured by the year-to-year pattern of earnings. The predictability of earnings reflects the depth of management control over operations. Second, after stability of earnings, is the level of earnings sustained over time, compared to other firms in the same industry and to general industrial performance. Beyond the figures, the professional analysts form a subjective opinion reflecting the level of their confidence in a firm's management.

Consider the pattern of results achieved by the two companies represented in Figure 1-1. The two companies are approximately the same size and compete directly in the same markets with similar products. According to their 1974 annual reports, Company A must pay the prime interest rate plus 2 percentage points for short-term borrowing while Company B can borrow at the prime rate. Additionally, the common stock of Company A trades at a price to earnings-per-share ratio of 7 while Company B's stock trades at a ratio of 11.

It does not necessarily follow that placing a great deal of emphasis on planning will lead to the desired results. One study[1] related corporate success in several financial parameters to qualitative factors which categorized companies as "planners" and "nonplanners" with regard to acquisitions. The study showed the financial results of the planners to be significantly higher (statistically) than those of the nonplanners. Direct linkages between planning and corporate results would be unlikely to be firmly established. We will depend on the weight of logic to support the alternative hypothesis that an effective planning process would scarcely inhibit the firm from reaching its objectives.

Why the emphasis on stability of earnings? This is often characterized as an overwhelming need to "avoid surprises." The financial analysts guide investors in the choice of firms and in the timing of their investments. A need to forecast future profits is inherent in the process of capital formation in this country's economic system. That is because investments are made in the anticipation of future profits, not for past performance. It is in the process of attempting to forecast future profit levels that the analysts depend on top corporate managers for assis-

[1] H. Igor Ansoff, et al., "Does Planning Pay? The Effect of Planning on Success of Acquisitions in American Firms," *Long Range Planning*, December 1970.

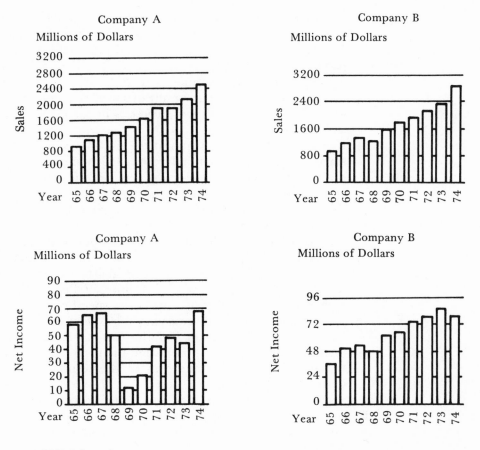

FIGURE 1-1

tance. In fact, corporate officers regularly provide public projections of anticipated profits and possible problems. These public pronouncements build a degree of credibility (good or bad) for the manager and the company with the investment community. The level of confidence in which the manager and his company are held is a major determinant of the company's stock market price and bank borrowing rates.

It is reasonable that financial analysts should prefer a stable and improving earnings pattern, which suggests a high degree of management control. Further, in any industry, some companies are consistently able to react to factors in their competitive markets and sustain higher earnings than their competitors, with essentially similar facilities and labor and raw material costs. In striving for stability in earnings, their managements overcome the factors which lower the level of earnings.

Other factors have also promoted the growth of formal planning during the last fifteen years.

1) *Growth of business organizations.* The sheer size of firms in terms of sales, products, employees, plant locations, and new investment

required has led managers to turn to formal planning as one way to give direction to the operation and to monitor performance.

2) *Product proliferation.* The increasing rate of introduction of new products and the general growth of the marketing function have made it imperative that management have some method of planning and controlling the phasing out of obsolete products and the timing of the introduction of new products in such a way as to preserve a stable profit pattern.

3) *Diversification.* Recognition of the risk inherent in dependence on a single or limited product line has led many managers to seek to diversify, either by developing new products or by merger and/or acquisition. The need to integrate the numerous diversified activities to produce a controlled pattern of results created a need for formal planning.

4) *Decentralization.* The traditional functional (e.g., marketing, finance, production, engineering) form of management organization was in many cases unwieldy in its ability to respond in numerous markets with large numbers of product lines. Managers came to realize that the ability to respond in specific market segments was greatly enhanced by diversifying — by delegating complete authority to conduct a segment of the firm to an autonomous general manager. This, in turn, committed the results of the firm as a whole to depend largely on the sum of the results of its decentralized units. Formal planning offered top corporate managers a tool to assist in their efforts to plan and control decentralized activities.

5) *Growth of international business.* The rapid spread of business operations around the world complicated management's job in terms of product variations, facility and skill differences, currency exchange rates and movement restrictions, and legal and other constraints. Formal planning offered the possibility of aiding in this process.

6) *Government regulation.* With enormous stakes at risk in automated facilities, long-range marketing strategy, and guaranteed annual wage and other supplementary unemployment benefits, business has had to cope with increasing government regulation in such areas as pollution abatement, safety requirements, and antitrust.

Each of these complicating factors has contributed to a difficult job for top managers. The demands of the bankers and analysts remain the same. Companies with high, sustained profit performance are more readily able to obtain the capital needed for future growth. Galbraith [2] characterized this process as "substituting planning for risk."

Some degree of "management of earnings" is feasible through various accounting and financial procedures, within the framework of generally accepted accounting principles. These include the manipulation of closing dates for various financial transactions, the definition of a variety of judgment variables, and the purchase of "sales" or "earnings" via acquisitions. Long-run dependence on such creative account-

[2] J. K. Galbraith, *The New Industrial State* (Boston: Houghton Mifflin Company, 1967).

ing methods has been capricious, however, and a number of apparently well-managed companies have eventually run out of the capability of such manipulations. In the long run, management must control the operational factors in sufficient detail to produce the preferred pattern of results.

Many companies have thus persevered in trying to effectively implement a formal planning system, in spite of organizational resistance to change and other impediments.

1.2   THE PLANNING PROCESS

ESTABLISHING CORPORATE STRATEGY

A typical corporate planning cycle is illustrated in Figure 1-2. The cyclical planning process applies pressure toward consistently earning an adequate return-on-assets (ROA). Regardless of the planning time span, establishing overall objectives and strategy is the first step in any planning program. A strategy can be offensive or defensive. Offensively, it can be directed at opening new markets or expanding existing ones. Alternatively, it can be devised to protect the existing situation, defending against competition. A strategy should recognize outside influences, including those brought on by the overall economic situation in which the company and its industry find themselves. A strategy should also recognize the organization's strengths and weaknesses. Finally, a strategy will reflect the personal interests and desires of the company's owners and management.

TRANSLATING STRATEGIC OBJECTIVES INTO PLAN- NING GOALS

A company's strategic objectives are usually expressed in general terms. Before a plan can be developed, it is necessary to refine these strategic objectives into planning goals. The process of converting strategic objectives into planning goals is illustrated in Table 1-1.

Are the goals derived realistic and attainable with a reasonable degree of risk? Consider the planning goal in Table 1-1 of improving return-on-assets from 12.8% to 20%. Management would question the means by which the return-on-assets would be steadily improved. What specific new products, advertising programs, inventory reduction programs, scheduling developments, and new facilities (perhaps automation) will be accomplished to insure the improved results? After sufficient examination to insure that each goal is feasible, the management adopts the set of planning goals for input to the next stage of the planning process.

DEVELOPING THE PLAN

Whether a long-range or a shorter-range plan is being developed, certain basic steps must be accomplished. One approach, based on the return-on-assets, is shown in Figure 1-3 and entails the following steps:

1) The return-on-assets goal for the planning period must be stipulated by the top management. It may reflect management's desire to equal or exceed the best performers in the particular market area involved.

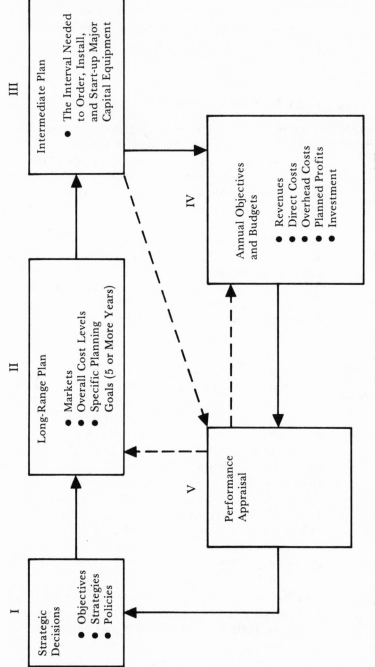

FIGURE 1-2 The Planning Cycle For Development of Long-Range, Intermediate, and Annual Plans

TABLE 1-1 Translation of Strategic Objectives into Planning Goals

Strategic Objectives	*Planning Goals*
1) To improve return on assets	1) Increase return on assets (after taxes) from 12.8% to 20%
2) To increase overall profit	2) Increase overall profit margin from 4% to 7%
3) To increase sales by: a) Improving market penetration in existing markets	3) a) Product A—increase market penetration from 15% to 20% Product B—increase market penetration from 20% to 25%
b) Opening up new markets, diversification	b) Move product development to production (planned market penetration, 5%) Purchase a company in the XYZ industry
4) To increase manufacturing productivity	4) Purchase new equipment Establish a methods engineering department
5) To improve management-union relations	5) Establish new industrial relations department and examine management's approach to labor problems

2) The total market for the profit center's product lines for the planning period must be projected.
3) Using the market projections, sales volumes for the years being planned must be established. A conservative volume level is normally set to induce tight planning of overhead expenses. The volume selected for corporate planning purposes is typically lower than realistic market projections, and below the objectives set for sales department performance measurement.
4) The overall return-on-assets goal must be translated into individual investment and profit targets at the level of sales selected.
5) The effects of internal and external factors which may influence the base plan must be projected. Wage and salary increases, changes in raw material and purchased part prices, and predicted changes in finished product selling prices are examples of such factors.
6) The effect of probable changes in the product mix must be forecast whether such changes are expected to result from market influences or planned management action.
7) Cost- and expense-reduction goals must be established which will reduce the overall cost level sufficiently to accomplish the desired rate of return-on-assets.
8) Overall support programs must be implemented to ensure the most

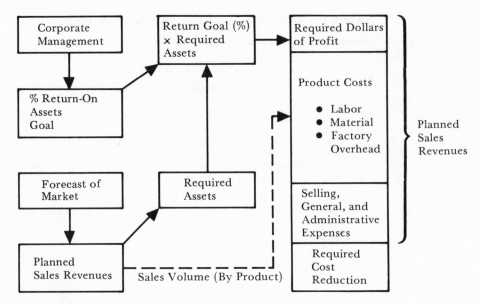

FIGURE 1-3 Planning for a Required Return-on-Assets

effective use of available funds in the areas of new product development, product redesign, methods and systems improvement, cost reduction, and market position improvement.

These are broad steps in the development of any plan. The sequence illustrates the basic philosophy of establishing the goal first, and then programming the action necessary to attain the goal, rather than building the programs and action first and allowing the goal to become whatever is left at the end. Employing this planning sequence may surface unrealistic profit or cost- and expense-reduction goals. This will necessitate backtracking to previous steps to discover feasible combinations of goals and actions.

1.3   SETTING OBJECTIVES AND GOALS

THE COMPARISON PROCESS   How, then, are realistic goals to be set? For the most part by internal comparisons of one operating unit with another, or with past performance, or by external comparisons with similar businesses. While a number of criteria may be used to measure business performance, including market share or the ratio of profit to sales, the single most widely accepted measure of management performance is the return on the invested capital. This, in the end, determines the willingness of an individual or institutional investor to make his capital available to the firm.

To devise detailed operational goals, a return-on-assets goal must be disaggregated to two factors, the profit on sales and the sales-to-assets ratio, often called the turnover rate. Thus:

$$\frac{\text{Profit}}{\text{Assets}} = \frac{\text{Profit}}{\text{Sales}} \times \frac{\text{Sales}}{\text{Assets}}$$

In a long-range plan the improvement in return-on-assets projected in Table 1-1 would be scheduled in detail, year by year, as shown in Table 1-2.

TABLE 1-2 Projected Return-on-Assets

Year	% Return on Sales	X	Turnover Rate	=	% Return-on-Assets
1	8.0		1.6		12.8
2	8.5		1.7		14.5
3	9.0		1.8		16.2
4	9.5		1.9		18.9
5	10.0		2.0		20.0

The components of the return on sales and the turnover rate must then be planned in more and more detail. Figure 1-4 shows the various elements which are combined to calculate the return-on-assets for a manufacturing business. The profit as a percent of sales is highly dependent on the extent of competition in the industry, the degree of labor intensity, characteristic wage and material costs, and overhead costs. The turnover rate for a product line is largely a function of the output per dollar of capital achievable in a given industry. Thus, the more capital-intensive an industry is, the more difficult it is to accomplish a high turnover rate. On the other hand, within a given industry the relative turnover rate among the competing companies is manageable through the organization's capability in scheduling, inventory control, wage and work rule systems, facility utilization, and man-hour levels.

PROFIT LEVEL VERSUS PROFIT STABILITY

In order to provide an explicit method for studying profits within a given industry, data were collected for 108 companies in 15 industries for 12 years (1962-1973). These data, from published financial statements, included sales, total assets, turnover rate, and profits after tax. A series of risk return curves were plotted for each industry, showing company detail. The ratio of profit after tax to total assets provided the measure of profitability, and the standard error of the estimate of the company returns for each year around the trend line of earnings during the 12 years was the risk measure. Figure 1-5 shows a plot of profitability versus the variation in profitability for a sampling of companies in the electrical appliance industry.

The pattern of data suggests that a lower level of earnings is associated with a more variable rate of profitability from year to year. Conversely, the companies which have the most stable pattern of

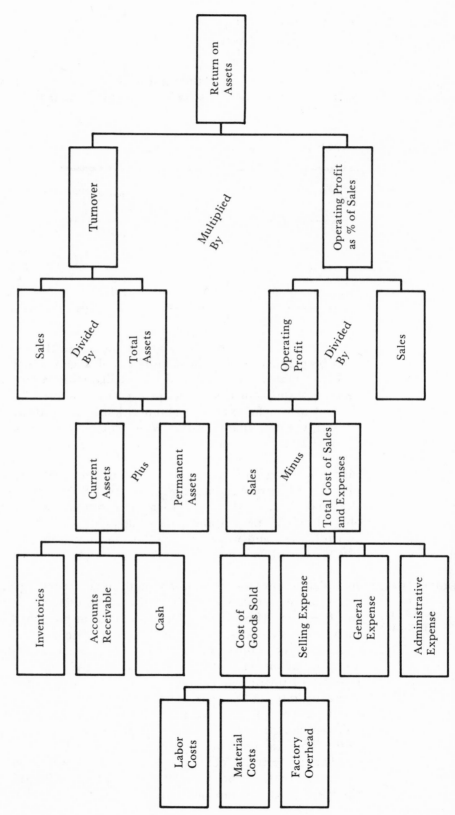

FIGURE 1-4 Relationship of Factors Affecting Return-on-Assets

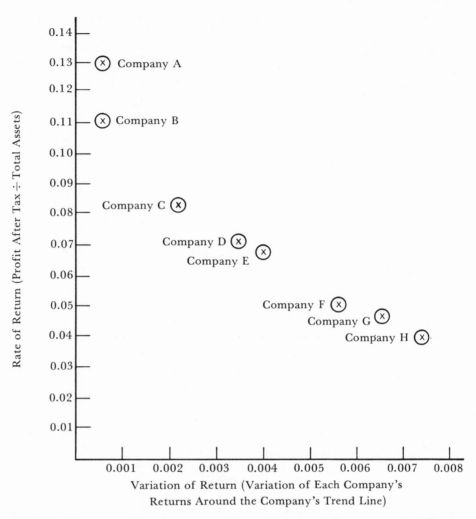

FIGURE 1-5 Average Return on Assets Versus Variation in Return — A Sampling of Electrical Appliance Manufacturers

earnings also have the highest level of earnings. This relationship was consistent within 12 of the 15 industries analyzed.

THE PROFIT-GROWTH INTERACTION Another important aspect of the goal-setting process is the interaction between the growth rate of the business and the level of profits. The growth rate of a business is commonly expressed as the percentage growth over some time period in either sales or earnings per share of stock outstanding. The same sample of 108 companies in 15 industries referred to earlier was analyzed in regard to their rates of growth in sales and return on assets during the past 10 years. These data were obtained from Forbes' 27th Annual Report on American Industry.[3] A quadrant arrangement has been used in Figure 1-6 to picture the joint

[3] "Measuring Management, 1974," *Forbes,* January 1975.

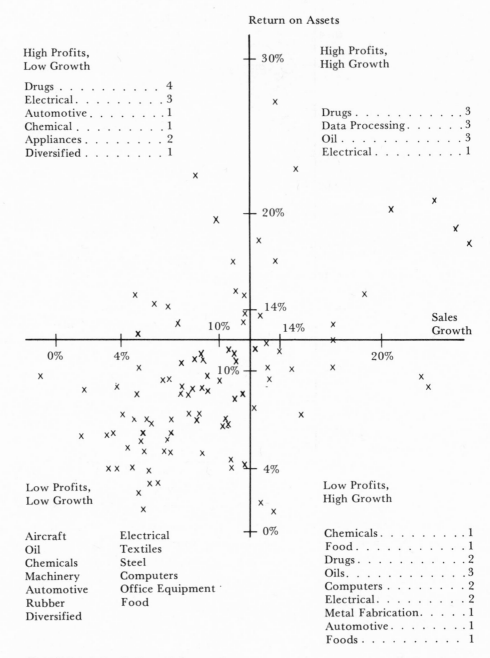

FIGURE 1-6 Profit-Growth Interaction

relationship between profit level and sales growth rate. The vertical line is placed at a 12% compound growth rate in sales over the ten-year period. The horizontal line is drawn at 12% return-on-assets. Thus, a point in the upper right quadrant represents a company which had both a high level of earnings and a high growth rate. The other three quadrants, moving clockwise, show companies with high growth and low profits, low growth and low profits, and low growth and high profits, respectively. The industries, and the number of sampled companies in each, that fall within the first, second, or fourth quadrants have been listed on the chart. A sampling of third-quadrant industries (low growth and low profits) has also been listed.

Industries can be broadly divided into those which are heavily capital-intensive and those which require very little capital. It is apparent that the prospects for high ROA results in capital-intensive businesses are less than in businesses with lower capital requirements, such as service businesses or banks. Even in manufacturing industries, there are wide differences in capital intensity — from steel, say, to electronic assembly.

Industries can be differentiated as to whether they are mature — growing at a rate similar to the gross national product (GNP) or the population — or are growing at a faster rate, or in some cases, a lesser rate. The level of aggregate sales of soap, or food products, or clothing will closely follow the growth (level) of the population. The same is generally true of most basic industries — steel, aluminum, plastics, textiles, etc. The only way a firm can grow at a rate faster than the mainstream of its industry is to introduce a preponderance of new products which capture a share of a new market, creating growth above the basic level (e.g., prepared food products, specialty steels, plastics as substitute materials).

It is logical that companies in basic, low-growth industries would fall to the left in the grid, with the well-managed companies in the upper left quadrant. Likewise, high-growth industries would fall to the right, with the well-managed companies in the upper right quadrant. Additionally, companies in the upper right quadrant would be expected to be highly marketing oriented, with emphasis on new products, advertising, and so forth.

Further, in the lower left quadrant it would be reasonable to expect to find very large companies, in basic industries, with little prospect for product differentiation, and in highly price-competitive situations. Thus, if companies and managements content themselves with the status quo, appropriate growth and ROA-level objectives and goals follow in a relatively straightforward way.

For a variety of reasons, companies adopt objectives and strategies involving movement away from the implied status quo, as the following examples illustrate. 1) A low-profit, low-growth company may attempt to move to the high-profit, high-growth quadrant by a spin-off of its steel mill (get rid of the heavy investment). 2) Low-profit, low-growth companies may try to move to the high-profit, high-growth quadrant by increasing sales and end up in the low-profit, high-growth quadrant because management cannot profitably manage the growth. 3) Many companies in basic industries have recently moved from the low-profit, low-growth category to the high-profit, low-growth quadrant by market control. Control of the market was spurred by short capacity resulting from plant closings (OSHA, pollution standards) and restricted capital investment (low stock prices, high interest rates).

There is evidence that a controlled growth policy provides an effective means for improving profits and profit stability through management control. For instance, one major corporation operated very profitably during the seven-year period from 1967 through 1973, when sales grew about 50%, or about 7% a year, very close to the rate of inflation. During that period the company earned an average of more than 14% return on total assets and more than 17% on stockholders' equity.

The analysis described provides guidance to top management on setting profit and growth goals — a sort of feasibility analysis for the performance which is achievable in an industry. The next step is to derive specific one-year and longer-range profit goals, either for the company or for operating divisions which compete within a given market segment. This step is largely subjective, with consideration given to such factors as recent performance, the maturity of the management team, and product dominance.

1.4   SUMMARY

The foregoing analysis indicates the difficulty of the planning problem, given the results expected. Considering the size, complexity, and other complicating factors facing businesses today, a planning and control system must be in place which will assist a firm in meeting its objectives regardless of exigencies. It was conjectured previously that professional financial analysts equate good management with the ability to forecast and attain stable results. The data presented above suggest that this criterion will lead the analysts to the most profitable firms in a given industry.

This chapter has described the corporate setting within which the production or operations manager must function. The intent has been to familiarize the student with the overall framework by which a manufacturing firm plans and controls its activities. It is expected that this profit-oriented structural framework will aid the student in better understanding the role of the detailed analytical techniques covered in this text and those not covered here which he will encounter in specialized production and quantitative courses. The remaining chapters explain the detailed procedures and techniques which are available to assist the operations manager in planning and controlling his segment of the business. Subsequent chapters also show the importance of the operations function to the overall profit result since the majority of the assets and costs are controlled in operations.

The chapters of the text are sequenced to match the profit planning cycle shown in Figure 1-3. Every firm with which the authors are familiar begins its annual planning process by a capital budgeting process which firms up much of the investment base for the following year. Sales forecasts allow both the development of the inventory and manpower plans and their fine-tuning through the aggregate planning (or master scheduling) process. Finally, within the capacity constraints in the form of fixed facilities and manpower levels, detailed scheduling procedures provide the means to increase the turnover rate by increasing the level of sales for a given asset base. Part II treats the portion of assets under the control of the operations manager: facilities

(Chapter 2) and inventories (Chapters 3 and 4). Part III covers manpower planning in structured (Chapter 5) and unstructured (Chapter 6) settings. Chapters 7 and 8 analyze the aggregate planning problem, which is the interface between manpower and inventory levels as the manager deals with demand fluctuations. Part IV covers the logic behind the use of detailed scheduling procedures to improve the asset-turnover ratio. Part V summarizes the various topics of the book, using the mechanism of widely used computer-based planning models.

1.5   BIBLIOGRAPHY

Ammer, Dean S. "The Side Effects of Planning." *Harvard Business Review*, May-June 1970, pp. 32-35 ff.

Andrews, Kenneth R. *The Concept of Corporate Strategy*. Homewood, Ill.: Dow Jones-Irwin, Inc., 1971.

Ansoff, H. Igor. *Corporate Strategy — An Analytical Approach to Business Policy for Growth and Expansion*. New York: McGraw-Hill Book Company, 1965.

Anthony, Robert N. *Planning and Control Systems; A Framework for Analysis*. Boston: Graduate School of Business Administration, Harvard University, 1965.

Boulden, James B., and Buffa, Elwood S. "Corporate Models: On-Line, Real-Time Systems." *Harvard Business Review*, July-August 1970, pp. 65-83.

Chambers, John C.; Mullick, Satinder K.; and Goodman, David A. "Catalytic Agent for Effective Planning." *Harvard Business Review*, January-February 1971, pp. 110-119.

Collier, James R. *Effective Long-Range Business Planning*. Englewood Cliffs, N.J.: Prentice-Hall, Inc., 1968.

Dzielinski, B. P. "A Guide to Financial Planning Tools and Techniques." *IBM Systems Journal*, no. 2 (1973), pp. 126-144.

Kingston, P. L. "Concepts of Financial Models." *IBM Systems Journal*, no. 2 (1973), pp. 113-125.

Knoepfel, Rudolph W. "The Politics of Planning: Man in the Decision Process." *Long Range Planning*, March 1972, pp. 17-21.

Litschert, Robert J., and Nicholson, Edward A., Jr. "Staffing Long Range Planning Groups." *Long Range Planning*, March 1972, pp. 37-39.

Mockler, Robert J. "Theory and Practice of Planning." *Harvard Business Review*, March-April 1970, pp. 148-159.

Pennington, Malcolm W. "Why Has Planning Failed?" *Long Range Planning*, March 1972, pp. 2-9.

Rudwick, Bernard H. *Systems Analysis for Effective Planning*. New York: John Wiley & Sons, Inc., 1969.

Seaberg, Ronald A., and Seaberg, Charlotte. "Computer Based Decision Systems in Xerox Corporate Planning." *Management Science*, December 1973, Part II.

Shank, John K.; Niblock, Edward G.; and Sandalls, William T., Jr. "Balance 'creativity' and 'practicality' in Formal Planning." *Harvard Business Review*, January-February 1973, pp. 87-95.

Skinner, Wickham, "Manufacturing — The Missing Link in Corporate Strategy." *Harvard Business Review*, May-June 1969.

Steiner, George A. *Top Management Planning*. New York: The Macmillan Company, 1969.

Vancil, Richard F.; Auguilas, Francis J.; and Howell, Robert A. *Formal Planning Systems — 1968*. Boston: Graduate School of Business Administration, Harvard University, 1968.

Warren, E. Kirby. *Long-Range Planning: The Executive's Viewpoint*. Englewood Cliffs, N.J.: Prentice-Hall, Inc., 1966.

Wilson, A. C. B. "Human and Organization Problems in Corporate Planning." *Long Range Planning*, March, 1972, pp. 67-71.

II

ASSET PLANNING
AND CONTROL

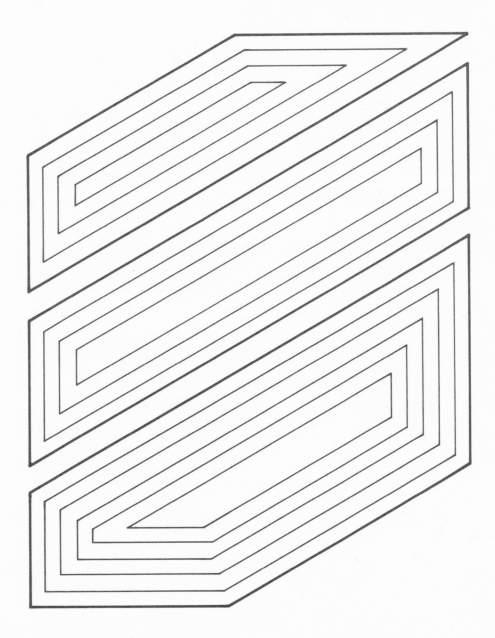

INTRODUCTION

Figure II-1 shows the segments of the overall management job with which Part II is concerned.

The determination of the planned profit level in Figure 1-3 followed from applying a stipulated return-on-assets goal to the investment base required to support a projected volume of sales. A given amount of cash is required to run any business, and accounts receivable are somewhat dependent on the fiscal habits and policies of customers. This part of the book concentrates on facilities and inventories which are largely managed by the operations function. In order to proceed with the detailed operational planning of inventory levels, manpower requirements, and expense budgets, the level of investment in plant and equipment must first be finalized. Decisions regarding investments in plant and equipment are discussed in Chapter 2. A supplement to Chapter 2 presents the most widely used methods for justifying capital expenses by estimating their likely level of profitability.

Chapters 3 and 4 cover inventories, the major portion of the asset base which is controllable by management in the short run. Inventory management includes controlling inventory costs and physical flows. Examples of relevant inventory costs include the costs of acquisition and storage and the cost of financing the inventory investment. Physical control includes insuring availability with minimum stock levels, transportation, and the movement of inventory from raw materials through work-in-process to finished goods.

Changes in the availability and costs of purchased materials, procurement lead times, production lead times and efficiencies, customer demand for service, and cash resources of the firm continually complicate the inventory-management problem. Materials comprise the major component of the cost of goods sold in most manufacturing industries. Measured as a percentage of the sales dollar, the material cost component averages 54% for all manufacturers. Examples of the material percentage of sales for various industries are shown in Table II-1.

Several factors influence the ability of the manager to maintain control over material costs. Production mistakes waste costly materials. Unplanned market price increases for raw materials and purchased components bring about significant variances in the cost of goods sold. Such expenses may be counteracted by final-product price increases, substitution of alternate materials, or product redesign – providing material cost movements can be properly anticipated. If the purchasing function is required to buy frequently in small lots, purchase discounts are foregone and transportation costs increase.

Portions of factory overhead and general administrative expenses are tied to various aspects of inventory management. Poor quality of materials or unplanned lead time extensions can cause the level of factory overhead costs, such as expediting, to increase. Excessive volume ordering of raw materials and other purchased items will lead to unplanned levels of inventory carrying costs – insurance, taxes, damage and spoilage, and warehouse costs.

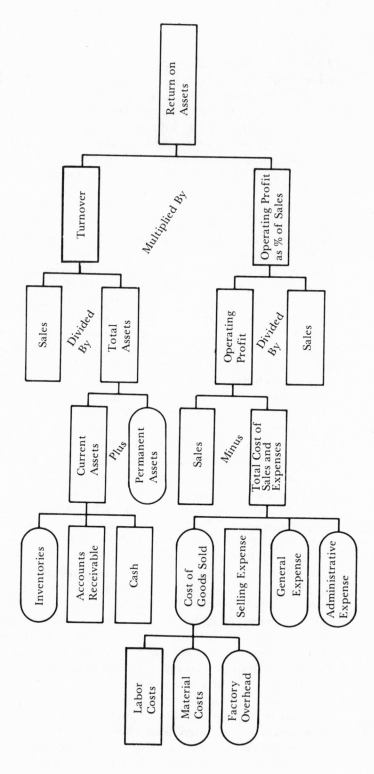

FIGURE II-1 Relationship of Factors Affecting Return on Assets

TABLE II-1 **Manufacturing Industries: Material as a Percent of the Sales Dollar**

Industry	Material %
Food	68
Textiles	60
Paper	55
Chemicals	45
Primary metals	58
Electrical machinery	44
Fabricated metals	50
Machinery	44
Average for all manufacturing industries	54

For all U.S. manufacturing corporations, from 1970-1974, inventories comprised 22.6% of total assets. Responsibility for inventory performance, however, is usually dispersed among several organizations. For example, the purchasing department usually sets material standard costs, negotiates prices, arranges for transportation, and expedites deliveries. The production scheduling function normally determines the quantities of items to be purchased and their delivery dates, based on inventory levels and either forecast item demand or a master production schedule. The scheduling function also plans the master production schedule, which may or may not call for the building of seasonal inventories or work-in-process parts storage. Finally, the scheduling function releases work to the shop, which can cause work-in-process inventories to fluctuate. The production function may influence work-in-process inventories because of bottleneck processes or other operating inefficiencies, such as multiple setups due to the expediting of hot orders. The marketing function is sometimes given the operating authority for controlling the movement of finished products from the factory through the firm's distribution centers.

The payoffs for coordinated inventory investment decisions are large; yet the payoffs are often elusive because of the compartmentalized authority for inventory management and the fragmented performance-measurement process. The challenge is therefore to improve the overall effectiveness of the inventory function. This challenge can be met by developing inventory investment goals and material ordering and distribution systems which will motivate the various responsible parties to achieve satisfactory performance.

Chapter 3 addresses the management task of determining a firm's proper levels of inventory investment. The chapter focuses on the basic functional uses of inventory — as pipeline stocks, cycle stocks, buffer stocks, and seasonal stocks. An analytical framework for setting rational inventory investment levels relative to the functional purposes served is presented. Chapter 4 presents the major techniques which initiate actions leading to the ordering of materials from suppliers, the releasing of manufacturing orders to the shop, and the shipping of products to distribution warehouses.

Facilities Planning

2.1 INTRODUCTION

This chapter addresses the major components of the facilities planning process. The decisions which flow from the facilities investment plan determine the nature of a firm's productive capabilities for a period of several years. The overall capacity of the firm is established and the boundaries of labor costs, material costs, and overhead expenses are dictated by facilities-investment decisions.

Figure 2-1 shows the aspects of the return-on-assets chart which are influenced by the facilities-planning process and the resulting decisions. In the assets segment, the Permanent Assets block is determined by the capital base invested in plant and equipment. It is decreased on a systematic basis by gradually allocating the investment cost to the production output of the firm. Accounting procedures provide the mechanism for this investment recovery in the form of depreciation expenses which are included in the Factory Overhead block. Investment planning also indirectly influences the Cost of Goods Sold block as labor cost and material cost improvements are realized by investing in more efficient space and equipment.

Facilities planning is vital to a company's success for the following reasons:

1) Capital investments may be critical to the successful achievement of a company's strategic goals.

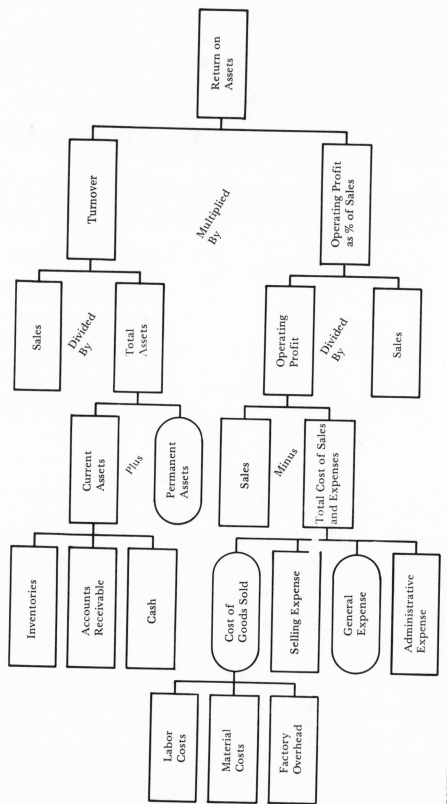

FIGURE 2-1 Relationship of Factors Affecting Return-on-Assets

2) Individual facilities projects may be large in relation to a company's total assets.

3) A large number of projects may be submitted and undertaken each year by a company.

4) A company is likely to have its capital spending restricted by the limited funds available.

5) Capital investments are often related to one another. An investment undertaken in one year may require a subsequent series of investments that involve large additional expenditures stretching out, in some cases, into future years.

6) The more capital-intensive a company, the more critical is effective facilities planning for all of the above reasons.

A management decision to commit resources to facilities projects follows a careful analysis of the expected costs and benefits to be derived from alternative proposals. Proposals are prepared and submitted by the operations manager, who provides an analysis of the various technical and cost factors attendant to each alternative. The analytical procedures and criteria for determining whether a given proposal will recover the investment cost and earn a suitable rate of return are usually covered in finance and/or accounting courses. A brief supplement at the end of this chapter provides an introduction to these techniques.

2.2   LONG-RANGE FACILITIES PLANNING

Long-range facilities planning is an integral part of strategy development and long-range planning. An obvious reason is that achieving corporate goals, such as obtaining a 10% market share or improving the return on assets to 15%, requires sufficient plant and equipment. The long-range corporate plan is a statement of the actions a firm will be taking over the next 5 to 10 years in order to meet its strategic goals. A plan typically includes market and sales projections and projected capacities, along with estimated cost and expense levels, profit forecasts, and funds-flow statements. Figure 2-2 shows the time-phased relationships between the overall corporate plan and facilities planning. Capital investments outlined in a long-range plan provide for new or additional manufacturing capacity, reflecting a corporate strategic decision to move into a new business or product, or to expand an existing product line. Capital investments proposed in the long-range plan should be justified by a statement of assumptions and a description of each project's relationship to corporate strategy.

EXPANSION OF EXISTING PRODUCTION CAPACITY   The long-range plan should forecast sales, by product, as well as product-line capacity for the planning period. This forecast is current capacity plus an average annual increase in capacity — even if the projects that will bring this increase about are not known at the moment. Charting the differences between the long-range sales forecast

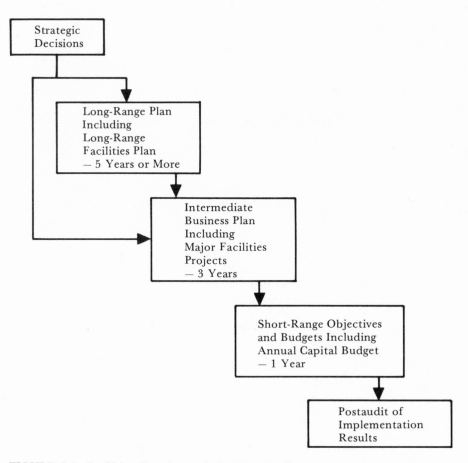

FIGURE 2-2   Facilities Planning and the Planning Process

and the capacity forecast will indicate the need for a facilities expansion project (see Figure 2-3). The detailed sales forecast, by product, should be analyzed by manufacturing center. The summary for each manufacturing center must then be compared with the capacity the center has or can expect to have over the planning period. The load forecast should be expressed as a percentage of the current year's actual load and compared (Figure 2-4) to both normal capacity (e.g., 5 days and 2 shifts) and maximum capacity. A lack of capacity in one or more manufacturing centers should trigger a facilities project or a reassessment of the sales forecast.

**STRATEGY-
BASED
CAPACITY
NEEDS**

The long-range plan may also include forecasts for entirely new products requiring completely new facilities. The acquisition of a new business would fall into this category. An estimate of the total amount of money required — capital and expenses — would be included in the long-range facilities plan. A brief description of the need for the project would be required. The need to modify facilities for such nonproductive reasons as limiting air or water pollution has become a common factor in facilities decisions in recent years. Major rearrangements and

FIGURE 2-3 Long-Range Facilities Planning, Sales and Capacity

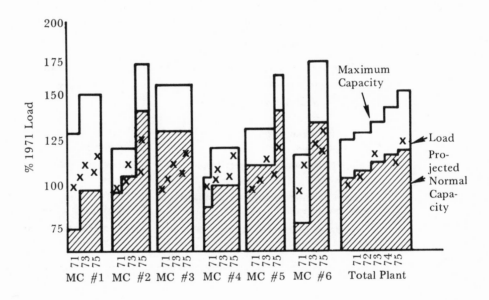

FIGURE 2-4 Manufacturing Centers

major expenditures for nonmanufacturing facilities such as office buildings are other examples.

There are advantages in handling existing product and strategy-based capacity issues separately. The analysis and justification for strategic projects are inherently unique to each particular investment. Management should treat them as special projects, until the decision is made to go ahead. Finally, a few key projects will account for a major portion of the long-range facilities expense. When these projects are approved, much of the total long-range facilities strategy has been approved.

All plans are, or should be, subject to change because of changing conditions inside or outside the company. It is therefore unwise to subject long-range facilities projects to detailed analysis and approval before funding is required. The management procedure for making the detailed analysis at the proper time is the company's facilities investment plan, or capital budget.

2.3   DEVELOPMENT AND APPROVAL OF CAPITAL BUDGETS

The capital budget is an integral part of a company's intermediate and annual financial plans. Table 2-1 contrasts the key ingredients of a long-range facilities plan with the more detailed capital budget.

For ease of identification, review, and approval, the most practical way to differentiate projects is by cost. For a small company a major project may be anything over $50,000. For a large company the amount may exceed $1 million. One definition, therefore, of a major facilities project is any project planned for any purpose in which the final cost to the company equals or exceeds some benchmark figure.

TABLE 2-1 How a Long-Range Facilities Plan Compares with a Capital Budget

Long-Range Facilities Plan	Capital Budget
Identifies projects required to achieve strategic goals	Undertaken only if strategy still implies project
Commits resources (subject to change in strategy)	Allocates funds
Project definition emphasizes description, not numbers	Emphasis on size, location, and specifications of project components
Long-range plan reflects projects to be funded during the period of the plan	Intermediate and annual budgets specify projects

MAJOR PROJECTS   If a major project is for product-line expansion, the following information is needed to justify the project:

1) Past and projected market and share-of-market data for the products to be manufactured in the new or expanded facility.
2) An analysis of competitors as to number, size, type, and position.
3) Past and projected product-line assets, costs, and profit performance in terms of profit margins, asset turnover, and return on assets.

This information should be analyzed to provide:

1) The likely accuracy of estimates incorporated in the projections with respect to price levels, wage rates, and material costs.
2) Cash flows indicated in the projected operations.
3) Maximum performance without the proposed expansion.
4) Added volume, assets, costs, and profits expected to result from the expansion.

If additional production capacity is justified, the problem may be whether to expand at the present factory location or to build a new plant in a different location. The timing of such a decision will depend upon many factors, including the necessary lead time for construction. Other factors which will need to be considered include the proximity of markets and raw materials; the availability, quality, and costs of land, labor, and utilities; living conditions and costs; and the local government's business incentives and taxation policies. More subjective factors include climatic conditions, location of competitors, and management preferences.

THE CAPITAL BUDGET   Facilities projects can also be classified according to purpose. Most organizations use at least four categories: 1) product volume, 2) product redesign, 3) cost reduction, and 4) necessity. The justification for each of the four classifications of short-range capital projects is closely related to its purpose.

1) *Product volume.* These projects are similar to major expansion projects except that the amount of money is less. Since the economic return on the additional investment is critical, information on incremental sales volume, investment, product and overhead costs, and profits must be submitted.
2) *Product redesign.* These projects are usually appraised in terms of marketing and engineering judgment regarding the competitive standing of the product line and needed improvements. Manufacturing facilities projects should be supported with information describing any product deficiency and the effect that it has on the product's competitive standing, the improvement planned, and the advantages that are expected to be obtained from improvement.
3) *Cost reduction.* These proposals must indicate savings that will yield an adequate rate of return on the money invested in the project. Both short-range and long-range cost-reduction goals, by product line, should be established according to the profit required in the corporate plans. Projects should result from continuing cost-reduction programs throughout the company which identify projects with returns sufficient to warrant implementation.
4) *Necessity.* These projects include:
   a) Service facilities such as offices, power plant substations, or a cafeteria when the expenditure is not directly related to expansion, product redesign, or cost reduction.

b) Facilities required for plant security and protection, improved working conditions, employee relations, or welfare and facilities required by law.
c) Forced replacements because of worn-out equipment or accidents, floods, and other calamities.
d) Projects which are required as a result of competitor actions.

In any procedure for choosing among numerous investment proposals, it is hazardous to use a single criterion such as return on assets as the basis for ranking investment alternatives and assigning priorities. Such a narrow approach fails to recognize strategic requirements, the inherent uncertainty contained in current and forecast data, possible competitive responses, and subjective assessments. Proposed facilities plans are usually submitted to corporate headquarters for review and approval, at which time the consolidated requirements for all plant locations are compared to the total funds available for facilities expenditures. The facilities plans are then adjusted, as necessary, to bring their total within the amount of available funds.

2.4   SUMMARY

This chapter has presented a qualitative description of the factors influencing investment decisions for varying amounts of capital and with different time horizons. The Supplement on Investment Decisions presents the techniques most widely used for evaluating and comparing investment alternatives.

As described in Chapter 1, the planning process concentrates on achieving a desired return on asset by first matching a sales or revenue target to a required asset base. The investment in plant, property, and equipment is the *least* controllable portion of the asset base in the short run. Cash, accounts receivable, and inventories are more amenable to management action than the more permanent investment in facilities. It is thus essential that the profit-planning process begin with a capital budget that fixes this important element of the capital base. The inventory portion of the investment base is covered in the next two chapters.

2.5   BIBLIOGRAPHY

Bierman, Harold, Jr., and Smidt, Seymour. *The Capital Budgeting Decision.* 4th ed. New York: The Macmillan Co., 1975.

Bower, Joseph L. *Managing the Resource Allocation Process: A Study of Corporate Planning and Investment.* Boston: Harvard University, 1970.

Chase, Richard B., and Aquilano, Nicholas J. *Production and Operations Management.* Homewood, Ill.: Richard D. Irwin, Inc., 1973.

Corke, D. K. "Long Range Planning for Production," *Long Range Planning,* December 1970, pp. 27-31.

Dean, Joel. *Capital Budgeting.* 3rd printing. New York: Columbia University Press, 1956.

Fair, Robert R. "Planning Your Facilities for Profit." *Metalworking Economics*, September 1971.

Friedman, B. M. "Financing the Next Five Years of Fixed Investment." *Sloan Management Review*, Spring 1975, pp. 51-74.

Fulton, Maurice. "New Factors in Plant Location." *Harvard Business Review*, May-June 1971.

Moore, Franklin G. *Production Management*. 6th ed. Homewood, Ill.: Richard D. Irwin, Inc., 1973.

Morris, William T. *The Capacity Decision System*. Homewood, Ill.: Richard D. Irwin, Inc., 1967.

Quiri, G. David. *The Capital Expenditure Decision*. Homewood, Ill.: Richard D. Irwin, Inc., 1967.

Schoeffler, Sidney; Buzzell, Robert D.; and Heany, Donald F. "Impact of Strategic Planning in Profit Performance." *Harvard Business Review*, March-April 1974.

Skinner, Wickham. "The Focused Factory." *Harvard Business Review*, January-February 1975.

————. "Manufacturing — Missing Link in Corporate Strategy." *Harvard Business Review*, May-June 1969.

Terborgh, George. *Administration of Investment Policy*. Washington, D.C.: Machinery and Allied Products Institute and Council for Technological Advancement, 1963.

Vancil, Richard F., and Lorange, Peter. "Strategic Planning in Diversified Companies." *Harvard Business Review*, January-February 1975.

Van Horne, James C. *Financial Management and Policy*. 2nd ed. Englewood Cliffs, N.J.: Prentice-Hall, Inc., 1971.

SUPPLEMENT ON INVESTMENT DECISIONS

INTRODUCTION

Capital-expenditure decisions, often called "capital budgeting," refer to those situations where funds may be invested in order to realize increased profits or savings in the future. The essential characteristic of these opportunities is that they involve some current investment of funds in order to realize expected future benefits. The key question in the analysis of capital expenditures is: are the expected future benefits large enough, compared to the initial investment, to warrant the expenditure?

Difficulties arise with these decisions because a choice must often be made among competing alternatives. An organization will usually have limited funds available for such expenditures and will want to insure that the maximum benefit is derived from their investment.

The terminology, capital budgeting, stems from the fact that an organization with a certain amount of available capital funds, a certain number of investment alternatives, and certain goals and objectives must carefully analyze and evaluate each alternative in order that the "best" selection of projects is made. This selection or listing of recommended projects is called the *capital budget*. The process of judging a particular alternative prior to its inclusion in the capital budget is called *project evaluation*.

BASIC ELEMENTS OF CAPITAL BUDGETING

The capital budgeting process can be viewed as consisting of five sequential steps: 1) developing alternatives, 2) estimating results, 3) evaluating alternatives, 4) considering risk, and 5) preparing the capital budget. Each of these elements is discussed below.

DEVELOPING
ALTER-
NATIVES

Promoting new ideas and developing alternative courses of action are the most important aspects of the capital budgeting process. If, through oversight, the best alternatives are not even considered, then only a poor decision can result, regardless of how much attention is paid to estimating cash flow, calculating paybacks, and the other elements of the evaluation process. Consider the idea of investing in a small computer to automate a manual payroll operation. It might appear there are two alternatives: invest in the small computer or continue the present operation. But further analysis will uncover additional alternatives, including 1) an improved manual operation, 2) partial automation via business machines, 3) a punched card or "unit record" system, 4) use of a computer service bureau, and 5) a large computer capable of automating other functions besides payroll — such as inventory control and production scheduling.

In fact, the best alternative might be to abandon the payroll process altogether and arrange for the bank to make direct deposits to employees' accounts. The selection process requires a thorough analysis of each alternative. Without a full spectrum of alternatives, the best action might be overlooked. Unfortunately, many capital projects are inhibited from the start because the best approach is never considered.

ESTIMATING
RESULTS

An essential step in project evaluation is developing an estimate of the results of each alternative. Future profits or cost savings must be estimated, along with future costs. Even determining the total cost of the initial investment may be difficult. For example, the price of a new piece of machinery can be determined from the seller, but the cost of freight, installation, wiring, and perhaps the resale value of the old equipment must be estimated. In preparing these estimates one normally attempts to establish the "most likely" figure for profit or savings. Sometimes a separate "conservative" or "optimistic" schedule of estimates is prepared and the results are then compared to those of the "most likely" estimate. In every case, however, it is important to be sure that the estimates are prepared carefully. Here is a useful set of guidelines to follow.

1) *Be objective.* Estimating future savings or costs is not the time to bring personal preferences or feelings into the analysis.
2) *Be consistent.* Don't mix conservative estimates with the most likely or the optimistic.
3) *Use rounded figures.* Estimates of future events cannot normally be made precisely. Figures to six decimal points or to the penny suggest a degree of precision that may be unwarranted.
4) *Collect data wisely.* Better data may provide a better decision; sometimes an organization will spend several thousands of dollars and many months of effort just to collect data for a decision. This is another "tradeoff" or balancing situation: collecting more data usually costs more money and takes time, thus introducing delay, but better data should yield a better decision.
5) *Don't estimate beyond a reasonable horizon.* Estimates should be made no further into the future than can be reasonably forecast;

that is, when considering the replacement of a new machine tool, estimates of savings beyond ten years are normally not made. The entire factory might be sold or scrapped by that time.

The last point is particularly important. Special attention should be given to what is called the "economic life" of a project or alternative. Very few capital budgeting alternatives involve unlimited life. The expected life of a machine or product often can be estimated and used as the economic life. Sometimes the decision is arbitrary: "We won't look beyond 60 months on this deal; the chances of keeping the product going past that time are just too low." Whatever time span is selected, the important thing is to *be sure that it is the same for each alternative.* In the example of the computer alternative mentioned above, the results of each alternative must be studied over the same time period, such as five years. Otherwise, the alternatives are not really comparable.

In capital budgeting decisions, estimates of the total investment, savings, costs, etc., are usually made in terms of cash flow rather than accounting income or savings. In many situations there is little difference between income-statement results and cash flow. Cash flow from sales closely follows accounting sales (on the income statement). Savings in labor, materials, supplies, etc., are frequently actual cash flow savings. The one major area where differences frequently occur between the income statement and cash flow concerns depreciation expense and book values. Depreciation is an expense item on the income statement (which tends to reduce net income), recognizing a portion of the cost of an asset over time. But depreciation is not a cash expense — cash was spent only at the time the asset was originally purchased. That cash outlay sometime in the past is a sunk cost and cannot be affected by any decision made now. Furthermore, book values seldom represent market values if the asset is to be sold or scrapped.

The book value of a machine which is scrapped when a new machine is purchased represents the unallocated amount of the original purchase price. Since we are interested in cash flows that result from a proposed decision, it is the scrap value or resale value that is relevant, not book value, unless they just happen to be the same. However, the book value will have an impact on taxes, and tax payments are cash flows. Generally the write-off of book value will come either all at once if the machine is scrapped or over time as a decpreciation charge. Thus, the difference is primarily one of timing. There will be more discussion of depreciation and book value in the section on Dealing With Taxes.

In estimating the expected results of a particular alternative it is usually necessary to specify only the differences which will result. For example, if we are considering the purchase of a semi-automatic or an automatic packaging machine to replace the existing manual operation, all we will be concerned with are the changes in future cash flows under each alternative. We do not need to concern ourselves with all future costs — just those that will be changed by the investment in either machine. Also, we do not need to estimate what the total plant costs will be five years from now — only what changes or differences there will be.

Several analytical techniques exist for evaluating capital budgeting alternatives. Each method has certain advantages as well as disadvantages and it is essential that the decision maker be aware of them while using a particular technique. The four techniques to be discussed here are 1) payback, 2) unadjusted rate of return, 3) net present value, and 4) internal rate of return.

Payback   The purpose of the payback method is to determine *when* the funds invested in a particular project will be recovered through profits or savings. The result is expressed as a period of time; i.e., three months, 6-1/2 years, etc. The payback technique addresses the question: If we spend $10,000 on a labor-saving machine, *how long will it take us to recover our investment through savings?* If we save $2,000 per year, the payback is thus *five years*. If the machine saves $5,000/year, the payback is *two years*.

When the savings are uniform each time period, payback can be calculated as

$$\text{Payback} = \frac{\text{Investment}}{\text{Savings}}$$

When the return is not the same each year, payback can be determined only by a process of counting or accumulation. For example, if our $10,000 machine is expected to yield the savings shown in Column (1) of Table 1, they may be accumulated as in Column (2).

TABLE 1   Payback Calculations

Year	*(1)* *Savings*	*(2)* *Accumulated* *Savings*
1	$1,000	$ 1,000
2	1,000	2,000
3	3,000	5,000
4	3,000	8,000
5	4,000	12,000
6	4,000	16,000
7	4,000	20,000

Payback is at that point where the investment is just recovered, in this case 4-1/2 years. At the end of year "4" we would have recovered $8,000 and, assuming an equal cash flow throughout the year, the remaining $2,000 would be received by midyear of the fifth year.

Payback has several advantages. The method is simple and the calculations are straightforward. More important, the concept of pay-back — the end result — is readily understood. The payback method is thus widely used to evaluate low-level, straightforward cost-reduction or product-redesign projects involving relatively small investments and a rapid payback interval. For instance, plant-level people in most organizations have the authority to carry out such projects as long as the payback period is 2 years or less. This implies a sufficiently high rate of return that more elaborate methods are not needed.

Unfortunately, the payback approach has several disadvantages, the most serious of which is that it ignores any revenue or savings beyond the payback period. The two investments in Table 2 both have the same payback, yet Alternative B earns revenue for several years beyond that of A and the total revenue is much higher.

TABLE 2 Comparative Payback Periods

Alternative A		Alternative B	
Investment: $15,000		Investment: $15,000	
Revenue:		Revenue:	
Year	Amount	Year	Amount
1	$5,000	1	$6,000
2	5,000	2	5,000
3	5,000	3	4,000
		4	3,000
		5	2,000
Payback: 3 years		Payback: 3 years	

From this example the reader will note that payback is a measure of return *of* investment (how soon we get back what we put in), not a measure of return *on* investment (how much we get back compared to what we put in). The other techniques all measure return *on* investment.

Unadjusted Rate of Return   Investors often calculate the return on investment (ROI) of a company by dividing the profit for the year by the company's investment in land, buildings, equipment, etc. When this approach is used to evaluate capital budgeting alternatives, it is called the unadjusted rate of return or the "accountant's method." It is calculated by dividing the annual average savings or profit minus de-preciation by the average investment outstanding. Average investment is often taken to be one-half of the purchase costs:

$$\text{Unadjusted rate of return} = \frac{\text{Average annual savings}}{\text{Average investment}}$$

For example, if a $10,000 investment is expected to yield $4,000 each year for five years, the unadjusted rate of return is:

$$\text{Return} = \frac{4{,}000 - 2{,}000}{(10{,}000/2)} = 40\% \text{ (The \$2,000 is the depreciation.)}$$

Savings are generally taken before taxes although in some companies the calculation is done on an after-tax basis. Gross investment (without dividing by 2) is sometimes used rather than average investment; it makes little difference in comparing alternatives as long as a company uses the same approach to evaluate each alternative.

Unadjusted rate of return is also simple to compute, easy to understand, and widely used. Its greatest weakness is that it operates under the assumption that money received or spent today is worth the same as money received or spent in the future. For example, look at the alternatives in Table 3.

TABLE 3 Unadjusted Rate of Return

Alternative C		*Alternative D*	
Investment: $10,000		Investment: $10,000	
Year	*Savings*	*Year*	*Savings*
1	$2,000	1	$6,000
2	3,000	2	5,000
3	4,000	3	4,000
4	5,000	4	3,000
5	6,000	5	2,000
Average annual savings:		$20,000/5 or $4,000	$20,000/5 or $4,000
Unadjusted rate of return:		$\dfrac{4{,}000 - 2{,}000}{5{,}000}$ or 40%	$\dfrac{4{,}000 - 2{,}000}{5{,}000}$ or 40%

Each alternative has an unadjusted rate of return of 40%, but clearly D is superior to C for we receive our money sooner and we can then presumably invest it somewhere else. However, the technique has ignored this "time value of money." In the above problem the advantages of receiving the money earlier are readily apparent by visual inspection and no one would be foolish enough to think the two alternatives were equal. But suppose another alternative were found, as shown in Table 4.

Here the unadjusted rate of return is less than 40%, and using the unadjusted rate of return method we would discard Alternative E from further study; but a quick inspection shows that this alternative earns savings of $18,000 during the first three years while D yields $15,000

TABLE 4 Unadjusted Rate of Return

Alternative E

Investment: $10,000

Year	Savings
1	$6,000
2	6,000
3	6,000
4	500
5	500

Average annual savings: $19,000/5 = $3,800

Unadjusted rate of return: $\dfrac{3,800 - 2,000}{5,000}$ = 36%

and C only $9,000. Isn't it possible that, if it is worth enough to us to have our money sooner rather than later, Alternative E would be preferable to D or C? This leads us to the consideration of what is termed "present value" and its use in the time-adjusted rate of return method.

Net Present Value   Consideration of net present value requires consideration of four aspects — the time value of money, its present value, taxes on income, and the replacement or scrapping of an asset. Each of these is illustrated in some detail.

1) The Time Value of Money   As we've already noted, the value of money to us changes over time. If we are to be paid $1,000, we'd prefer to have it today rather than next year, since if we had it today and could invest it in a bank paying 5% interest, by next year we'd have $1,050. In fact, we'd have to invest only $952 today to have $1,000 next year. (Five percent interest on $952 would give us $48 [0.05 × 952]. This, together with the return of our $952, totals $1,000.) This leads us to a very important conclusion: receiving $1,000 one year from now is not "worth" $1,000 to us now; it's "worth" only $952. Another way of viewing this is that at 5% we're indifferent as to a $952 payment now or $1,000 in one year. This $952 amount is called the *present value*, and this approach is called *discounting*.

Also, note that present value works whether we're *being paid* or *paying someone*. At 5% we're indifferent as to *paying* $952 now or $1,000 a year from now. We're also indifferent as to *receiving* $952 now or $1,000 one year from now.

If we had other opportunities to invest that would yield more than 5%, the $1,000 future payment would be worth even less than $952. Thus, present value is dependent upon some interest rate — in our example 5%. It is also clear that if the $1,000 were to be received 10 years from today, it would be "worth" even less than $952. Thus, present value is dependent upon some *time period* as well. Therefore, to be precise, we say:

The present value at 5% of $1,000 received one year from now is $952.

Tables exist which provide a present-value factor for a large combination of interest rates and periods of time.[1] Table 12 in the Appendix of this supplement gives present-value factors for interest rates from 2%-30% and from 1-40 years. To use this table, one must first locate the present-value factor corresponding to the interest rate and time period in question. The factor from the table is then multiplied by the amount to be received to yield the present value.

For example, suppose a company is to receive $5,000 at the end of 12 years and money, to them, is worth 8%. What is the present value of that future payment? Looking at Table 12 we find the present-value factor for 12 years at 8% to be *0.40*. Multiplying this times the $5,000 yields a present value of $2,000.

In another case suppose that we are to receive 3 equal payments of $5,000; the first at the end of year 1, the second at the end of year 2, and the last at the end of year 3. What is the present value of these payments at 8%? The following calculation makes use of Table 12.

(1) End of Year	(2) Cash Flow	(3) Table 12 Present-Value Factor	(4) (Col. 2 x 3) Present Value
1	$5,000	0.93	$ 4,650
2	5,000	0.86	4,300
3	5,000	0.79	3,950
Total	. . . .		$12,900

The present value at 8% of $5,000 each year for three years is thus $12,900.

Since we frequently find capital budgeting problems involving *equal annual cash flows* (as above), tables exist to make this calculation

[1] The mathematics for determining present value are quite simple:

$$\text{Present value} = \frac{\text{Future payment}}{(1 + i)^n}$$

when i is the rate of interest and n is the number of years until the time of payment. In our sample problem i was 0.05 and n was 1 (one year) so that

$$\text{Present value} = \frac{\$1,000}{(1.05)} = \$952$$

For most problems the decision maker has access to a table of present-value factors or a computer program for these calculations.

directly. Such present value factors are shown in Table 14 of the Appendix. Thus, from Table 14 the present-value factor for 3 equal yearly payments at 8% is 2.58; and 2.58 times $5,000 is $12,900.[2] Table 14 saves time and calculations when the cash flows are equal.

In each of the above examples the cash flow occurred as a single payment or payments *at the end of the year.* What about situations where the cash flows occur evenly throughout the year as would normally happen with profits from a new product or savings from a new machine? Approximate present-value factors for continuous cash flows are provided in Table 13 (for a midyear payment during any one year) and Table 15 (for equal annual cash flows occurring during the year). Since it *does* make a difference, the decision maker must be careful to determine the actual timing of the expected cash flows for each problem and then to use the appropriate table.

2) Present Value   How is present value used as a technique to evaluate capital budgeting alternatives? The steps are as follows:

1) *Determine the required investment rate* which is that "hurdle rate" representing the organization's cost of funds or the earnings rate a new investment must exceed in order to be approved. For some companies this rate is set at the average cost of money (both from debt and equity) for the firm. In other organizations the hurdle rate is set higher as a means of eliminating all but the most profitable investment alternatives. Organizations often separate capital expenditures into one of several categories according to the riskiness of the project and then establish different hurdle rates for each category. Ordinarily the same hurdle rate is used for all capital budgeting decisions within the same risk category and remains the same over a long period of time. The determination of this invest-ment rate is a very important step in the use of the present-value method, but any further discussion of it is beyond the scope of this supplement.

2) *Estimate the total cash investment* for each alternative. Because the investment is usually made at the beginning of a project, no discounting is necessary because cash is paid immediately. This is usually referred to as a cash flow in time period 0 (hence a discount or present-value factor of 1).

3) *Estimate the resulting cash savings* in the future, period by period.

4) *Discount or present-value these future cash flows* using present-value factors for each year at the required interest rate.

5) *Add the discounted figures* together. The result is the *sum of the discounted cash flows.*

6) *Subtract the original investment from the sum of the discounted cash flows.* The result is called *net present value.* If the net present value is positive, it means that the investment rate or hurdle rate

[2] The reader will note that 2.58 is simply the sum of three present-value factors: *0.92; 0.86;* and *0.79.* Indeed, that is how Table 14 was derived.

has been exceeded for this alternative. If negative, the investment fails to meet the required return.

For example, using the previous examples and assuming that 8% is the "hurdle rate," or minimum acceptable rate of return, we produce Tables 5 and 6.

TABLE 5 Net Present-Value Calculations for Alternative C

(1) Time Period	(2) Unadjusted Cash Flow (+ Savings) (−Investment)	(3) Present-Value Factor 8% (from Table 12)	(4) Cash Flow [Col. (2) x Col. (3)]	(5) Adjusted Cash Flow
0	−$10,000	1.0		−$10,000
1	+ 2,000	0.93	$ 1,860	
2	3,000	0.86	2,580	
3	4,000	0.79	3,160	
4	5,000	0.73	3,650	
5	6,000	0.68	4,080	
Sum of the discounted cash flows			$15,330	+$15,330
Net present value				$ 5,330

TABLE 6 Net Present-Value Calculations for Alternative D

(1) Time Period	(2) Unadjusted Cash Flow (+ Savings) (−Investment)	(3) Present-Value Factor 8% (from Table 12)	(4) Discounted Cash Flow [Col. (2) x Col. (3)]	(5) Adjusted Cash Flow
0	−$10,000	1.0		−$10,000
1	6,000	0.93	$ 5,580	
2	5,000	0.86	4,300	
3	4,000	0.79	3,160	
4	3,000	0.73	2,190	
5	2,000	0.68	1,360	
Sum of the discounted cash flows			$16,590	+$16,590
Net present value				$ 6,590

From these examples we can see that since both alternatives have a positive net present value, both projects exceed the 8% investment rate requirement. We also see that at the 8% rate Alternative D has a higher net present value. Other things being equal, and if the alternatives are mutually exclusive (i.e., only one of the alternatives can be selected), D would be preferred.

3) Dealing with Taxes   All of the discussions to date have dealt with current investments and future cash flows as if income taxes were not an issue in the decision. Indeed, many organizations that face capital budgeting decisions do not pay taxes: schools, hospitals, governmental agencies, foundations, etc. Most business organizations pay both federal and state income taxes, however; and since taxes affect investment decisions, they must be considered.

Taxes enter the evaluation of capital budgeting decisions in two ways: 1) some or all of the savings may be subject to tax, and 2) some or all of the initial investment may be depreciated or amortized in the future, serving to reduce taxable earnings at that time. The latter consideration often causes confusion because, while depreciation serves to reduce taxable income and thus reduce cash outflow (that otherwise would have gone to pay taxes), depreciation itself is not a cash expense. For example, assume that the investment in Alternative E had an expected life of five years for tax purposes. Note that this also corresponds to the length of expected savings and is the economic life. Suppose, also, that a straight-line method of depreciation is to be used. Calculation of the net present value under these conditions is shown in Table 7.

TABLE 7   Net Present-Value Calculations for Alternative E

(1) Time Period	(2) Unadjusted[1] Cash Flow (+ Savings) (−Investment)	(3) Present-Value Factor 8% (from Table 12)	(4) Discounted Cash Flow [Col. (2) x Col. (3)]	(5) Time-Adjusted Cash Flow
0	−$10,000	1.0		−$10,000
1	+ 4,000*	0.93	$ 3,720	
2	4,000*	0.86	3,440	
3	4,000*	0.79	3,160	
4	1,250**	0.73	912	
5	1,250**	0.68	850	
			$12,082	+$12,082
Net present value				$ 2,082

[1] Derivation of unadjusted cash flow, Column (2) above:

Description	*Years 1—3	**Years 4—5
Total savings	$6,000	$ 500
Depreciation	−2,000	−2,000
Taxable savings	$4,000	($1,500) (Loss)
Taxes	2,000	(750) (Taxes avoided)
Therefore:		
Total savings	$6,000	$ 500
less taxes	2,000	(750) (Taxes avoided)
Unadjusted cash flow	$4,000	$1,250

Note that during the first three years the $6,000 before-tax savings amounts to $4,000 savings after tax. Again, this is the result of two factors:

1) Taxes on $6,000 savings at 50% are $3,000, leaving $3,000 after-tax cash flow.
2) But depreciation of $2,000/year "saves" $1,000 in taxes, leaving $4,000 ($3,000 + $1,000) as the *total after-tax cash flow.*

An alternative form of calculation is shown in Table 8, taking data from Alternative D. Again, a tax life of 5 years and income tax rate of 50% are assumed. Table 8 is designed to prevent the kinds of errors in analysis that can occur when the tax rate is different from 50%. These matters can become very tricky: at a 40% tax rate, every $1 of savings before tax leaves 60¢ after tax, but every $1 of depreciation saves only 40¢ in taxes.

4) Replacement or Scrapping Replacing one asset with another often results in a situation where the old asset is sold for either a profit or a loss with respect to taxes. Scrapping an old asset also may yield tax advantages. There are three basic situations in replacement problems concerning disposition of the old asset:

1) Scrapping an old asset (disposing of an old asset and receiving nothing for it).
2) Loss on sale of old asset (selling an old asset but at some price less than book value).
3) Gain on sale of old asset (selling an old asset at some price greater than book value).

Each situation is illustrated separately.

1) Scrapping an Asset

Old asset:	Original cost: $15,000 Accumulated depreciation: $10,000 Scrap value: $0 Remaining life: 5 years
New asset:	Cost: $20,000 Expected life: 5 years Expected salvage at end of 5 years: $0
Savings on new asset:	$6,000/year for 5 years
Required investment rate:	12%

These calculations are shown in Table 9. There is an important point to observe from this example. When an asset is scrapped and there is a remaining book value (accumulated depreciation is less than the original cost), a loss may be reported for tax purposes equal to the book value. In this case $5,000. If the tax rate is 50%, this will save

TABLE 8 Net Present-Value Calculations for Alternative D with Taxes Considered

	(1)	(2)	(3)	(4)	(5)	(6)	(7)	(8)	
	Time Period	Savings	Depreciation	Taxable Savings	(4) x Tax Rate Tax	(2) − (5) After-Tax Cash Flow	Table 12 8% Present-Value Factor	(6) x (7) Discounted Cash Flow	Totals
Description									
Investment	0					10,000	1.0		−10,000
	1	+6,000	2,000	4,000	2,000	+4,000	0.93	+3,720	
	2	5,000	2,000	3,000	1,500	3,500	0.86	3,010	
	3	4,000	2,000	2,000	1,000	3,000	0.79	2,370	
	4	3,000	2,000	1,000	500	2,500	0.73	1,825	
	5	2,000	2,000	-0-	-0-	2,000	0.68	1,360	12,285
Net present value									2,285

TABLE 9 The Effect of Scrapping an Asset

Description	(1) Time Period	(2) Savings	(3) Depreciation	(4) Taxable Savings	(5) (4) x Tax Rate Tax	(6) (2) – (5) After-Tax Cash Flow	(7) 12% Present-Value Factor	(8) (6) x (7) Discounted Cash Flow
New investment	0					–20,000	1.0	–20,000
Tax savings on scrappage	0			(5,000)[1]	(2,500)	+2,500	1.0	+2,500
Future depreciation lost	1–5		(1,000)	(1,000)[2]	500	–500	3.81	–1,905
Savings	1–5	6,000	4,000	2,000	1,000	+5,000	3.81	+19,050
Net present value								–355

[1]
$15,000 Original cost
–10,000 Accumulated depreciation
$ 5,000 Book value

Thus, $5,000 before-tax loss on scrappage yields $2,500 tax savings.

[2] Tax savings on future depreciation given up.

$2,500 in cash flow that would otherwise have been paid in taxes. But had we continued to use the asset, we would have eventually been able to depreciate it to zero and thus realize the full $5,000 in depreciation (and hence saved $2,500 in taxes) sometime. By scrapping the asset and taking this "tax loss" now, we forego taking depreciation and the resulting tax savings in the future ($1,000/year for 5 years or $5,000). Hence we save $2,500 in taxes whatever we decide to do, but there is an advantage to immediate scrapping because of the time value of money. From above: immediate scrapping saves $2,500 in taxes now, but we give up $500/year for 5 years which is "worth" only $1,905 at 12% now. (The present value of $500/year for 5 years at 12% discount rate is $1,905.)

2) Loss on Sale of Asset

Old asset:	Original cost: $20,000
	Accumulated depreciation: $10,000
	Sales value: $5,000
	Remaining life: 5 years
New asset:	Cost: $20,000
	Expected life: 5 years
	Expected salvage value at end of 5 years: $0
Savings:	$6,000/year for 5 years
Required investment rate:	10%

These calculations are shown in Table 10. Here we see that sale of the old asset yields an immediate $5,000 in cash flow plus a $5,000 book loss (old book value was $20,000 – $10,000 = $10,000). The $5,000 loss saves $2,500 in taxes so that the cash flow effect of the sale is $7,500 ($5,000 + $2,500). Had we not sold the asset, we would continue depreciating it at $2,000 per year, thus saving $1,000/year in tax. The depreciation tax savings given up is thus $1,000 per year for five years, which at 10% is "worth" $3,980.

3) Gain on Sale of Asset

Old asset:	Original cost: $20,000
	Accumulated depreciation: $10,000
	Current sales value: $15,000
	Remaining life: 5 years
New asset:	Cost: $20,000
	Expected life: 5 years
	Expected salvage value at end of 5 years: $0
Savings:	$6,000/year for 5 years
Required investment rate:	10%

The calculations are shown in Table 11.

TABLE 10 The Effect of Losses on the Sales of an Asset

Description	(1) Time Period	(2) Savings	(3) Depreciation	(4) Taxable Savings	(5) (4) x Tax Rate Tax	(6) (2) – (5) After-Tax Cash Flow	(7) 10% Present-Value Factor	(8) (6) x (7) Discounted Cash Flow
Investment	0					–20,000	1.0	–20,000
Sale of old asset[1]	0					+5,000	1.0	+5,000
Tax savings on loss[2]	0			(5,000)	(2,500)	+2,500	1.0	+2,500
Future depreciation lost[3]	1–5		(2,000)	(2,000)	(1,000)	–1,000	3.98	–3,980
Savings	1–5	6,000	4,000	2,000	1,000	+5,000	3.98	+19,900
Net present value ·								3,420

[1] Sales value of old asset.
[2] Tax savings on loss on sale of old asset.
[3] Tax savings on future depreciation given up.

TABLE 11 The Effect of a Gain on the Sale of an Asset

Description	(1) Time Period	(2) Savings	(3) Depreciation	(4) Taxable Savings	(5) (4) x Tax Rate Tax	(6) (2) – (5) After-Tax Cash Flow	(7) 10% Present-Value Factor	(8) (6) x (7) Discounted Cash Flow
Investment	0					-20,000	1.0	-20,000
Sale of old asset[1]	0					+15,000	1.0	+15,000
Tax on gain[2]	0			5,000	2,500	-2,500	1.0	-2,500
Future depreciation lost[3]	1–5		(2,000)	(2,000)	(1,000)	-1,000	3.98	-3,980
Savings	1–5	6,000	4,000	2,000	1,000	+5,000	3.98	+19,900
Net present value								+8,420

[1] Sales value of old asset.
[2] Taxes of gain on sale of old asset.
[3] Tax savings on future depreciation given up.

Advantages/Disadvantages   Net present value represents a significant improvement over the unadjusted rate of return approach in that it recognizes the time value of money and explicitly incorporates it into the calculations. However, it has several disadvantages:

1) The calculations are more difficult.
2) The meaning and importance of the "time value of money" must be thoroughly understood by the decision maker.
3) The required investment rate must be known.
4) The answers are difficult to interpret.

This last item is perhaps the most serious. For example, suppose the net present values for three mutually exclusive alternatives are as follows:

	Alternatives		
	X	Y	Z
Investment	$20,000	$20,000	$20,000
Discounted cash flow	18,000	22,000	25,000
Net present value	(2,000)	2,000	5,000

Obviously X does not meet the required investment rate, while Y and Z do. Between the two of them Z is preferable. But, suppose the situation was as follows:

	Alternatives	
	E	F
Investment	$10,000	$16,000
Discounted cash flow	12,000	19,000
Net present value	2,000	3,000

Which alternative is preferable? Alternative F has a higher net present value than E, but the required investment is also higher. The internal rate of return method is designed to overcome this problem.

Internal Rate of Return (adjusted rate of return)   Consider the following example:

Investment	$10,000
After-tax savings	$ 2,000/year for 10 years

Now $2,000/year for ten years discounted at 6% is $15,160 (7.58 × $2,000). At 8% it is $13,940 (6.97 × $2,000). As the discount rate is increased, the total discounted cash flow is reduced. Obviously if we keep going higher, there is some rate at which the discounted cash flow is just equal to $10,000. Put another way: there is some discount rate where the net present value is zero. This is called the *internal rate of return*. For example:

Interest Rate (%)	After-Tax Savings 1—10 Years	Present-Value Factor	Total Discounted Cash Flow
6	$2,000	7.58	$15,160
8	2,000	6.97	13,940
10	2,000	6.44	12,880
12	2,000	5.98	11,960
14	2,000	5.57	11,140
16	2,000	5.21	10,420
18	2,000	4.88	9,760

The internal rate of return for this project is thus somewhere between 16% and 18%. With more detailed present-value tables or a computer we could calculate the exact rate. (Actually it is 17.24%.)

If we had, say, three alternatives, the internal rate of return could be calculated for each. If all three return rates were higher than the company's required earnings rate, all three could be approved. If they were mutually exclusive, that project with the highest adjusted rate of return would be preferred.

Advantages/Disadvantages   This method overcomes the problem of the net present-value approach in that a definite return is calculated for each investment alternative and the rates can be compared one to another and to the organization's "hurdle rate." The major disadvantage with this method is the complexity of the calculations, essentially a process of hunting for a particular discount rate. Computer programs are now readily available to make these calculations, but as the reader will note, it is a long way from the simple payback calculation with respect to ease of use.[3]

CON-SIDERING RISK   Risk has been mentioned at several points in this supplement, and several ways in which it might be handled have been mentioned.

1) In addition to the "most likely" forecast of results, a conservative or optimistic schedule may also be studied.
2) Very short payback periods may be required of risky investments, regardless of the other criteria employed.
3) If one of the return-on-investment methods is used, different risk categories may be established — each with its own hurdle rate.
4) Short "economic lives" may be used to constrain the decision.

[3] There is one simple case where the internal rate of return can be calculated easily, i.e., where the after-tax savings are uniform each year. The procedure is to divide the investment by the yearly after-tax savings. The results are then used to find a corresponding interest rate in Table 14 or 15. For example, in the problem on page 80:

$20,000/$4,000 = 5

In Table 15, for 10 years, it will be seen that 5 falls somewhere between 16% and 18%.

While these approaches have merit, they are not as good as more refined methods. When people discuss risk, what they really mean is the uncertainty of future events and the resulting difficulty in trying to predict the impact of various alternatives. Much work has been done in this area to develop practical approaches to decision making under conditions of uncertainty. While a detailed discussion of these methods is well beyond the scope of this book, the basic approach can be discussed.[4]

There is general agreement among financial theorists that the best means of dealing with uncertainty lies in trying to establish probabilities of various outcomes of a particular alternative. Instead of: "What is the most likely estimate of savings?" we try to determine: "What are the chances of the savings being less than $2,000 (say) per month? or $3,000? or $5,000?" and so on. Of course, it is much more difficult to collect this type of information, particularly when the chances of one thing happening are related to the chances of something else, etc. Indeed, one of the disadvantages of this approach is the cost and energy which the decision maker must spend to gather the refined predictions. However, with these predictions it is then possible to state an answer in terms of: "the chances of the ROI being below 12% are only 6%, below 15% it is 20%, etc.," as opposed to the single "most likely" answer. One can see from the following hypothetical results table how a probability-type answer could provide much more useful information to the decision maker.

Hypothetical Alternative

"Most Likely" Estimate	*"Probability-Type" Answer*	
		Of a Return
Internal Rate of Return	*Probability*	*Less Than*
12%	35%	6%
	40%	8%
	45%	10%
	55%	12%
	90%	14%
	95%	16%

Here we see that while the "most likely" return is 12%. Using the additional estimates and their probabilities, the formal risk methods yield ROI "results" which show that the chances of it being less than 12% are very great, while there is not much chance of it being more than 12%.

PREPARING THE CAPITAL BUDGET   The last step in the capital budgeting process is to pull together the results of each project evaluation into a set of spending plans for the organization. This does not mean that the results of each project are

[4] For further material in this area the reader is directed to Robert Schlaifer, *Probability and Statistics* (New York: McGraw-Hill Book Company, 1959).

automatically included in the capital budget. Sometimes projects are included even if they fail to meet the evaluation criteria (such as a payback too long or return on asset too low) for some of the reasons mentioned at the beginning of this supplement. On the other hand, sometimes a project will be deleted from the budget even if it passed the return criteria. This often happens when an organization has more good project ideas than money to fund them. Evaluating and ranking the proposed projects is just part of the capital budgeting process. The final decision will be influenced by matters of long-run strategy which necessarily affect the validity and importance of individual capital-expenditure projects.

APPENDIX: PRESENT-VALUE FACTORS[5]

TABLE 12 Present Value of $1 Received at End of Year Indicated

$$P.V. = 1 \div (1 + i)^n$$

End of Year	2%	4%	6%	8%	10%	12%	14%	16%	18%	20%	25%	30%
1	0.98	0.96	0.94	0.93	0.91	0.89	0.88	0.86	0.85	0.83	0.80	0.77
2	0.96	0.92	0.89	0.86	0.83	0.80	0.77	0.75	0.71	0.70	0.64	0.59
3	0.94	0.89	0.84	0.79	0.75	0.71	0.67	0.64	0.61	0.58	0.51	0.46
4	0.93	0.86	0.79	0.73	0.68	0.63	0.59	0.55	0.52	0.48	0.41	0.35
5	0.90	0.82	0.75	0.68	0.62	0.57	0.52	0.47	0.44	0.40	0.33	0.27
6	0.89	0.79	0.71	0.63	0.56	0.51	0.46	0.41	0.37	0.34	0.26	0.20
7	0.87	0.76	0.66	0.59	0.51	0.45	0.40	0.36	0.31	0.28	0.21	0.16
8	0.85	0.73	0.63	0.54	0.47	0.41	0.35	0.30	0.27	0.23	0.17	0.12
9	0.84	0.70	0.59	0.50	0.42	0.36	0.31	0.26	0.22	0.19	0.13	0.10
10	0.82	0.68	0.56	0.46	0.39	0.32	0.27	0.23	0.19	0.16	0.11	0.07
11	0.81	0.65	0.52	0.43	0.35	0.29	0.23	0.20	0.16	0.14	0.09	0.06
12	0.79	0.63	0.50	0.40	0.32	0.26	0.21	0.17	0.14	0.11	0.07	0.04
13	0.77	0.60	0.47	0.37	0.29	0.23	0.18	0.14	0.12	0.09	0.05	0.03
14	0.76	0.58	0.44	0.34	0.26	0.20	0.16	0.13	0.10	0.08	0.04	0.03
15	0.74	0.55	0.42	0.31	0.24	0.18	0.14	0.11	0.08	0.07	0.04	0.02
20	0.67	0.45	0.31	0.22	0.15	0.10	0.07	0.05	0.04	0.03	0.01	0.01
25	0.61	0.37	0.23	0.15	0.09	0.06	0.04	0.03	0.02	0.01	*	*
30	0.55	0.31	0.17	0.10	0.06	0.03	0.02	0.01	0.01	*	*	*
35	0.50	0.25	0.13	0.07	0.04	0.02	0.01	0.01	*	*	*	*
40	0.45	0.21	0.10	0.05	0.02	0.01	*	*	*	*	*	*

[2] These tables were reprinted from Almand R. Coleman, *Financial Accounting*, (New York: John Wiley & Sons, Inc., 1970). Tables prepared by Almand R. Coleman, Professor of Accounting, October, 1959; revised August, 1960. All rights reserved by University of Virginia Graduate School Sponsors.

TABLE 13 Present Value of $1 Received at Middle of Year Indicated

$$P. V. = 1 \div (1 + i)^{n - \frac{1}{2}}$$

Middle of Year	2%	4%	6%	8%	10%	12%	14%	16%	18%	20%	25%	30%
1	0.99	0.98	0.97	0.96	0.95	0.95	0.94	0.93	0.92	0.91	0.89	0.88
2	0.97	0.94	0.92	0.89	0.87	0.84	0.82	0.80	0.78	0.76	0.72	0.67
3	0.95	0.91	0.86	0.83	0.79	0.75	0.72	0.69	0.66	0.63	0.57	0.52
4	0.93	0.87	0.82	0.76	0.72	0.67	0.63	0.60	0.56	0.53	0.46	0.40
5	0.92	0.84	0.77	0.71	0.65	0.60	0.55	0.51	0.48	0.44	0.37	0.31
6	0.90	0.81	0.72	0.65	0.59	0.54	0.49	0.44	0.40	0.37	0.29	0.23
7	0.88	0.77	0.69	0.61	0.54	0.48	0.43	0.38	0.34	0.31	0.23	0.18
8	0.86	0.75	0.64	0.56	0.49	0.43	0.37	0.33	0.29	0.25	0.19	0.14
9	0.84	0.71	0.61	0.52	0.44	0.38	0.33	0.28	0.24	0.21	0.15	0.11
10	0.83	0.69	0.58	0.48	0.40	0.34	0.29	0.25	0.21	0.18	0.12	0.08
11	0.81	0.66	0.54	0.45	0.37	0.31	0.25	0.21	0.18	0.15	0.10	0.07
12	0.80	0.64	0.51	0.41	0.33	0.27	0.22	0.18	0.15	0.12	0.07	0.05
13	0.78	0.61	0.48	0.38	0.30	0.24	0.20	0.15	0.12	0.10	0.06	0.04
14	0.76	0.59	0.46	0.36	0.28	0.22	0.17	0.14	0.11	0.09	0.05	0.03
15	0.75	0.57	0.43	0.33	0.25	0.19	0.15	0.11	0.09	0.07	0.04	0.02
20	0.68	0.47	0.32	0.22	0.16	0.11	0.08	0.05	0.04	0.03	0.01	*
25	0.61	0.38	0.24	0.15	0.10	0.06	0.04	0.03	0.02	0.02	*	*
30	0.56	0.31	0.18	0.10	0.06	0.04	0.02	0.01	0.01	0.01	*	*
35	0.50	0.26	0.13	0.07	0.04	0.02	0.01	0.01	*	*	*	*
40	0.46	0.21	0.10	0.05	0.02	0.01	*	*	*	*	*	*

TABLE 14 Present Value of $1 Received at End of Each Year for N Years

Period in Years	2%	4%	6%	8%	10%	12%	14%	16%	18%	20%	25%	30%
1	0.98	0.96	0.94	0.93	0.91	0.89	0.88	0.86	0.85	0.83	0.80	0.77
2	1.94	1.88	1.83	1.79	1.74	1.69	1.65	1.61	1.56	1.53	1.44	1.36
3	2.88	2.77	2.67	2.58	2.49	2.40	2.32	2.25	2.17	2.11	1.95	1.82
4	3.81	3.63	3.46	3.31	3.17	3.03	2.91	2.80	2.69	2.59	2.36	2.17
5	4.71	4.45	4.21	3.99	3.79	3.60	3.43	3.27	3.13	2.99	2.69	2.44
6	5.60	5.24	4.92	4.62	4.35	4.11	3.89	3.68	3.50	3.33	2.95	2.64
7	6.47	6.00	5.58	5.21	4.86	4.56	4.29	4.04	3.81	3.61	3.16	2.80
8	7.32	6.73	6.21	5.75	5.33	4.97	4.64	4.34	4.08	3.84	3.33	2.92
9	8.16	7.43	6.80	6.25	5.75	5.33	4.95	4.60	4.30	4.03	3.46	3.02
10	8.98	8.11	7.36	6.71	6.14	5.65	5.22	4.83	4.49	4.19	3.57	3.09
11	9.79	8.76	7.88	7.14	6.49	5.94	5.45	5.03	4.65	4.33	3.66	3.15
12	10.58	9.39	8.38	7.54	6.81	6.20	5.66	5.20	4.79	4.44	3.73	3.19
13	11.35	9.99	8.85	7.91	7.10	6.43	5.84	5.34	4.91	4.53	3.78	3.22
14	12.11	10.57	9.29	8.25	7.36	6.63	6.00	5.47	5.01	4.61	3.82	3.25
15	12.85	11.12	9.71	8.56	7.60	6.81	6.14	5.58	5.09	4.68	3.86	3.27
20	16.35	13.59	11.47	9.82	8.51	7.47	6.62	5.93	5.35	4.87	3.95	3.32
25	19.52	15.62	12.78	10.68	9.08	7.85	6.88	6.09	5.47	4.95	3.99	3.33
30	22.40	17.30	13.76	11.26	9.43	8.06	7.01	6.18	5.52	4.98	4.00	3.33
35	25.00	18.67	14.49	11.65	9.64	8.18	7.07	6.21	5.54	4.99	4.00	3.33
40	27.36	19.80	15.04	11.92	9.78	8.25	7.11	6.23	5.55	5.00	4.00	3.33

TABLE 15 Present Value of $1 Received at Middle of Each Year for _N_ Years

Period in Years	2%	4%	6%	8%	10%	12%	14%	16%	18%	20%	25%	30%
1	0.99	0.98	0.97	0.96	0.95	0.95	0.94	0.93	0.92	0.91	0.89	0.88
2	1.96	1.92	1.89	1.85	1.82	1.79	1.76	1.73	1.70	1.67	1.61	1.55
3	2.91	2.83	2.75	2.68	2.61	2.54	2.48	2.42	2.36	2.30	2.18	2.07
4	3.84	3.70	3.57	3.44	3.33	3.21	3.11	3.02	2.92	2.83	2.64	2.47
5	4.76	4.54	4.34	4.15	3.98	3.81	3.66	3.53	3.40	3.27	3.01	2.78
6	5.66	5.35	5.06	4.80	4.57	4.35	4.15	3.97	3.80	3.64	3.30	3.01
7	6.54	6.12	5.75	5.41	5.11	4.83	4.58	4.35	4.14	3.95	3.53	3.19
8	7.40	6.87	6.39	5.97	5.60	5.26	4.95	4.68	4.43	4.20	3.72	3.33
9	8.24	7.58	7.00	6.49	6.04	5.64	5.28	4.96	4.67	4.41	3.87	3.44
10	9.07	8.27	7.58	6.97	6.44	5.98	5.57	5.21	4.88	4.59	3.99	3.52
11	9.88	8.93	8.12	7.42	6.81	6.29	5.82	5.42	5.06	4.74	4.09	3.59
12	10.68	9.57	8.63	7.83	7.14	6.56	6.04	5.60	5.21	4.86	4.16	3.64
13	11.46	10.18	9.11	8.21	7.44	6.80	6.24	5.75	5.33	4.96	4.22	3.68
14	12.22	10.77	9.57	8.57	7.72	7.02	6.41	5.89	5.44	5.05	4.27	3.71
15	12.97	11.34	10.00	8.90	7.97	7.21	6.56	6.00	5.53	5.12	4.31	3.73
20	16.51	13.86	11.81	10.20	8.93	7.91	7.07	6.38	5.81	5.33	4.42	3.78
25	19.72	15.93	13.16	11.09	9.52	8.30	7.34	6.56	5.94	5.42	4.45	3.80
30	22.62	17.64	14.18	11.70	9.88	8.53	7.48	6.65	5.99	5.46	4.46	3.80
35	25.25	19.04	14.93	12.11	10.11	8.66	7.55	6.69	6.02	5.47	4.46	3.80
40	27.63	20.19	15.50	12.39	10.26	8.73	7.58	6.71	6.03	5.48	4.47	3.80

3

Managing The
Inventory Investment

Inventories provide certain essential benefits for a firm and its customers, but the holding of inventories may tie up a considerable portion of available assets. When a large percentage of a firm's assets are invested in inventories, it is essential that management exercise effective planning and control of both physical and financial inventories. On December 31, 1974, General Motors Corporation held $6.4 billion of inventories, and the Westinghouse Electric Corporation held $758.4 million. If either of these stocks could be reduced without damaging the efficiency of operations or the company's level of service, the return-on-assets of the company would be raised.

An indication of the importance of the inventory investment in relation to total assets can be gained from Table 3-1. The reasons for the large differences in inventory-holding practices are the differences in the benefits that inventories can provide to the firms and the costs of maintaining inventories.

The general problem in managing inventories is to maintain those stocks of physical units which provide for suitable internal production operations and external distribution of the products, but which do not tie up an excessive amount of the firm's limited dollar resources. The study of inventory management typically focuses on those tools that are useful in assisting the manager in determining how much of an item to order and when the order should be placed. Many managers are familiar with the economic lot size or economic order quantity (EOQ)

TABLE 3-1 Inventory-Holding Practices of Different Industries:
December 31, 1973[1]

Industry	Inventory Investment as a Percentage of Total Assets
Manufacturers of men's work clothing	42.7%
Manufacturers of fertilizers	22.1%
Wholesalers of dry goods	42.1%
Wholesalers of sporting goods and toys	51.0%
Retailers of drugs	54.7%
Retailers of cameras and photographic supplies	35.4%
Retailers of flowers	27.3%
Motels	2.3%
Radio stations	.1%

[1]Source: Robert Morris Associates, *Analysis of Financial Statements 1974.*

concept as it applies to the purchase of raw materials and components and the scheduling of production orders. In the last few years the concept of material requirements planning (MRP) has been widely implemented in large manufacturing situations. Both of these approaches will be covered in Chapter 4. This chapter treats the broader management problem of the aggregate level of inventories which is needed to support a firm's operations.

3.1 ANALYSIS OF TOTAL INVENTORIES

PHYSICAL TYPES OF INVENTORIES Inventories exist in virtually all production and/or distribution systems. In a production system, operations or transformation processes are being carried on for the purpose of creating goods or services. The need for inventories is brought about by management's desire to operate the various purchasing, manufacturing, distribution, and sales operations somewhat independently of each other. For example, by providing finished-goods inventories, management can allow the shipment rate for customers' sales to differ from the production rate of the manufacturing process. In effect, the shipping rate and the manufacturing rate can be varied independently of one another and are coupled only partially through the finished-goods inventory.

Using a rectangle to represent an inventory accumulation and an arrow to represent a flow, the total inventory situation for most manufacturing operations could be drawn as shown in Figure 3-1. In this representation total inventories have been subdivided for analysis by location in the production/distribution process: 1) raw materials, 2) supplies, 3) work-in-process, and 4) finished goods.

Raw materials, work-in-process, and finished goods are all major items of approximately equal financial size for many manufacturers. The raw materials category includes all items purchased for manufacture and assembly into the product the firm sells but which have not

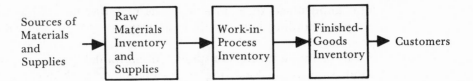

FIGURE 3-1   Total Inventories in a Manufacturing Operation

yet been entered into the production process. Materials for a firm might thus include purchased components or subassemblies, basic materials and commodities, and hardware. Work-in-process includes all those items intended to become finished products which have been introduced into the production process but have not yet been completed and placed into finished inventories. Finished goods are those items produced for sale on which the physical processing has been completed.

Supplies are generally of much less significance financially than the other three types and comprise items which do not become part of the finished product but are necessary for the operation of the business. Examples of supplies are oil for the heating plant and paper for the office. The low level of inventories for the two service industries listed in Table 3-1 — motels and radio stations — reflects the requirement for service businesses to carry only supplies in their inventory.

The magnitude in dollar values of stocks of the three types (supplies are lumped with materials) of inventories for manufacturing firms is given in Table 3-2.

While the dollar investment in these categories is somewhat similar for "All Manufacturers," the categories become unbalanced when the firms are classified as manufacturers of "durable" and "nondurable" goods.

It is seen that the longer manufacturing cycle times in durable goods industries, combined with a tendency for such goods to be made to order, leads to the preponderance of inventories being in work-in-process. Effective scheduling and control of work-in-process are thus of

TABLE 3-2   Manufacturers' Inventories by Types: December 31, 1974[1]

Type	Durable-Goods Manufacturers Amount (millions)	Percent	Nondurable-Goods Manufacturers Amount (millions)	Percent	All Manufacturers Amount (millions)	Percent
Materials and supplies	$33,393	34	$20,727	40	$ 54,120	37
Work-in-process	41,506	42	8,044	15	46,479	31
Finished goods	23,068	24	23,666	45	46,734	32
Totals	$97,967	100	$52,437	100	$147,333	100

[1]Source: U.S. Department of Commerce, *Survey of Current Business*, vol. 55, no. 3.

vital importance to a durable-goods manufacturer. Chapter 9 on Job Shop Scheduling is particularly appropriate to the control of work-in-process.

In manufacturing consumer (nondurable) products, on the other hand, short manufacturing cycles combined with demanding competition for rapid deliveries leads to most of the inventory being positioned as finished goods. Large raw material inventories combined with very short manufacturing cycles (and low work-in-process) allow for the rapid replenishment of finished-goods levels as consumer demand shifts from time period to time period.

FUNCTIONAL COMPONENTS OF TOTAL INVENTORIES   Inventories serve functional purposes when used as pipeline stocks, cycle stocks, buffer stocks, or anticipation (seasonal) stocks. With an understanding of the functional purposes of inventories, the manager is better able to evaluate the costs and benefits of incremental changes in the level of each type of inventory and in the level of total inventories.

As a means of illustrating this approach, consider the system shown in Figure 3-2.[1]

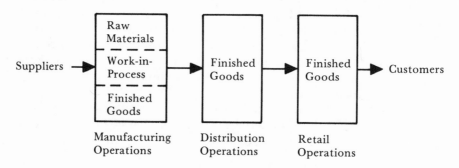

FIGURE 3-2   **Production − Distribution System**

A variety of production-distribution firms could be placed within this schematic representation. By specifying certain characteristics such as extent of vertical integration, nature of the product, size of operation, time delays necessary to move a unit from one point to another, and volume of product movement, a manager could begin to lay out the functional aspects of his firm's total inventory position.

Figure 3-3 illustrates some of the characteristics of a hypothetical consumer goods manufacturer. In order to make the analysis as broad as possible, this manufacturer is assumed to retain ownership of all inventories from the time the raw materials are ordered to the consumer's purchase of finished goods. Furthermore, the manufacturing firm distributes its products through several distribution warehouses to numerous retail operations. The following sections describe how a functional analysis can be used in studying the underlying structure of a firm's investment in inventories.

[1] Adapted from Elwood S. Buffa's treatment of aggregate inventory analysis in *Operations Management* (New York: John Wiley & Sons, Inc., 1968).

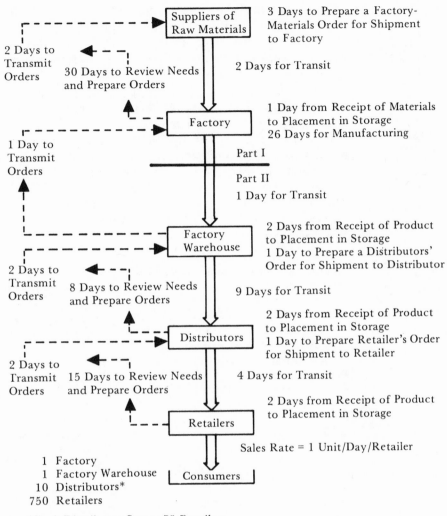

1 Factory
1 Factory Warehouse
10 Distributors*
750 Retailers

*Each Distributor Serves 75 Retailers

FIGURE 3-3 Hypothetical Consumer Goods Manufacturer

PIPELINE
STOCKS
Pipeline stocks reflect the time delays for producing, handling, and distributing a product. They represent the minimum amount of material or product needed between and within the various stages in the production — distribution system. Considered in their functional role, pipeline stocks have a variable financial significance, depending on the degree of vertical integration in a firm.

In the hypothetical firm of Figure 3-3, pipeline stocks exist in raw materials, work-in-process, and finished-goods inventories. The times shown in Figure 3-3 are the average time requirements for the processing, transport, and handling at each point in the flow or pipeline. Since 22 days are needed to move a unit of finished-goods inventory from the factory to the consumer (through Part II of the pipeline) and 750 units are sold each day at the end of the pipeline, the pipeline-stock portion of the total finished-goods inventory is equal to 16,500 units. None of these units is available for sale. Rather, this pipeline stock is the minimum amount of equivalent finished goods inventory necessary to keep the supply pipeline full and to sustain a distribution rate of 750 units per day.

Only those units that have completed manufacturing operations are considered finished goods. A portion of the firm's investment in work-in-process and raw materials inventories can be represented by pipeline stocks. Twenty-six days are required for production and six days are needed for the receipt and storage of raw materials. Thus, 32 days of equivalent finished-goods units must be in Part I of the pipeline to support a constant flow of finished product to the factory warehouse. The pipeline-stock portions of the total raw materials and work-in-process inventories are shown in Table 3-3, along with the finished-goods segment.

TABLE 3-3 Pipeline-Stock Calculations

Physical Type	Average Time Requirements (days)	Equivalent Finished Goods (unit sales/day)	Pipeline Stock (units)
Work-in-process	26	750	19,500
Raw materials	6	750	4,500
Finished goods	22	750	16,500
Total			40,500

Thus, for this system the total pipeline inventories of 40,500 units are the minimum investment required for the firm to carry on its daily operations. One can see that shortening the pipeline delay by one day would free 750 units of pipeline inventories and the holding costs associated with them. This reduction of the pipeline length might be possible with improved processing methods in the factory or faster transportation of goods between the links in the system.

CYCLE STOCKS   The pipeline delays for producing and distributing a product represent the minimum level of inventory that must be flowing through the pipeline at all times. There are also delays associated with information flows and with decision making about order quantities which make it necessary to carry additional inventories, over and above the pipeline stocks. As shown in Figure 3-3, the typical retailer prepares and places an inventory-replenishment order to a distributor on a 15-day review cycle. If the order quantity depends on the sales rate during the previous cycle, each retailer needs to order at least 15 days' worth of product to offer for sale between reordering points A and B as shown in Figure 3-4.

Figure 3-4 shows the inventory patterns for a 15-day stock-replenishment cycle. Since it takes nine days to receive an order after it

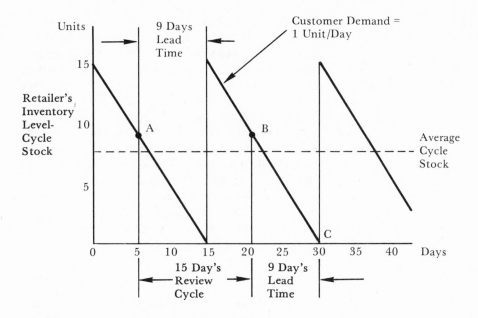

FIGURE 3-4 Retailer's Inventory Pattern

is prepared by the retailer (two days to transmit the order to a distributor; one day for the distributor to prepare the shipment: four days in transit; and two days for the retailer to receive, unpack, price, and place on shelves), this time must be allowed for. In this idealized replenishment ordering system a new order of units becomes ready for sale just as the old order quantity is depleted from the shelf. Units ordered at Point B are received at Point C.

With an assumption of continuous demand of one unit/day at each retail store, each of the 750 retail stores would place replenishment orders for 15 units every review cycle and would sell these at the average rate of one per day. The *average* cycle stock for the typical retail store would be 7.5 units (or half of the total ordered every review cycle). For all 750 retailers, an average of 5,625 units of cycle stock would be held in the system, as a result of the particular periodic review cycle being used by the retailers. These cycle stocks at the retail stores occur because of the noncontinuous ordering practice — order every 15 days — and they thereby act as a decoupling mechanism between customer demand and distributor shipments. The retailers may order cyclically because of the costs of preparing the orders or because of the lower shipping charge per unit for larger shipments. Analysis of the costs of more frequent and smaller orders compared to the costs of carrying additional cycle stocks leads to an optimum level of cycle stocks. These can be determined by utilizing the optimum-lot-size techniques presented in Chapter 4.

With 75 retailers in each distributor's area reviewing their replenishment needs every 15 days, it is reasonable to assume that the flow of retailers' orders to a distributor is approximately uniform over time. That is, each distributor receives an average of 5 orders, each for 15 units, every day and ships those orders to the retail outlets in his geographical area. If a distributor follows an 8-day review cycle, his average cycle-stock level would depend on the average shipment rate to the retailers during a review period. Since a distributor ships 15 units of product from his inventory to 5 retailers in his area each day, he would order 600 units per replenishment order from the factory warehouse every 8 days (5 retailers times 15 units required times 8 days) to cover shipments between the receipts of goods from the factory warehouse. The distributor's lead time from the factory warehouse is 14 days, so the distributor will have placed another replenishment order before he receives the shipment from his previous order. Figure 3-5 shows the inventory pattern for a distributor's cycle stock. The average distributor's cycle stock is 300 units, so for all 10 distributors there are 3,000 units of finished-goods cycle stock in the system. Units ordered at Point B are received at Point C.

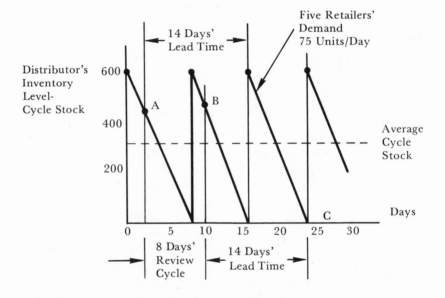

FIGURE 3-5 Distributor's Inventory Pattern

With only 10 distributors in the system, it is difficult to predict the exact distributor ordering pattern to the factory warehouse. Assuming more or less uniform ordering, the warehouse would receive an average of 1.25 orders per day for a total daily demand of 750 units. When the factory is producing and placing goods in the warehouse at the rate of 750 units/day, little or no cycle stock would be required to decouple the factory production rate and warehouse shipping rate.

On the other hand, cycle stocks would be at a maximum if the factory warehouse received all of the distributors' orders on the same day. In this case 6,000 units of inventory (10 distributors times 600 units per order) would be needed to cover all the distributors' orders received on that day, and the warehouse would therefore carry an average cycle stock of 3,000 units. These two extreme possibilities are shown in Figure 3-6. If it is assumed that a more realistic ordering pattern lies between these extremes, the average cycle-stock level at the factory warehouse would be, say, 1500 units.

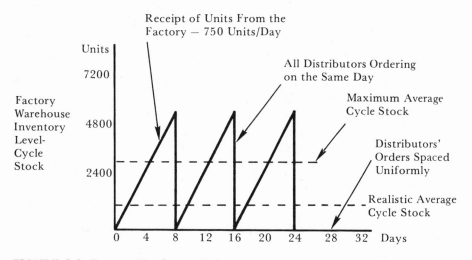

FIGURE 3-6   Factory Warehouse Finished-Goods Inventory Pattern

Cycle stocks of work-in-process inventory do not exist in the example of Figure 3-3, since 750 units are demanded each day and 750 units are produced each day. Finally, the decoupling function of cycle stocks applies to the raw materials inventory in the factory. Based on a 30-day review period for raw materials and a daily demand of 750 units, the factory would maintain an average cycle-stock level of 11,250 equivalent finished goods units of raw materials.

Thus far, no variability in the product demand has been assumed. In most situations consumer purchases will fluctuate over time, causing variations in the retailers' orders, distributors' orders, factory output, and raw material purchases. The variation results from a number of factors, some of which can be predicted and some of which cannot. The predictable factors are frequently described as the trend and seasonal components of a time series pattern. The unpredictable ones are usually termed random fluctuations.

Dealing with the trend component requires an evaluation of the available capacity in the pipeline to absorb the anticipated changes in product demand. Long-term growth in demand creates a proportional increase in the flow of inventory through the system pipeline and an increase in the average cycle stocks at each point in the system. The trend component poses important long-range planning questions for management in assessing the impact of growth upon its production and distribution capabilities.

SEASONAL STOCKS   Seasonal stocks are held in the various raw material, work-in-process, and finished-goods inventories to absorb the predictable variations between sales, shipping, and production rates in the system. Seasonal variations can be met in either of two basic ways (or any combination of them): 1) by varying replenishment orders or factory output to meet the anticipated demand, and 2) by ordering or producing evenly and carrying seasonal inventories. Seasonal inventories are thus built up in the slack season and depleted during the peak season. Their consideration is an important element in the master-scheduling problem of planning production to meet a seasonally varying product demand. Chapter 7 treats the analysis of seasonal stocks.

BUFFER (OR SAFETY) STOCKS

Random fluctuations in the demand pattern can cause the actual demand to be larger than the 750 units per day that have been assumed in the hypothetical production — distribution system. To protect themselves against running out of stock during a reorder cycle, retailers maintain additional inventories called buffer stocks to fill unanticipated customers' orders. Buffer stocks of finished goods can be maintained at each of the points within Part II of the production — distribution system shown in Figure 3-3. In the case of work-in-process inventories in the factory, buffer stocks protect against uncertainty in availability or delivery from the suppliers or variations in the usage rates within the factory.

For illustrative purposes, variations on the requirements of the retailer, distributor, and warehouse in the hypothetical system will be considered. The level of buffer stocks is determined by the amount of random variation the requirements can be expected to exhibit and the level of service that is desired.

The level of service rendered should be based on the tradeoffs between the costs of stocking out and the costs of carrying inventory. The costs of stockouts are extremely difficult to determine and differ greatly for different businesses. For some firms these costs are low since their customers do not require or expect quick service. If they stock out one week, the order is filled the next week with very few sales lost and little customer ill will. Other businesses may have very high costs of stockouts. If the product is not available for sale when the customer wants it, not only that sale, but additional future business from that customer may be lost.

Because of the difficulty in assigning a cost to stockouts, buffer stocks are usually set such that the risk of stockout is acceptable to management. Common risk levels are 10%, 5%, and 2%. A 5% stockout percentage indicates that management expects demand to exceed inventory in 5% of the replenishment order cycles, defined as the review time plus the supply lead time. Stockout risks of 10%, 5%, and 2% correspond to service levels of 90%, 95%, and 98%.

At the retail level, with demand constant at one unit per day, the cycle-stock inventory would satisfy demand between replenishment orders. With random variations in demand, however, the retailer will carry buffer stocks such that there is a 5% risk of stockout during a replenishment cycle. The retailer reviews his inventory every 15 days and orders an appropriate level of cycle stock to service demand during the 15-day time lag to the next reorder point. After the retailer places his replenishment order, say at Point A in Figure 3-4, he must wait 9 days for its arrival from the distributor. Thus, a period of 24 days elapses, during which time random demand fluctuations could cause the retailer to run out of stock. Although he places a second order at Point B in Figure 3-4 during the 24-day replenishment cycle, this order does not affect the possibility of a stockout during the replenishment cycle time from Point A to Point C. The second order will affect the stockout possibilities during the following replenishment cycle starting at Point C.

Assuming that the maximum demand expected during the replenishment cycle was 28 units, the retailer would maintain a buffer stock of four units in his finished-goods inventory. In total, a buffer stock of 3000 units (four units times 750 retailers) would be held at the retail level. Similarly, the buffer-stock function applies to the distributors and factory warehouse. Table 3-4 shows a hypothetical level of buffer inventories for the distribution stages in the system. Chapter 4 expands upon the concept of buffer stocks.

TABLE 3-4 Calculation of Total Buffer Stocks

	Assumed Maximum Demand during Replenishment Cycle (units)	–	Average Demand during Replenishment Cycle (units)	=	Buffer Stocks (units)	Total Buffer Stocks (units)
Retailer	28		24[1]		4	3,000
Distributor	2,550		1,650[2]		900	9,000
Factory warehouse[3]	26,500		22,500[4]		4,000	4,000

[1] 1 unit/day × (15 days' review + 9 days' lead time) = 24 units
[2] 75 units/day × (8 days' review + 14 days' lead time) = 1,650 units
[3] Average replenishment time assumption = Factory lead time plus 2 days for order transmittal and shipment plus 2 days' storage time = 30 days
[4] 750 units/day × (30 days' lead time) = 22,500 units

TOTAL INVENTORY ANALYSIS The inventory types and the methods of functional analysis which have been described illustrate the nature and purposes of a firm's investment in inventories. Inventories serve to decouple successive operations or stages in the production-distribution process and thereby make it possible for these operations to vary relatively independently. In the hypothetical system of Figure 3-3 various stocks were studied for the purpose of understanding the total inventory investment in a firm. The stocks summarized in Table 3-5 were developed by analyzing the levels of inventories that were needed to carry on the operations within the system under the hypothesized conditions.

3.2 SUMMARY

Management analysis of the inventory investment within a firm should be based on the foundation provided by a functional analysis of inventories. From this foundation a structure of effective inventory

TABLE 3-5 Summary of Inventory Requirements

Functional Purpose	Raw Materials Equivalent Units of Finished Goods	Work-in-Process	Finished Goods	Total
Pipeline stocks	4,500	19,500	16,500	40,500
Cycle stocks				
Retailers			5,625	
Distributors			3,000	
Factory warehouse			1,500	
Factory	11,250	0	0	21,375
Seasonal stocks	0	0	0	0
Buffer stocks				
Retailers			3,000	
Distributors			9,000	
Warehouse			4,000	16,000
Total				77,875

management can be built by assessing the financial savings and risks in each type of inventory which would be brought about by changes proposed in current production techniques, distribution routes, information systems, or ordering policies.

Chapter 4 provides a more detailed analysis of cycle and buffer inventories. Chapters 7 and 8 present a framework for analyzing the tradeoff between work-force fluctuations and seasonal inventories. Chapter 9 on Job Shop Scheduling presents an approach to determining the most effective level of pipeline work-in-process inventories.

3.3 BIBLIOGRAPHY

Buffa, Elwood S. *Operations Management*. New York: John Wiley & Sons, Inc., 1968.

Buffa, Elwood S., and Taubert, William H. *Production-Inventory Systems: Planning and Control*. Homewood, Ill.: Richard D Irwin, Inc., 1972.

Landel, Robert D. "Managing the Inventory Investment." *Journal of Systems Management*, July 1971.

Inventory Planning and Control

4.1 INTRODUCTION

Inventory planning and control systems have undergone significant changes in the last 15 or 20 years. The strongest impetus for change has been the widespread application of computerized stock-ordering and record-keeping systems, making feasible a battery of techniques along the spectrum of procurement, production, and distribution activities in the firm.

Four inventory-related activities take place on a day-to-day basis in most manufacturing or distribution operations:

1) The quantity and delivery-time requirements for inventory items are determined, based on analyses of item demand and stocks on hand and on order.
2) Shop orders or purchase orders are prepared, depending on the make-or-buy policy for the item.
3) Items are received from vendors, subcontractors, or manufacturing facilities and are inspected and placed in storage.
4) Inventory transactions are recorded at time of stock receipt and at time of stock issue.

This chapter focuses on Activity (1). Activities (2) − (4) are discussed in more specialized texts on materials management. The management task relative to Activity (1) is to select and implement a stock-ordering system which sets in motion the flow of orders and movement of inventories into and through the firm's manufacturing and distribution processes. Action documents generated on the basis of item demand and stocks on hand and on order initiate orders either to purchase raw materials and parts, or to fabricate parts and subassemblies, or to place finished goods in distribution warehouses.

4.2   ABC ANALYSIS

A stock-ordering system should provide for varying degrees of inventory control, depending on an individual item's importance to the firm. In virtually every firm a few stock items account for most of the annual dollar value of materials and parts usage. It follows that a firm's inventory investment could be categorized on the basis of annual usage value, with more planning and control effort devoted to the high-value items.

An ABC analysis categorizes a firm's inventory items into groups reflecting their relative value. The first step in an ABC analysis is to forecast the total annual outlay for each stock item. The total annual dollar usage must be estimated by applying an average cost per item to the forecast production requirements for material, parts, and components. The items are then ranked by total annual costs, with the largest-dollar-volume item at the top, and then separated into three groups.

> Group A — the top 10% of the stock items.
> Group B — the next 20% of the stock items.
> Group C — the bottom 70% of the stock items.

The following dollar-volume relationships are typical:

> Group A items will account for about 70% of the annual dollar volume.
> Group B items will account for about 20% of the annual dollar volume.
> Group C items will account for about 10% of the annual dollar volume.

Figure 4-1 shows the relationship between value and the number of inventory items.

While the precise relationship will vary from firm to firm, the idea behind ABC analysis can be generally applied. The bulk of management planning and control efforts, aimed at effecting improvement in prices, transportation costs, quality, and demand forecasting, can be committed to the Group A and B items. Successful improvement activities will then have a substantial positive impact on the level of inventory investment. Occasionally management may decide that items should be moved from the Group C category — a loose-control category — to the

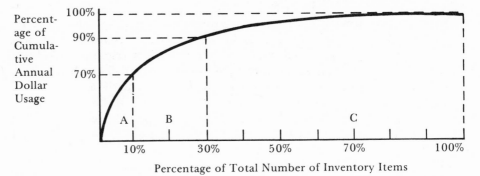

FIGURE 4-1 ABC Analysis

Group A category — a tight-control category — because of recent vendor delivery problems or manufacturing quality difficulties. Some items move from Group C to Group A because the computer can control them at a very low cost. Moreover, management may elect to establish additional categories based on criteria other than dollar usage. For example, the astute distributor distinguishes new products, obsolete products, and one-customer products from the more standard products and accordingly establishes different levels of emphasis for inventory planning and control.

4.3 STOCK REPLENISHMENT PLANNING VS MATERIAL REQUIREMENTS PLANNING

The many variations of stock-ordering systems in use fall into one of two basic classes: stock-replenishment planning systems or material-requirements planning systems. The choice of a stock-ordering system depends on the nature of the orders being placed against the firm's inventories.

FORECAST DEMAND Orders may arrive at unpredictable intervals and call for quantities whose magnitude cannot be precisely predicted ahead of time. Examples of such orders include service parts orders, distributor orders placed upon a factory warehouse, or customer demand at a retail facility. When the arrival time and quantity required for each order are unknown, stocks must be held in anticipation of demand. The principal management concern is to maintain the proper quantity of each item held — given that too much stock absorbs a disproportionate share of the firm's assets and too little stock reduces customer service. Forecasts are thus necessary and must be based on historical order rates and anticipated changes in future usage.

One approach to forecasting the next period's demand is based upon the prior period's demand. A simple average of historical data can be calculated and used as an estimate of the next period's demand. Such an averaging approach smoothes the random fluctuations and provides a usable estimate when demand is stable. More frequently, however, demand is growing or declining over time. In such situations the historical data are analyzed for trend movements, using moving-average techniques or least squares regression techniques. These two techniques require considerable quantities of historical data and numerous computations. For companies with a large number of items to forecast on a frequent basis, the cost of data storage and computational time for such analyses would be prohibitive. For recurring forecasts of large numbers of items, the exponential smoothing technique provides forecasts at a much lower cost.

The day-to-day planning and control of inventory under forecast demand conditions is accomplished by a stock-replenishment planning system. The inventory planning and control objective is to keep enough stock on hand to cover expected demand for each item between successive replenishment orders (cycle stocks) and to provide additional stock as protection against unpredictable demand variations (buffer stocks). By checking the level of stock on hand and on order every time an item transaction occurs, or by periodically reviewing inventory levels, a decision can be made as to whether there is enough inventory to cover projected average usage during the expected stock-replenishment lead time.

The key tasks in a stock-replenishment planning system are to:

1) Project item demand, using statistical forecasting methods.
2) Calculate replenishment order quantities and the timing of reorder execution by considering quantity discount and freight rate schedules, ordering and receiving costs, inventory holding costs, and service performance standards.
3) Determine buffer stock requirements, based on replenishment lead time, a specified level of order service, and forecast demand.
4) Report on a timely basis the stock status and performance history of each item of inventory.

SCHEDULED REQUIRE-MENTS DEMAND   Inventory systems may be managed on the basis of complete knowledge of the timing and quantity of future inventory withdrawals. This knowledge is derived from a predetermined schedule of the firm's production and/or shipping requirements. Examples include purchase orders for materials and parts to meet a firm shipping schedule, shop orders calling for the fabrication and assembly of finished goods built in advance of a seasonal peak in customer demand, or shipping orders that will place finished products in distribution warehouses on a known schedule. Inventory stock withdrawals are calculated in advance according to a known backlog of orders. This type of demand is called scheduled requirements demand.

Analysis of a shipping schedule for final products produces a detailed list of all of the raw materials, subassemblies, and parts needed and the times at which they are needed. This analysis is called "exploding" the master schedule, and the requirements generated are called "time-phased requirements." The delivery of the purchased items or the completion of the fabrication and subassembly work required for final assembly can be planned precisely. The receipt of purchased and manufactured items at each stage of production is timed to coincide with specific needs as derived from a preset production plan.

The day-to-day process of determining time-phased requirements and preparing action documents to meet these requirements is called material requirements planning (MRP). Because items are ordered to match discrete period-by-period planned usage rates, the need for buffer stock is reduced considerably compared to the forecast demand situation where order uncertainties must be covered. The key tasks in a material requirements planning system are to:

1) Project product demand based on historical data and the backlog of orders in hand.
2) Adjust demand for planned inventory build-up or depletion in the distribution channels.
3) Prepare a time-phased master production schedule.
4) Explode the schedule into the quantities of materials, parts, and subassemblies required to support the master production schedule.
5) Allow for on-hand and on-order stocks and for shrinkage and scrap considerations.
6) Write purchase orders and shop production orders for the net requirements and time their delivery to phase with the master production schedule.
7) Replan outstanding purchasing-production orders as the master schedule, engineering drawings, and manufacturing process times are altered.
8) Schedule finished-product shipments to customers and/or distribution warehouses.
9) Provide daily stock status reports and summary trend reports to management.

4.4   MANAGING THE CYCLE-STOCK COMPONENT

This section deals with the techniques that are used to manage the cycle-stock inventory component under forecast demand and/or scheduled requirements demand. With either type of demand, a lot size quantity is calculated such that the costs of ordering and the costs of holding the item in inventory are minimized.

LOT SIZE COST CONSID- ERATIONS Inventory cost analyses are developed under the relevant cost principle. The relevant costs are the outflows of cash or the costs of foregone opportunities which are influenced by the inventory activity under consideration. The relevant costs can be thought of as "marginal" or "incremental" costs and should be calculated by eliminating the cost elements which will not change if inventory levels change. Exhibit 4-1 shows the costs usually included as relevant inventory costs. Determination of the magnitude and relevancy of each cost category in a given situation is a matter of interpretation and judgment.

EXHIBIT 4-1
Relevant Inventory Costs

Costs of Ordering

Purchased lots: Managerial, clerical, and computer costs associated with order requisition, purchase order preparation, expediting, and receipt; inspection; updating inventory records and accounts payable records; quantity discounts, freight consolidation breaks, and anticipated price change schedules.

Manufactured lots: Managerial, clerical, and computer costs associated with order requisition and shop order preparation; direct and indirect labor associated with the preparation of equipment, tools, and fixtures for the manufacturing activities required; expediting; inspection; inventory records updating; contribution loss due to limited machine capacity or lost sales.

Costs of Holding Inventory

Storage facility costs: Property taxes; insurance; depreciation; rental fees; maintenance; operational costs and personnel costs necessary for storage space and material handling equipment.

Possession costs: Taxes; insurance; obsolescence; spoilage; deterioration; pilferage; record keeping; labor costs.

Capital costs: Interest on money tied up in inventory or returns earned if cash were invested in opportunities other than inventory; storage facilities and associated equipment.

COSTS OF ORDERING The costs of ordering shown in Exhibit 4-1 are assumed to be fixed, regardless of the quantity of parts ordered, and are incurred each time a purchase order or shop order is placed. For example, the cost, S, for the order requisition, purchase order preparation, receipt, inspection, and the updating of accounting records might be $25.00 per order. If the forecast annual requirements, R, were for 2,000 units, the following formula could be used to determine the annual cost of ordering:[1]

Annual costs of ordering = Number of orders per year × ordering cost

$$= \frac{R}{Q} \times S$$

where R = annual demand forecast, Q = lot size per order, R/Q = number of orders per year, and S = ordering cost per order.

Annual costs of ordering = $\frac{2000}{500} \times \$25.00 = \$100.00$
(quarterly basis)

[1] Note that these costs do not include the purchase price of the item.

Annual costs of ordering $= \dfrac{2000}{1000} \times \$25.00 = \$50.00$
(semi-annual basis)

Figure 4-2 shows the inverse relationship between the annual costs of ordering and the lot size quantity per order.

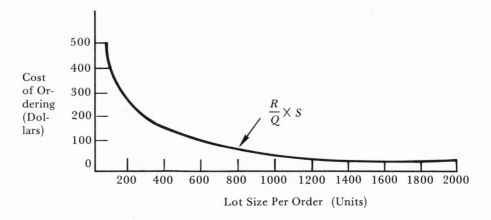

FIGURE 4-2 Annual Costs of Ordering

The same general relationship exists between the setup costs and lot sizes for internally manufactured parts. Ordering costs therefore favor large lot sizes and hence "a few orders per year."

COST OF HOLDING INVENTORY   It is generally assumed that a linear relationship exists between average inventory and the relevant holding costs in Exhibit 4-1. Suppose that an analysis of a firm's annual expenditures for holding a unit of the item in the previous example is $0.50 per unit, or 25% of its purchase price of $2.00.

Under these assumptions the sawtooth pattern in Figure 4-3 would characterize the behavior of the inventory. The average inventory is $Q/2$, assuming the unit usage rate per time period is steady. The inventory will be at the maximum level, Q, just after the order is received and then will drop to zero just before the next order quantity is received. If the order quantity were to be doubled, without a change in the usage rate, then the average inventory would also double. The total holding cost can be calculated as follows:

Annual cost of holding inventory = Average inventory on hand $\times$ Cost per item $\times$ Holding cost percentage

$$= \frac{Q}{2} \times C \times K$$

where $Q/2$ = average units of inventory carried during the year, C = unit cost, and K = total of all holding cost charges as a percentage of the unit cost.

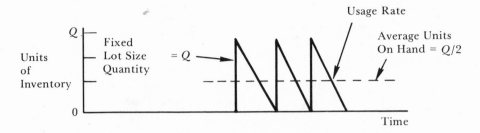

FIGURE 4-3 Inventory Behavior

If the forecast annual requirements were for 2000 units and if quarterly and semi-annual purchasing were being considered, the following annual holding costs would result:

Ordering on a quarterly basis:

Annual cost of holding inventory $= \dfrac{Q}{2} \times C \times K$

$$= \dfrac{500}{2} \times \$2.00 \times 25\% = \$125$$

Ordering on a semi-annual basis:

Annual cost of holding inventory $= \dfrac{Q}{2} \times C \times K$

$$= \dfrac{1000}{2} \times \$2.00 \times 25\% = \$250$$

The annual inventory holding costs increase as the lot size increases, as shown in Figure 4-4. This leads to the conclusion that a firm should attempt to carry low levels of inventories by ordering frequently in small lots. The analysis of the cost of ordering in Figure 4-2 indicated the opposite policy.

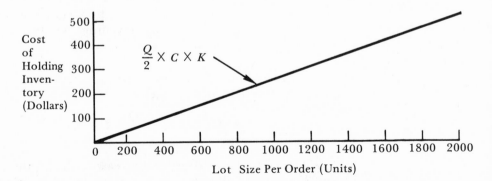

FIGURE 4-4 Annual Costs of Holding Inventory

LOT SIZES FOR FORECAST DEMAND The lot size quantity, Q, can be set on the basis of management judgment, such as "always order the minimum quantity allowed by the supplier." It is usually determined, however, on the basis of the appropriate relevant costs. The economic order quantity (EOQ) lot size is the quantity, Q^*, which can be purchased and held in storage at a minimum total annual cost. Figure 4-5 combines the ordering and holding costs discussed earlier and shows that there is a lot size quantity which minimizes total cost.

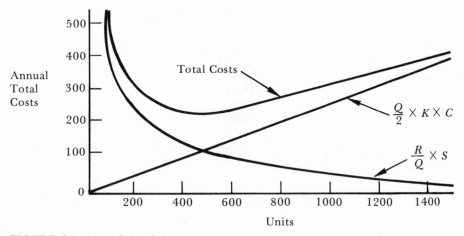

FIGURE 4-5 Annual Total Costs

The optimal economic order quantity, Q^*, can be determined by locating the lowest point on the total annual cost curve of Figure 4-5 and then reading the lot size from the horizontal axis. It can also be determined from Table 4-1 with some difficulty.

The EOQ is best determined by a formula for locating the lowest point on the total cost line in Figure 4-5.[2]

$$Q^* = \sqrt{\frac{2RS}{KC}} = \sqrt{\frac{2(2000)\,(25.00)}{(.25)2.00}} = 447$$

LOT SIZES FOR SCHEDULED REQUIREMENTS DEMAND Manufacturers with a backlog of firm orders plan operations for as much as six months in advance and thereby place rather stable production requirements upon the factory. Inventory transactions are planned to control the flow of purchased materials, parts fabrication, and subassembly manufacturing to meet known production and assembly requirements. Lot size calculations for scheduled requirements demand are dependent upon the net requirements that have been generated from a bill-of-materials explosion process.

Using a computerized bill-of-materials processor, the delivery schedule is exploded to yield gross requirements, by time period, for every

[2] James H. Green, *Production and Inventory Control* (Homewood, Ill.: Richard D. Irwin, Inc., 1974).

TABLE 4-1 Calculation of Annual Total Costs

Lot Size (units) Q	Ordering Cost ($) R/Q × S	Holding Cost ($) Q/2 × K × C	Annual Total Cost ($) (R/Q × S) + (Q/2 × K × C)
100	500.00	25.00	525.00
200	250.00	50.00	300.00
300	166.67	75.00	241.67
400	125.00	100.00	225.00
450	111.11	112.50	223.50
500	100.00	125.00	225.00
600	83.33	150.00	233.33
800	62.50	200.00	262.50
1000	50.00	250.00	300.00
1200	41.67	300.00	341.67
1400	35.71	350.00	385.71
1600	31.25	400.00	431.25
1800	27.80	450.00	477.80
2000	25.00	500.00	525.00

Where R = forecast annual demand = 2000 units, S = ordering costs = \$25.00, K = holding cost percentage = 25% per year, and C = unit cost = \$2.00.

subassembly, part, and raw material required at each stage of the manufacturing process. Gross requirements by time period are adjusted for inventories on hand and on order, and for predicted spoilage and scrap percentages to produce net inventory requirements. Lead time data for purchased items are used to plan the order release and receipt of each purchased part and raw material. The fabrication and assembly operations in the firm are scheduled, using manufacturing lead times and previously determined capacity information.

In the EOQ stock replenishment planning system an order is timed such that an item will be received just as on-hand stock reaches the buffer-stock level. If the lead time of an item varies or if its production needs are changed, the system relies upon the safety stock. Material requirements planning relies upon rescheduling to match availabilities to need when changes occur in lead times or the production schedules.

Consider the master schedule for Product A shown in Table 4-2. Using a bill of material for Product A, the gross requirements for all component parts can be determined. Assume that Product A is made from several purchased and internally manufactured parts.

TABLE 4-2 Master Schedule—Product A

Weeks	1	2	3	4	5	6	7	8	9	10
Quantity required	0	30	40	0	0	45	0	50	0	60

Each unit of Product A requires one unit of Part A-1, a purchased component. Net requirements for Part A-1 are determined in Table 4-3, using on-hand and on-order information.

TABLE 4-3 Net Requirements—Part A-1

Weeks	1	2	3	4	5	6	7	8	9	10
Gross requirements	0	30	40	0	0	45	0	50	0	60
On-hand	10									
On-order	10		60		50					
Net requirements	+20	−10	+10	+10	+60	+15	+15	−35	−35	−95

For Part A-1 exisiting purchase orders would be revised or new purchase orders would be placed such that the appropriate quantities of Part A-1 would be available for the assembly of Product A in each of the specified time periods shown in the master schedule of Table 4-2. Actions which could be taken to improve the delivery schedule of Part A-1 include:

1) Increasing the on-order quantity in Week 1 to 20 units and delaying receipt until Week 2.
2) Decreasing the on-order quantity in Week 3 to 40 units.
3) Decreasing the on-order quantity in Week 5 to 45 units and delaying receipt until Week 6.
4) Placing new orders for 50 and 60 units to be received in Weeks 8 and 10, respectively.

These order revisions and new orders would produce the revised schedule as shown in Table 4-4.

TABLE 4-4 Revised Schedule of Orders

Weeks	1	2	3	4	5	6	7	8	9	10
Gross requirements	0	30	40	0	0	45	0	50	0	60
On-hand	10	0	0	0	0	0	0	0	0	0
On-order		20	40	0	0	45	0	50	0	60
Net requirements	+10	0	0	0	0	0	0	0	0	0

Net requirements for manufactured parts would be calculated in a similar manner, resulting in time-phased due dates for all raw material and purchased-components requirements needed to support the manufacturing activities. As in the case of Part A-1, positive or negative net requirements trigger an action for new or revised orders. Lot-sizing techniques based on balancing the costs of ordering and holding inventory can be used with MRP systems.

In Table 4-4 orders for Part A-1 were rescheduled to be received in weeks 2, 3, 6, 8, and 10. It might be advantageous to combine the requirements to produce fewer orders since the pattern shown could result in excessive ordering costs from five separate orders. If the order requirements for weeks 2 and 3 were combined, then a purchase order would be written for 60 units to arrive at the beginning of week 2. Thus 40 units of Part A-1 stock would be carried in inventory for one week in advance of the actual requirement, and an inventory holding cost would be incurred.

ALTER-NATIVES FOR COMBINING REQUIRE MENTS

1) Combine requirements for Weeks 2 and 3; order 60 units and carry 40 units for 1 extra week.
2) Combine requirements for Weeks 2-6; order 105 units and carry 40 units for 1 extra week and 45 units for 4 extra weeks.
3) Combine requirements for Weeks 2-8; order 155 units and carry 40 units for 1 extra week, 45 units for 4 extra weeks, 50 units for 6 extra weeks.
4) Combine requirements for Weeks 2-10; order 215 units and carry 40 units for 1 extra week, 45 units for 4 extra weeks, 50 units for 6 extra weeks, and 60 units for 8 extra weeks.

Table 4-5 illustrates an approach to deciding whether requirements should be combined to effect deliveries of stock in advance of actual need, by examining the tradeoffs of inventory ordering and holding costs.

TABLE 4-5 Lot Size Cost Calculations

Week	Revised Order Schedule From Table 4-4	Cumulative Order Lot	Extra Inventory	Weeks Extra Inventory Is Held	Incremental Holding Cost ($)	Ordering Cost ($)
1	0	0	0	0		
2	20	20	0	0		50.00
3	40	60	40	1	4.00	
4	0					
5	0					
6	45	105	45	4	18.00	
7	0					
8	50	155	50	6	30.00	
9	0					
10	60	215	60	8	48.00	

Assumptions:

Ordering cost	=	$50.00 per order
Holding cost	=	26% per year or 1/2% per week
Value of part A-1	=	$20.00
Holding cost/week	=	$0.10/unit

The inventory holding costs associated with these alternatives are shown in Table 4-5. A purchase order for 20 units *must* be placed in Week 2. As an alternative to a subsequent mandatory order for 40 units in Week 3, the 40 units could be added to the order which must be placed in Week 2. In fact, each of the future requirements could be included in the order to be placed in Week 2, as long as the incremental costs of holding the additional inventory are less than the cost of placing an additional order. This procedure would lead to the purchase of the requirements for Weeks 2-10 in Week 2. The purchase of the requirements for Week 10 in Week 2 would add incremental holding costs of $48.00, about the same as the $50.00 cost of a second purchase order in Week 10. It would probably be advantageous to wait for a later purchase for the Week 10 requirements, on the basis that many factors could change in the eight-week interval and management can retain its options by deferring the purchase. This approach and other lot-sizing techniques are discussed in greater detail in more specialized texts.[3]

4.5   MANAGING THE BUFFER-STOCK COMPONENT

SERVICE POLICY AND BUFFER STOCKS

Lot size calculations address the cycle-stock question, How much to order? Buffer stocks provide protection against the unpredictable elements in demand and lead time. If both item demand and lead time were known with 100% reliability, buffer stocks would not be required. An order would be placed just at that point where the existing stocks were sufficient to cover usage during the replenishment cycle.

In Table 3-4 a reasonable rate of maximum demand during the replenishment cycle was arbitrarily set. This maximum demand could be determined on the basis of management's observation of the range of actual item usage during equivalent replenishment-cycle periods. For example, if, during 12 four-week periods, actual demand ranged from 80 to 200 units and averaged 130 units, management might set the reasonable level of maximum demand at 200 units for a four-week replenishment cycle. Thus, buffer stock would be set at a level of 70 units (the difference between the maximum and the average demand).

Another method for determining buffer-stock protection is based on a predetermined service policy which states the frequency with which demand should be served by the on-hand inventory. For example, with a 90% service policy, management plans its buffer-stock levels with the expectation that a stockout condition will be incurred during 10% of the reorder cycles. A 95% or 98% service policy is commonly encountered in finished-goods distribution operations and in raw materials and parts inventory situations. A firm's service-level policy is usually determined by top management on the basis of the consequences of being out of stock. With a service guideline, the buffer stock

---

[3] For a detailed treatment of MRP, the reader is referred to Joseph Orlicky, *Material Requirements Planning* (New York: McGraw-Hill Book Company, 1975; and Oliver W. Wright, *Production and Inventory Management in the Computer Age* (Boston: Cahners Publishing Company, 1974).

can be set by using a statistical measure of demand variability during the lead time. The range between peak and lowest observed value was used above as a crude means of estimating demand variability. An alternative method uses the standard deviation of demand during the replenishment cycle or lead time to establish a reasonable level of maximum demand.

To illustrate the technique of setting buffer stocks on the basis of service policy, assume that demand during the lead time was found to follow a normal distribution and its average and standard deviation were calculated as 150 units and 35 units, respectively. Based on a 95% service level (a stockout condition is allowable in 5% of the order periods), the maximum rate of demand during lead time could be calculated as follows:

Maximum demand = Average demand + Z × Standard deviation
during lead time   during lead time   of demand during
                                                          lead time

where Z = one-tail standardized normal deviate from statistical tables of area under a normal curve = 1.65. For this situation during the replenishment period:

Reasonable maximum demand = 150 + 1.65 × 35 = 150 + 57.8

= 207.6, or approximately 208 units

The buffer stock carried, 58 units, would be the difference between the stock needed to cover average demand and the stock needed for a 95% service policy during the replenishment reordering cycle.

Tables 4-6 and 4-7 show the effect of service-level policy on buffer-stock investment. Management should carefully weigh the advantages of very high service (low stockout chances) against the discretionary costs of buffer stocks. Unless a favorable marketing position is secured by more favorable service levels, a firm should provide service consistent with that of competitors.

TABLE 4-6 Effect of Service Policy on Buffer Stock

Service Policy	Standard Z Value	Buffer Stock (units)
90%	1.28	approximately 45
95%	1.65	approximately 58
96%	1.75	approximately 61
97%	1.88	approximately 66
98%	2.05	approximately 72
99%	2.33	approximately 82

TABLE 4-7 Incremental Effect of Increasing Service Policy

Increasing Service Policy	Incremental Effect
From 90% to 95%	45 to 58 units, or 29% increase in stock
From 95% to 99%	58 to 82 units, or 38% increase in stock
From 90% to 99%	45 to 82 units, or 82% increase in stock

WAREHOUSE LOCATION AND BUFFER STOCKS

In addition to purchasing or manufacturing a product which satisfies consumer needs, a firm must also plan and control distribution operations to place the proper product mix at the proper location at the right time. Buffer-stock policy, then, takes on a particularly important role in the firm which operates a network of distribution centers. It has been shown that inventory investment levels vary with lot size quantities, review and lead time periods, and service policy. The total buffer-stock investment for an item is also dependent on the number of distribution centers.

In a distribution network, inventories are placed in major demand centers in order to provide quick, convenient service to customers. Since inventories tie up resources and incur carrying costs, a firm will frequently evaluate whether or not it is cost-effective to keep all types of inventories (Groups A, B, and C) at each of its warehouses or to place certain slow movers from Group C at fewer locations. At other, less frequent, intervals the firm will analyze whether the proper number of warehouses is being maintained. Building upon the production-distribution example of Chapter 3, the relationship between inventory investment and the number of stock locations can be developed. In the example of Chapter 3, ten distribution outlets served 750 retailers, each of whom was experiencing an average demand of 1 unit per day. The cycle stocks and buffer stocks necessary to support the distributor segment were:

Average cycle inventory for 1 distributor	= 300 units
Average cycle inventory for 10 distributors	= 3000 units
Buffer-stock inventory for 1 distributor	= 900 units
Buffer-stock inventory for 10 distributors	= 9000 units

Suppose the number of distributors were to be decreased from 10 to 5, such that each distributor would provide service to 150 retailers in its surrounding geographical area. As discussed in the example, it is reasonable to assume that the flow of retailers' orders to a distributor will be approximately uniform over time. Each of the 5 distributors would therefore now receive 10 orders, each for 15 units, every day and ship those orders to the 10 retailers ordering in his area.

The average cycle stock at a distributor depends only on the average shipment rate to the retailers. Therefore, assuming that lead times, review periods, and demand were not altered by a proposed reduction in distribution outlets, the average cycle stock would be calculated as follows:

Maximum cycle stock = Shipments per day per retailer $\times$ Number of retailers ordering $\times$ Review period

$$= 10 \times 15 \times 8 = 1200 \text{ units}$$

Average cycle stock = 1/2 Maximum cycle stock = 1/2 $\times$ 1200

$$= 600 \text{ units}$$

Average cycle stock for 5 distributors = 5 $\times$ 600 = 3000 units

Notice that the average cycle-stock investment for this product was not changed by a reduction in the number of distributor facilities.

The investment in buffer stocks will be altered, however, by a change in the number of distributors. It has been shown that buffer stocks are set to cover a reasonable level of demand variation during the replenishment cycle. In Table 3-4 the buffer stock at one distribution outlet was calculated to be 900 units. That figure was based on the judgment that a reasonable level of maximum demand during replenishment would be 2550 units. As shown in the preceding section, buffer stocks can be calculated by multiplying the standard deviation of demand during the replenishment cycle times the Z value associated with a desired service level.

Using the production-distribution example of Chapter 3 (a ten-distributor network with each distibutor serving 5 retailers per day and carrying 900 units of buffer stock), the standard deviation and variance of the demand at each distributor would be calculated as follows. Assuming buffer stock = Z value $\times$ standard deviation of demand during replenishment cycle, and assuming $Z = 1.65$ for a 95% service policy, then at each distributor:

Standard deviation of demand = 900 $\div$ 1.65 = 545.5 units

Variance of demand = $(545.5)^2$ = 297,520 units

With 10 distributors, 9000 units of buffer-stock inventory were needed to provide for a 95% service level at each distributor's facility. To determine the total inventory of buffer stock required with 5 distributors, the standard deviation of demand must be recalculated to reflect the fact that each distributor would serve a larger number of retail outlets and the characteristics of the demand variability would be changed.

The variance and standard deviation of demand of each of 5 distributors may be calculated as follows.   The total variance in the ten distributor network is 10 X the variance of demand at each of the distributors; or, 10 X 297,520 = 2,975,200 units.

Variance for each = Total variance ÷ Number of distributors
distributor in a
five-center
network

$$= 2,975,200 ÷ 5 = 595,040 \text{ units}$$

Standard deviation for each distributor in a five-center network = 771.4 units

Thus, the buffer stock for each of 5 distributors in the five-distributor network would be:

Buffer stock = Z X Standard deviation of demand

$$= 1.65 \times 771.4 = 1273 \text{ units}$$

The total inventory of buffer stock required with 5 distributors is:

Total buffer stock = 5 X 1273 = 6365 units

While the buffer-stock level at each distributor has increased from 900 units to 1273 units, the total buffer stock required to provide a 95% service level has been decreased from 9000 units to 6365 units. Figure 4-6 shows the relationship between buffer-stock requirements and the number of distribution facilities as the number of facilities is changed.

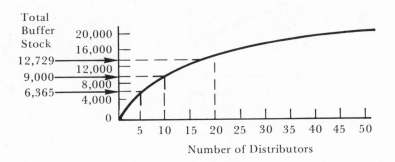

FIGURE 4-6 Total Buffer Stock

It should be apparent that regardless of other attributes in a distribution system, the number of stocking locations will require a specific quantity of buffer stocks. In fact, the total buffer stock required is proportional to the square root of the number of stocking locations ($9000/\sqrt{10} = 6365/\sqrt{5} = 12{,}729/\sqrt{20} = 2846$ units of buffer stock required for one stocking location).

4.6   DETERMINING THE REORDER POINT

The economic-order-quantity technique maintains adequate cycle stocks by reviewing the level of an item's inventory each time a demand occurs. When the inventory level of an item reaches a predetermined point, an order is placed for the optimal lot size, Q^*, as shown in Figure 4-7. If item demand could be forecast precisely, the reorder point (ROP) would equal the amount of stock needed to cover demand during the replenishment lead time. For example, if demand was 10 units/week and lead time was 4 weeks, the reorder point would be 4 weeks $\times$ 10 units per week, or 40 units. Thus, when the inventory level reached 40 units, an order for replenishment stock would be placed. If actual demand was subsequently 10 units per week and if the lead time was exactly 4 weeks, the level of inventory would reach zero just as the replenishment order of 40 units arrived. No firm would gamble on week-to-week demand being predictable, or on lead time being constant. Since both demand and lead times vary, the joint variation of demand during the lead time must be estimated to determine the buffer-stock level and the reorder point. Specialized texts on inventory management give analytical methods for determining various attributes of order-point, order-quantity systems.[4]

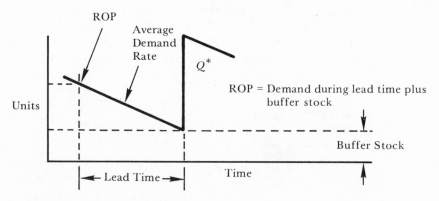

FIGURE 4-7   Reorder Point

4.7   ADDENDA

EOQ ASSUMPTIONS Since EOQ and buffer-stock techniques are employed in many computerized inventory planning and control systems, it is important to understand the following underlying assumptions.

1) *Forecast of Demand.* The EOQ formula is derived on the assumption that item demand can be forecast. While buffer stocks are

[4] Green, op. cit.

intended to cover variations in demand, if a seasonal or trend component of demand has been omitted from the forecast, the buffer stock will rapidly be depleted. Management must insure that item forecasts are monitored for accuracy, since no inventory technique will provide satisfactory results if forecasts are unreliable.

2) *Unit Cost.* The cost of the ordered item is assumed to remain constant over the range of order quantities being considered. In reality, price breaks or quantity discounts are typically offered by a vendor, or transportation rate schedules vary with quantity shipped, or manufacturing costs change with high-volume versus low-volume processing procedures. The EOQ technique can be modified to account for such deviations from the unit-cost assumption. The adaptations to the basic formula are covered in detail in more specialized texts.

3) *Inventory-Holding Cost and Ordering Cost.* Inventory-holding costs are assumed to vary proportionally with increases in the average quantity, $Q/2$. In some situations inventory-holding costs may increase at a greater than proportional rate because of such things as a sliding scale for fire insurance, additional warehousing space, or higher interest costs on money which must be borrowed to cover larger order quantities. The holding cost percentage must be determined for a period of time equivalent to the period of forecast demand. Ordering costs are assumed to be a fixed amount for each order. In some situations, however, components of the ordering cost — such as inspection costs — can vary significantly with the quantity ordered.

SENSITIVITY OF Q^*

The costs of ordering and holding inventory produce the type of total-cost curve shown in Figure 4-5, which is relatively flat around the Q^* quantity. Modest deviations from the economic lot size will not induce large increases in costs. It can also be seen that order quantities larger than the Q^* quantity bring about relatively lower error costs than order quantities which are equivalently smaller than the Q^* quantity.

LEAD TIME

The reorder-point level is based upon an assumption of predictable lead time. If lead times change frequently, their estimates must be updated regularly to avoid nonoptimal levels of inventories. Long lead times are usually more variable than short lead times, so less confidence can be placed on long replenishment-cycle times; and greater buffer-stock levels are required.

RELATION-SHIPS AMONG ORDERS

In the case of manufactured products, shop orders released on the basis of reorder points having been triggered may impose conflicting demands upon a given facility. The lead time for some shop orders may be extended while waiting for processing. Thus, schedules must be monitored closely when EOQ quantities are competing for the same facilities.

In the case of purchased items, vendors may offer discounts on sales of similar products within a given commodity class. The EOQ technique would not provide the best results in such a case, since replenishment orders would be placed at random times. It would be preferable to use an ordering procedure in which replenishment orders for all items in a given commodity class would be placed at one time.

4.8   SUMMARY

The fundamental tasks in inventory planning and control are to set in motion the flows of purchase, production, and shipping orders, and to control the movement of raw materials, work-in-process, and finished goods through manufacturing and distribution processes. Management's objective is to select and implement stock-ordering and buffer-inventory policies and techniques which provide for optimal inventory service and cost levels, and then to insure the ability of the firm to achieve a desired return on assets.

4.9   BIBLIOGRAPHY

Ammer, Dean S. *Materials Management.* Homewood, Ill.: Richard D. Irwin, Inc., 1968.

Bowersox, Donald J.; Smykay, Edward W., and Lalonde, Bernard J. *Physical Distribution Management.* New York: The Macmillan Company, 1968.

Brown, Robert G. *Smoothing, Forecasting and Prediction of Discrete Time Series.* Englewood Cliffs, N. J.: Prentice-Hall, Inc., 1963.

_____. *Statistical Forecasting for Inventory Control.* Englewood Cliffs, N. J.: Prentice-Hall, Inc., 1959.

Buchan, Joseph, and Koenigsberg, Ernest. *Scientific Inventory Management.* Englewood Cliffs, N. J.: Prentice-Hall, Inc., 1963.

Buffa, Elwood S., and Taubert, William H. *Production-Inventory Systems: Planning and Control.* Homewood, Ill.: Richard D. Irwin, Inc., 1972.

England, Wilbur B., and Lenders, Michiel R. *Purchasing and Materials Management.* 6th ed. Homewood, Ill.: Richard D. Irwin, Inc., 1975.

Fetter, Robert B., and Dalleck, Winston C. *Decision Models for Inventory Management.* Homewood, Ill.: Richard D. Irwin, Inc., 1961.

Green, James H. *Production and Inventory Control.* Homewood, Ill.: Richard D. Irwin, Inc., 1974.

Hadley, G., and Whitin, J. M. *Analysis of Inventory Systems.* Englewood Cliffs, N. J.: Prentice-Hall, Inc., 1963.

Hassmann, Fred. *Operations Research in Production and Inventory Control.* New York: John Wiley & Sons, Inc., 1962.

International Business Machines, Inc. *Wholesale IMPACT — Advanced Principles and Implementation Reference Manual.* White Plains, N. Y.: IBM, 1969.

Orlicky, Joseph. *Materials Requirements Planning.* New York: McGraw-Hill Book Company, 1975.

Wright, Oliver W. *Production and Inventory Management In the Computer Age.* Boston, Mass.: Cahners Publishing Company, 1974.

MANPOWER PLANNING
AND CONTROL

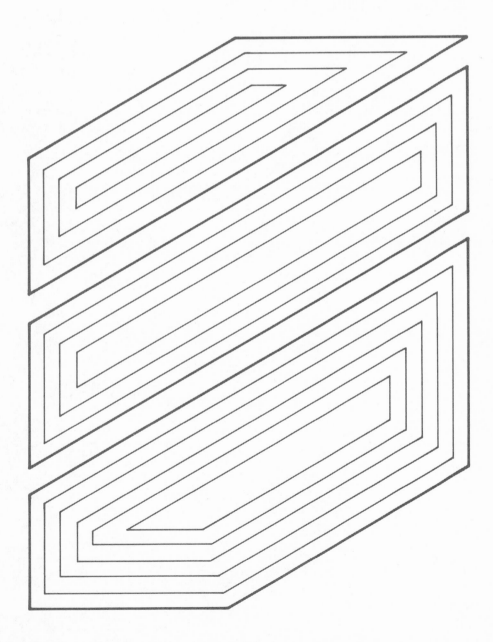

INTRODUCTION

The operations manager plans for and controls the firm's use of most of its equipment, materials and labor resources. A means of measuring the output capability of each resource is essential to the management task. When a certain type of machine is set to run — with a given set of tools, fixtures, scrap and waste considerations, feeds, speeds, etc. — the output rate is predictable and consistent. Similarly, the weights, densities, and size requirements for the materials in a given product can be measured to a required degree of precision.

The output capability of labor has been difficult to measure, however. Measurement difficulties arise because of the substantial impact on labor capability of such factors as:

- working or environmental conditions.
- the skill level of the workers.
- work methods and work station layout.
- allowances for unavoidable interruptions, personal time, or fatigue.
- the level of effort expended.
- the repetitiveness of the work task.
- the mental attitude of the worker.
- random demands for service.
- tasks of unpredictable duration.

Since most of the employees in any business are employed in the operations function, as pointed out in Chapter 1, it is important to develop a capability to measure labor capacity in both production- and service-oriented operations.

The chart in Figure III-1 shows the elements of return on assets which the chapters in this section address.

Labor performance is normally measured on the basis of labor cost per unit of output produced. Labor cost per unit of output is based on two factors: the wage rate paid and the productivity of the workers. There are two ways to improve the relative cost of a firm's labor resources — increase productivity and/or decrease wages. Wage rates, however, generally tend to move only upward and usually have a strong relationship to area wage conditions, union pressures, and historical precedence in the firm. The most manageable facet of wage costs is the productivity element. In order to increase the productivity of labor, most managers rely heavily upon some form of measurement of the time required to perform given work tasks.

The overwhelming contributor to the efficient use of labor in factory settings is the ability of management to organize and schedule the work to the worker. The work place layout and methods can then be planned to employ the workers in the most effective manner, and the work can be scheduled to the work place to minimize worker idle time. We refer to activities organized in factory-type work place settings as structured activities.

Service operations, on the other hand, are usually complicated by an inability of the management to specify either the time of arrival or

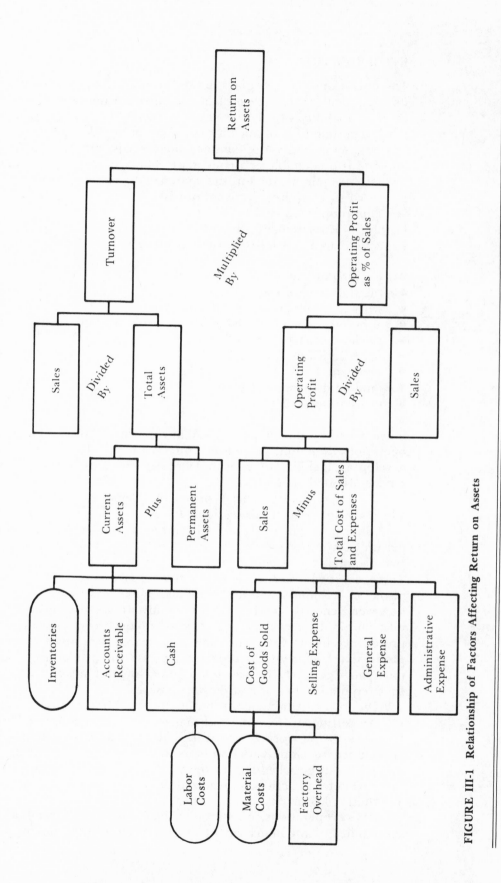

FIGURE III-1 Relationship of Factors Affecting Return on Assets

the work content of the task to be performed. In a bank, for instance, customers arrive at unpredictable times and require services of widely variable work content. We refer to activities in such service-oriented operations as unstructured activities.

Chapter 5 treats the management uses for time estimates and the four techniques most commonly used to establish estimates of the time required to perform tasks in structured situations. Chapter 6 expands the operational setting to unstructured activities and presents methods for planning and controlling activities with highly variable work content and unschedulable demands.

When the work content of an operational situation is known and performance standards are available, the next task in the planning process is to determine the pattern of manpower which will be needed during the planning period to meet the operation's output objectives. First, the overall capacity of the operation must be controlled relative to the level of output desired. In the long run, if the management expects to ship, or sell, or complete 10,000 man-hours of product per week, say, then at least 10,000 man-hours of capacity must be provided. Since products or services demanded are not smooth from time period to time period, and productivity (or output) levels are not consistent, more than 10,000 actual man-hours will be needed to accomplish an average 10,000 man-hours of output.

Second, additional controllable variables must be introduced to assist the manager in the workload-smoothing process. The order backlog can be allowed to fluctuate. The level of work-in-process inventory can be manipulated to achieve worker utilization and desired lead times (throughput times). Finished-goods inventories can be used to achieve a smoother workload and workflow. The process of planning and controlling the various aspects of the total flow of work is herein referred to as manpower planning. The terms, *aggregate production planning* or *master scheduling,* are frequently used in the literature to refer to this process.

Chapters 7 and 8 develop a framework for the general aggregate planning problem which extends the planning process introduced in Chapter 1 and provides the setting within which the various detailed scheduling methods, presented in Part IV, must operate. A research study outlining the results of Simulation Studies of the Manpower Decision Framework completes this section.

Analysis of Structured Activities

5.1 INTRODUCTION

Work measurement is the process by which the time it should take to do a delineated task is established. The labor-measurement difficulties cited in the Introduction to Part III make the work-measurement task less than scientific. Because of the importance of the problem and the inherent difficulties, much attention has been devoted to the establishment of the best procedures to be followed by a person developing a time estimate. In fact, research and development of the work-measurement process extends back to 1835. Following Frederick Taylor's[1] introduction of time studies in 1881, the use of work measurement by management went through a period (1911-1915) in which workers and unions openly resisted its use. Work measurement is accepted today by labor union leaders and management as a systematic process for handling a difficult mutual problem.

5.2 MANAGEMENT APPLICATIONS OF TIME ESTIMATES

MANPOWER PLANNING A production unit, or a service facility in a factory, or a work center in an office, bank, or hospital should be staffed with a number of workers sufficient to perform the anticipated workload. In a production unit,

---

[1] F. W. Taylor, *The Principles of Scientific Management* (New York: Harper & Bros., 1915), p. 60.

the workload estimate may be derived from a six-month production schedule. In a factory service operation such as shipping, estimates of the workload may be formulated from the shipping schedule. In an office, bank, hospital, or similar service-oriented setting, the anticipated workload forecast may have to be based on the workload in prior periods. With such forecasts of workload, time estimates for each task associated with the workload can then be used to plan the number of workers needed.

PRODUCTION SCHEDULING AND CAPACITY PLANNING   Given a level of production capabilities, the scheduling function develops a timetable for the movement of materials, work-in-process, and finished goods through the manufacturing and distribution activities of the firm. The coordination of the activities throughout the plant depends largely upon the availability of time estimates for the completion of each work task performed on each order at each work center. With time estimates available, the precise period-by-period workload in each work center of the plant can be determined. The shop foreman and operations manager are interested in the work scheduled into their facilities because the resulting workload directly influences their performance in relation to cost and schedule goals. The marketing function is interested in time estimates, since product delivery dates must be estimated from production schedules. Once the shop load is determined from the production schedule and time estimates, the labor requirements can be compared with the regular-time and overtime capabilities of each work center and assembly area. This comparison is usually developed on the basis of time units. The requirements and capacity should be closely balanced. If not, production backlogs and delays will occur when there is insufficient capacity, or excessive equipment and idle-manpower costs will be incurred under a situation of too much capacity. The time standards information is often useful in management decisions regarding equipment replacement and additions, new material handling processes, and plant layout designs.

LABOR COST PLANNING AND CONTROL   The formulation of cost center budgets, selling prices, and competitive bids, and the relevant labor costs in make-or-buy situations are dependent upon time estimates for the appropriate labor activities. Time estimates are developed both for direct labor and indirect labor, and they often become the basis for overhead expense distribution.

Time estimates are fundamental for the control tasks of the foreman, office manager, and operations manager. They provide a basis for monitoring each work unit's operations and judging the effectiveness with which labor resources have been utilized. Period-by-period reporting of the actual time spent on a job versus the time estimate for the job provides a criterion by which performance of the worker and the supervisor can be judged.

WAGE PAYMENTS   Time estimates serve as the basis of the production worker's wages in those situations where a wage incentive system is used. This application of time estimates is covered later in this chapter.

WORK METHODS IMPROVEMENT Methods analysis is the first step in a work-measurement study of a given task. The objective of methods analysis is to improve job performance through better work motions and procedures, tools and fixtures, product configurations, work-place layout and equipment, and other working conditions such that worker productivity increases without an accompanying increase in worker fatigue. Given an effective work method, a time estimate is developed on the basis of executing the given method. The productivity potential of any change in method is evaluated by measuring and comparing the times required to perform the job using the old method and the new method.

5.3   WORK-MEASUREMENT TECHNIQUES

Several different methods of measuring the work content of jobs have been developed. Each is best suited for certain job situations and management needs. The techniques to be discussed here are 1) stop-watch time study, 2) standard data, 3) predetermined time standards, and 4) work sampling. Before examining these techniques, it should be recognized that time estimates are developed in many situations without using any of the above approaches. Time estimates for doing a job can be developed on the basis of past experiences with the job or with the individual work tasks that comprise the job. A company may not have the expertise to employ one of the more precise techniques listed above. The value of the standard may not warrant the expense required for elaborate methods. The usefulness of estimates depends on the experience and judgment of the person developing the time estimates. Rough estimates can be effectively applied to some manpower planning and scheduling situations in which there is a large degree of variability already present in the environment, such as the first production run on a newly developed product. It is very rare, however, to use gross time estimates for the establishment of wage incentive base rates. The need for precision dictates whether management can be satisfied with time estimates based on prior experience and judgment.

Each of the four more elaborate techniques has as its objective the measurement of the time it should take to complete a given task under the following conditions:

1) The best work methods, procedures, tools, fixtures, and working conditions have been designed and made available to the worker.
2) The time reflects the capabilities of an average worker who is qualified and trained for the task.
3) The time has been established with due allowances provided for unavoidable delays such as the time required for machine maintenance, supervision, rest breaks, and personal needs.

When these conditions are met, the time estimate is usually thought of as being a time standard. A time standard is therefore a fair and comprehensive representation of the time it should take an average worker who has received proper instructions to perform a given task.

As indicated previously, time measurement begins with an analysis of the best way to perform the activity of interest. Successful work-methods analysis requires substantial knowledge of the motion-study principles relating to the use of the human body, to the arrangement of the work place, and to the design of tools and equipment. Such principles were first developed by Frank and Lillian Gilbreth[2] and later refined by Ralph M. Barnes.[3] Methods analysis requires specialized skill in the decomposition of a job into basic motion elements. The analysis of detailed work motions assists in constructing improved ways of performing the job by such means as eliminating or combining hand and body motions, using new tools and fixtures, and rearranging the work-place layout. The manager should insure that appropriate attention has been given to the improvement of work methods, independently of the work-measurement techniques chosen to establish time estimates.

STOPWATCH TIME STUDY
The stopwatch time study technique was, in the past, the most widely used method for deriving time estimates. As the name implies, a stopwatch is used to measure the time intervals for completing a given sequence of work-motion elements. With a worker utilizing the best sequence of motions for doing a job, each of the basic motion elements is timed for a large number of work cycles. The element timing constitutes the drawing of a random sample of times for performing each element of the work task. The average time for each element is found by dividing the sum of the time values for all observations of each element by the number of work cycles observed.

The average time for each element of the work represents the work time for the person actually observed. Since the objective is to establish a time standard which is applicable to the average worker putting forth average effort under normal working conditions, the average time values for each element may have to be adjusted or leveled. The stopwatch time study technique places the responsibility on the analyst to judge whether the worker being measured is working at a normal pace. If the time study observer believes that he is witnessing a nonnormal performance, the average cycle time for the job must be revised. For example, if the worker is felt to be working at only 90% of normal pace, the average cycle time should be multiplied by 0.90 to yield the time that should normally be required to complete the job. This process is known as rating.

After the normal work time is established, further adjustments are made in order to account for unavoidable work delays. Factors typically included are personal time, equipment breakdown and/or maintenance, supervisory time, and fatigue. The total normal time is usually adjusted by an allowance for unavoidable delays, expressed as a percentage factor. An allowance of 15% is widely used in business for this adjustment. Once adjusted, the resulting total time becomes the standard time for the job.

[2] F. B. and L. M. Gilbreth, *Applied Motion Study* (New York: Sturgis & Walton Co., 1917), p. 43.

[3] R. M. Barnes, *Motion and Time Study*, 3rd ed. (John Wiley & Sons, Inc., 1949), p. 18.

STANDARD
DATA

Standard data techniques provide another approach for establishing time standards. These techniques make use of historical actual time data to set new work standards. To use the standard data method, it is necessary for the file of historical job times to be broken into very specific elements, as in the stopwatch study technique. The different elemental standards are then applied to a new work procedure to establish a composite time estimate for the new job. This composite time estimate is then adjusted by the necessary allowances for unavoidable delays to establish the required standard time.

This technique works very well in those situations where work tasks are similar from job to job. It provides a means by which new standards can be derived without the very difficult process of observing workers. As with the time-study method, the best work method is assumed to be used when the elemental times are applied. The time standards developed with standard data techniques are only as good as the validity of the standard data. If the work conditions, work-place layout, or other factors change to the extent that they no longer represent existing job conditions, then the new time standards will not be adequate.

PRE-
DETERMINED
TIME
STANDARDS

The third approach for establishing time standards uses predetermined time data for such basic body movements as "reach," "grasp." or "hold." For each movement a normal time has been calculated by using stopwatch techniques and other more complex procedures such as motion pictures and electronic measurement devices. These data can be found in reference books or can be obtained from industrial engineering consulting companies. The best known of the commercially available systems is the Methods-Time-Measurement (MTM) system. In the MTM system the times for basic body movements are measured in units of 0.0006 of a minute. The times for the different movements are tabulated in accordance with work-place parameters, such as the distance an arm must move or the degree of difficulty assigned to grasping a part.

To derive a standard time for a new job, the operations comprising the job must be broken into elements, and the basic body movements which comprise each element must be established. Normal time values are then found in tables of predetermined time data. Unavoidable allowances are then added to the sum of the predetermined elemental time values to obtain the time standard.

The use of predetermined time standards, as with standard data, does not require the person setting the new time standard to make direct measurements of the worker. Regardless of the work-measurement technique employed, establishing a viable time standard requires that the analyst must have enough experience with the work cycle to be able to understand and precisely describe the process, tools, and methods being used. Judgmental factors are inherent in the predetermined data since the creators of the data specified the normal times for the basic body movements. When the person setting the standard decides what degree of difficulty should be assigned to such tasks as grasping a washer out of a bin or locating a hole in which a screw must be inserted, he also introduces judgment. Since different times are assigned for different degrees of difficulty, the analyst must assign units to the different body movements. Finally, the allowance for unavoidable delays introduces additional judgment.

WORK SAMPLING   Work sampling[4] differs from the previous three techniques in that its purpose is not to arrive at a precise time standard. Work sampling provides an economic means to analyze how effectively resources are being used in complex, intermittent, or nonrepetitive operations. It usually consists of brief, random observations of equipment or employees over an extended period of time. These observations then provide data such as the following: a certain machine is not in use 18% of the time, or 43% of the time that a clerk spends waiting on customers is spent searching for the desired item. The level of detail to which a work-sampling program is carried depends on the requirements for the study. The accuracy of these data is directly dependent on the number of observations that are made. Work sampling provides a method for analyzing the activities of people or machines with low relative cost, a predictable degree of accuracy, and little negative effect on the objects of the study.

5.4   WAGE PAYMENT SYSTEMS

Time standards are used for measuring the worker's output for purposes of wage payment, in both production and service operations. The worker may receive a pay premium for output above a planned or agreed-upon level, providing an opportunity for the worker to earn extra pay. The opportunity for extra pay provides the incentive for additional production and the possibility of lower total cost per unit produced. This lower unit cost should result in additional profit and a higher return-on-assets. Incentive systems, when properly designed and administered, contribute to an overall increase in productivity and lead to more intensive use of fixed plant and equipment.

INDIVIDUAL INCENTIVES   In order to develop and apply incentives, management needs to determine the relationship between the worker's normal and incentive paces. The normal pace should relate to management's definition of normalcy used in establishing time standards. The incentive pace is the rate at which the worker produces when motivated by incentive pay. Specific terms are usually laid down regarding the worker's financial reward for maintaining the higher incentive work pace.

While there are many versions of wage incentive plans, the basic idea is to pay the worker his normal hourly rate for producing at the required pace and an additional percentage of his rate for production above the standard rate. If the standard required the production of 100 items per hour, for instance, and the worker produced 120 items during the hour, he would have earned a 20% bonus, in addition to his base hourly wage. In this case the employee receives 100% credit for all

[4] Ralph M. Barnes, *Work Sampling*, 2nd ed. (New York: John Wiley & Sons, Inc., 1957).

production in excess of normal. In some incentive plans, the worker receives a fraction (or share) of the additional productivity achieved. The 100% participation ratio is simple and straightforward, and is the one that most employees would naturally favor. The ratio at which increased productivity above a normal pace will be shared must be specified as part of the plan.

GROUP INCENTIVES

When a given operation can be performed on an individual basis without depending on other operations, it is usually desirable to establish incentives on an individual basis. When operations such as an assembly line or a crew working on a single piece of equipment cannot be individualized, incentive payments based on group performance may be applied. To establish group incentives, it is necessary to study each individual operation to be performed by the group in order to determine the proper staffing level and to insure effective balance between operators on the line or in the crew. Time standards are then summarized for the group, and the normal output is established. Total group output compared to normal output determines the amount of incentive pay. Each worker's compensation is increased by the group percentage earned.

Group incentives tend to level the output of the workers involved. The better workers may not work as hard as possible, but the performance of the poorer workers is improved by the group's peer pressures, the morale of the group, and the personal help of the more skilled operators.

MEASURED DAYWORK

Wage incentives are used where management believes that the worker is entitled to higher pay because his productivity is increased through his own effort. When worker productivity is largely controlled by workplace factors, no incentive should be paid. In many more-or-less-automated industries today, the worker cannot influence processing time. In such cases the worker is paid for his time, assuming his performance meets the basic skills required. This form of payment is called measured daywork.

SALARIED INCENTIVES

Work measurement has recently begun to be applied to salaried or clerical workers, usually as an adaptation of the measured-day work system. Time studies may be used to determine and control the amount of clerical production expected, but they are not normally used for pay purposes. Some salaried employees are compensated by incentive systems not related to work measurement as normally practiced in the factory. Most common are salesmen paid in proportion to sales consummated. Sales commissions thus earned relate to the salesman's productivity, not necessarily to his level of effort.

Management employees are frequently paid additional compensation for meeting or exceeding personal or corporate objectives. Payments in the form of bonuses and deferred compensation provide positive incentives to achieve agreed-upon objectives.

Under proper conditions wage and salary incentives can increase output and lower costs. Successful incentive systems require:

1) A full explanation of the incentive plan prior to installation.
2) A plan that is simple and easy for the worker to understand.
3) A comprehensive work-methods study and properly established time standards.
4) A complete evaluation of all jobs involved.
5) A proper allowance for conditions that affect the worker's ability to perform.
6) A clear system for inspection and accounting for employee's output.
7) A system for updating standards when methods change.
8) A continuing following-up to see that production methods and standards are being adhered to.
9) A procedure for the employees to question the system and its application.

5.5   SUMMARY

Whether work-measurement data are used as a wage incentive time standard or for alleviation of a scheduling bottleneck, the time estimates are not exact figures which represent actual performance in every case. If a well-performed work-measurement program results in a time standard of 5 parts an hour being set for a certain assembly task, this does not mean that everyone who works on that task works at a rate of 5 parts an hour. There are likely to be workers who, because of dexterity or youthful stamina, can surpass the rate without undue strain. There are also workers who can work at that pace only for a brief time and do not have the agility to sustain a rate of 5 pieces per hour. Similarly, a work-sampling study to estimate the down time of machines may show that the lathes are not in use 45% of the time, on the average. A closer inspection of the individual lathes may show that down times range from 10% to 90% on individual machines.

The major problem encountered with the use of work-measurement techniques is that management gains additional control over employee activities. In the workers' eyes, management benefits more from this extra degree of control than the workers. For the most part, the members of the work force have little interest in the establishment of accurate production standards. This lack of common goals between labor and management can cause a feeling of animosity which can be a serious threat to management's goal of improving labor productivity. Companies often have a policy that once a time standard is established, management will change the standard only if a methods change is introduced which makes the old time standard obsolete. This policy serves to protect the worker from a slow process of tightening the time standard values each time worker skills improve.

For these reasons caution must be used by managers in considering proposed time standards and the results of work-sampling studies.

Efforts should be made to use new time standards equitably so that a majority of the workers are treated fairly. It is possible that a situation could arise in which few people are actually working within a reasonable range of the new time standard. A significant number may be working substantially above or below the standard. In such cases efforts should be made to find the cause of the variation before the standard is finally adopted and to correct the situation that has caused the disparity.

Finally, it should be recognized that competition in most industries provides an effective feedback on the relative productivity of the work force, in aggregate. A firm will have great difficulty continuing to compete if its methods or work pace are far behind its competitors. In most mature businesses in the U.S., the process of mechanization has proceeded to the point where direct labor costs (those labor costs most amenable to measurement and control) are 12% or less of the sales dollar. Management should recognize that the value of time standards lies not so much in extracting a faster pace or more production from the workers as in their value for estimating, pricing, manpower planning, and scheduling. Management can thus achieve the greatest possible utilization of its investment in inventories and plant and equipment.

5.6   BIBLIOGRAPHY

Aquilano, Nicholas J. "A Physiological Evaluation of Time Standards for Strenuous Work as Set by Stopwatch Time Study and Two Predetermined Motion Time Data Systems," *Industrial Engineering*, September 1968.

————. "Why IE's Can't Measure Fatigue." *Industrial Engineering*, March 1970.

Barnes, Ralph M. *Work Sampling*, 2nd ed. New York: John Wiley & Sons, Inc., 1957.

————. *Motion and Time Study: Design and Measurement of Work*, 6th ed. New York: John Wiley & Sons, Inc., 1968.

Beegle, B. B., and Bricker, T. J. "One-Man Incentive Plan," *Industrial Engineering*, August 1972.

Belcher, D. W. *Wage and Salary Administration*, 2nd ed. Englewood Cliffs, N.J.: Prentice-Hall, Inc., 1962.

Brown, James. "How to Measure Group Performance." *Industrial Engineering*, September 1969.

Burri, George. "A Standard for Measuring Fluctuating Work," *Industrial Engineering*, March 1969.

Cornman, Guy, Jr. "Fatigue Allowances — A Systematic Method." *Industrial Engineering*, April 1970.

Doney, Lloyd, and Gelb, Thomas. "Regression Short-Cuts Cycle-Time Estimating." *Industrial Engineering*, February 1971.

Fein, Mitchell. "Work Measurement: Concepts of Normal Pace." *Industrial Engineering*, September 1972.

————. "Work Measurement Today." *Industrial Engineering*, August 1972.

Frank, Eric. "Low-Cost Standards for Indirect Labor." *Industrial Engineering*, August 1970.

Geisel, John M. "A Method for Measurement and Analysis of Supervisory Work." *Industrial Engineering*, April 1968.

Gibson, David. "Work Sampling Monitors Job-Shop Productivity." *Industrial Engineering*, June 1970.

Herzberg, F., Mausner, B., and Snyderman, B. B. *The Motivation to Work*, 2nd ed. New York: John Wiley & Sons, Inc., 1959.

Jinich, Carlos, and Niebel, Benjamin. "Synthetic Leveling — How Valid?" *Industrial Engineering*, May 1970.

Khalil, Tarek M. "Design Tools and Machines to Fit the Man." *Industrial Engineering*, January 1972.

Konz, Stephan. "Fitting the Job to the Man." *Industrial Engineering*, January 1971.

Mandel, B. J. "Work Sampling In Financial Management — Cost Determination in Post Office Department." *Management Science*, February 1971.

Martin, John. "A Better Performance Rating System." *Industrial Engineering*, August 1970.

Mundel, Marvin E. *Motion and Time Study*. Englewood Cliffs, N.J.: Prentice-Hall, Inc., 1960.

Nadler, Gerald. *Work Design*. Homewood, Ill.: Richard D. Irwin, Inc., 1970.

Niebel, Benjamin W. *Motion and Time Study*, 5th ed. Homewood, Ill.: Richard D. Irwin, Inc., 1972.

Saluto, George, Jr. "How to Pay the Worker Whose Job Changes." *Industrial Engineering*, June 1969.

Thompson, David A., and Applewhite, Philip B. "Objective Effort Level Estimates in Manual Work." *Industrial Engineering*, February 1968.

Travis, Charles. "Auditing Time Standards." *Industrial Engineering*, November 1969.

Wheeler, Kenneth E. "Small Business Eyes the Four-Day Workweek." *Harvard Business Review*, May-June 1970.

Analysis of Unstructured Activities

6.1 INTRODUCTION

This chapter treats the management of work activities in an unstructured setting. The methods and procedures described in Chapter 5 implied an orderly presentation of the work to the worker, such as is normally found in a factory setting. In such a situation, the rate at which work arrives at a work station and the load of work at the time of arrival are carefully planned and controlled. The rapid growth of service industries has complicated the work-measurement task by presenting numerous situations in which the work to be accomplished arrives at the work station at unpredictable times and presents a series of tasks with widely varying work content, and thus variable work times. These conditions (unpredictable workload arrivals of widely varying work content) lead to situations in which work lines form in front of work stations, such as the checkout counters in a supermarket. This chapter presents an approach to managing such unstructured activities in a number of situations.

Waiting-line situations are encountered widely in business. A better understanding of waiting lines would result, in many cases, in increased efficiency, significant cost savings, and a greater knowledge of the service activity being studied. A method is outlined in this chapter through which answers may be obtained to questions about the characteristics of waiting-line systems by the use of time estimates and the tables and charts provided.

The term, *waiting-line system,* should be understood as it is used in this chapter. A waiting-line system is a situation in which servers, behind a counter or in a service facility of some sort, provide service of variable duration to customers who arrive at random or unscheduled times. There are a number of queuing situations in which the waiting time of customers cannot be considered a direct cost to the organization providing the service. Such situations are found in unemployment offices, post offices, banks, auto-rental agencies, information centers, railway or airline ticket counters, barber shops, etc. Nevertheless, business may be lost in many cases if waiting lines become too long. Thus, it is desirable to know how long the waiting lines and the waiting times are likely to be for various facility service rates. On the other hand, engineers waiting at the window of a blueprint room constitute a situation in which both the customer's waiting time and the server's idle time are costly to the organization.

The manager of such waiting-line systems must understand several key notions. No matter how many servers are provided, there is some probability that a large number of customers will arrive and a line will form. Waiting time cannot entirely be eliminated. Alternatively, if few servers are provided and long waiting lines prevail most of the time, the servers will still be idle some of the time.

The objective in applying waiting-line analysis to such systems is to minimize the total of the various costs associated with operating the system. That is, for instance, "What number of servers (in a particular situation) leads to an average waiting time for the customers and an average idle time for the servers, such that the total cost of the system is minimized?" This clearly will depend on the relative costs (in a particular situation) of customers and servers. Utilizing the information available from the tables in Appendix 6-1, particular costs can be applied, as appropriate, in analyzing a specific situation. The examples included in the chapter are intended to illustrate the use of the tables, and to give some idea of the range of their possible applications. It is expected that a familiarity with specific business situations and the information presented here will suggest additional uses not included.

Appendix 6-2 includes families of curves which graphically present the information given in the tables of Appendix 6-1. The curves may be used when the information sought cannot be found directly from the tables. The curves also provide the user with an insight into the dynamics of waiting-line systems not readily apparent from the tables. In solving waiting-line problems, a given user may find one or the other more acceptable or convenient. The mathematical formulas are included in Appendix 6-3. An understanding of the mathematical derivations of the formulas is not a necessary prerequisite for the use of the tables and curves presented. For those who are interested in a more thorough explanation of the theory, the Bibliography presents appropriate source material. Sample exercises are provided for those wishing to test their understanding of the material.

6.2   SCOPE OF APPLICATIONS

The material presented here treats one type of waiting-line situation. Arrivals for service are assumed to follow a Poisson distribution. Service times are exponentially distributed, and arrivals form single queues or lines while waiting for service.[1] Arrivals to the service facility take their place in a single line, and are taken on a first-come, first-served basis as channels in the service facility (for instance, teller windows at a bank) become available. Where more than one channel is provided at a service facility, lines may form in front of each channel. This is not a departure from the single-queue situation as long as the channels are in close physical proximity to one another and customers are free to move into an empty channel as soon as one becomes available.

The condition of statistical equilibrium on which the formulas depend exists only when the ratio of the average arrival rate (A) to a service facility's total average service rate is less than one. Where S is the average service rate for a single service channel and M is the number of channels, the average total service rate (MS) *must* exceed the average arrival rate (A). Therefore $\frac{A}{MS}$ must be less than one.

The portion of queuing theory treated may be used to analyze situations found in manufacturing plants, banks, hospitals, drug stores, cafeterias, supermarkets, toll booths, ticket windows, department stores, government service bureaus, repair shops, barber shops, or computer centers. Other situations which have been treated theoretically (but are not addressed here) include consideration of constant service times, customers who leave the system if they wait a certain length of time, service rates which are dependent upon the queue length, and a variety of other special cases.

6.3   SYMBOLS AND DEFINITIONS

Facility — A total servicing unit. A facility may be composed of several channels or as few as one.

Channel — A servicing point within a facility.

A — Average arrival rate of customers into the system.

S — Average service rate of each service channel.

M — Number of channels in the facility.

MS — Average service rate of the service facility.

n — Number of customers in the system.

P_n — Probability of n customers in the system.

$\bar{n}$ — Average number of customers in the system: those being serviced plus the waiting line.

$\bar{w}$ — Average number of customers waiting in line ($\bar{n} - A/S$).

$\bar{T}_w$ — Average waiting time ($\bar{w}/A$).

[1] For a discussion of the assumptions underlying queuing theory and the derivation of the formulas, see P. M. Morse, *Queues, Inventories and Maintenance* (John Wiley & Sons, New York, 1958).

T_o — Idle-channel time units/unit of facility operating time.
A/MS — Utilization factor.
P_o — Probability of a facility (all channels) being completely idle.

6.4   MEASURABLE CHARACTERISTICS OF A WAITING-LINE SYSTEM

The following characteristics of waiting-line situations are both measurable and of some value for decision-making purposes. The ratio of A/MS, called the utilization factor or service density, is perhaps the most obvious factor over which the decision-maker has control. The total average service rate of the facility (MS) can be changed by adding or removing service units. In some situations S might be altered by methods improvement. The average arrival rate (A) might be altered by scheduling arrivals to some degree, such as staggering lunch periods to reduce congestion in a plant cafeteria.

The average number in the system ($\bar{n}$) may be changed by altering A, M, S, or a subset of them. In the case of lines at water fountains, rest rooms, or other personal facilities, the estimated hourly wages of people waiting, multiplied by $\bar{n}$, gives the total hourly waste cost of the system.

The average number waiting in line ($\bar{w}$) is exclusive of those actually being serviced. In many situations the service time is necessary and should not be considered a waiting-time cost. Lines at blueprint rooms or tool rooms are examples of this type of service system. This contrasts with the system in which the service time comprises a waiting-time cost. Similarly to $\bar{n}$, $\bar{w}$ times the hourly wage gives the hourly cost of the waiting line. In cases where the cost of waiting time cannot be estimated (such as customers waiting in a bank), the average waiting time may be a useful criterion for decision-making.

T_o is the total of idle-channel time units for one service-facility time unit. This means that if the service facility has two channels and $T_o = 1.4$, each service channel will be idle, on the average, 0.7 hour for each hour of operation. The two channels combined give a total of 1.4 hours of channel idle time for each hour that the facility is in operation. This quantity is useful for calculating the cost of idle facility time since T_o times the hourly wage rate of service clerks equals the hourly cost of facility idle time.

6.5   DECISION CRITERIA

A system may be altered by changing M, the number of service channels of average service rate S, if $\bar{n}$ is too long, if the average waiting time is excessive, or if facility idle time (T_o) is excessive. Several other useful criteria are apparent from the curves in Appendix 6-2 as discussed below.

For A/MS equal to or less than 0.80, the occurrence of a line of length n which has a very slight probability of existing might indicate that a shift in arrival rate has transpired. This characteristic is useful where no single distribution of arrival times exists. There may be serveral periods of peaks and lulls in the demands on the service facility. In some such cases a day is actually composed of several arrival distributions. The observance of a line length which has a probability of occurrence of 0.10 or 0.05 could be considered to indicate that action should be taken in the form of adding another service channel. In such situations service personnel perform some other routine work during lull periods, and the problem is one of when they should cease the other work and commence to serve arrivals to the facility. Note that when the formulation of a line of any appreciable length is undesirable, the ratio of A/MS must be approximately 0.80 or below, depending on M.

The average arrival rate can often be found from available records. For instance, the number of blueprint requisitions for a given time period provides an estimate of the arrival rate. The average service rate (S) is usually more difficult to obtain. Suppose a sampling study were arranged whereby the average number in the system $(\bar{n})$ or the average number waiting $(\bar{w})$ could be observed by means of sampling at random times. This parameter could be estimated to a desired degree of statistical significance and used with the curves to estimate A/MS. Knowing M and A, an estimate of S can be found.

There are instances where similar queues form at similar but physically separated service facilities. The average number waiting in the system is materially reduced by simply combining two such service facilities. This is because the overall efficiency of each system is increased by enlarging the system. In the former instance one facility might be idle while the other is accumulating a waiting line. Merging the two systems eliminates the possibility of such a situation.

6.6   DESCRIPTION OF TABLES AND GRAPHS

Twenty-four tables are included in Appendix 6-1. These tables provide a value for any of the desired parameters relating to the steady state of an appropriate waiting-line situation.

Table 6-1   Values of $\bar{n}$ are given for different utilization factors and different numbers of service channels. The utilization factors (from 0.05 to 0.95) are in intervals of 0.05, and values for channels 1 through 10 are provided.

Table 6-2   Values of $\bar{w}$ are given for different utilization factors and different numbers of service channels. The utilization factors (from 0.05 to 0.95) are in intervals of 0.05, and values for channels 1 through 10 are provided.

Table 6-3   Values of T_o are given for different utilization factors and different numbers of service channels. The utilization factors (from

0.05 to 0.95) are in intervals of 0.05, and values for channels 1 through 10 are provided.

Table 6-4   Values of P_o, the probability of the facility being completely idle, are given for different utilization factors and different numbers of service channels. The utilization factors (from 0.05 to 0.95) are in intervals of 0.05, and values for channels 1 through 10 are provided.

Tables 6-5—6-14   These tables show P_n for different utilization factors and different n's. Table 6-5 does this for $M = 1$, Table 6-6 for $M = 2$, and so on, through Table 6-14 for $M = 10$. The P_ns are listed until they are less than 0.01.

Tables 6-15—6-24   show cumulative P_n values.

USE OF THE TABLES   The use of the twenty-four tables in Appendix 6-1 can be illustrated by the following example. Consider a facility with two service channels, an average arrival rate of 70 per hour, and an average service rate of 50 per hour per channel.

The A/MS ratio is thus 0.70. The tables provide the following:

a) Using Table 6-1, the average number of customers in the system $(\bar{n})$ is found to be about 2.73.
b) Using Table 6-2, the average number waiting $(\bar{w})$, excluding those being serviced, is shown to be 1.33.
c) Using Table 6-3, T_o is seen to be 0.60.

$$\left[T_o = M \left(1 - \frac{A}{MS} \right) = 2 \left(1 - 0.7 \right) = 2 \left(0.3 \right) = 0.60 \right]$$

This figure multiplied by the cost per channel of operating the facility will yield the cost of idle time. If each operator earned $2.00 per hour, the cost of idle time would be $1.20 for each hour the two-channel facility operates.

d) Using Table 6-4, an A/MS ratio of 0.70 with two service channels yields a probability of 0.18 that the two servers will be completely idle.

DESCRIPTION OF THE CURVES   The four sets of curves given in Appendix 6-2 could have been used in the above example. The tables were used because they can be read more accurately than the curves. For utilization factors not listed in the tables, however, the graphs provide an alternative approach through interpolation.

6.7   THE ANALYSIS OF WAITING-LINE SYSTEMS

In addition to illustrating the use of the tables in various situations for which they are appropriate, the following problems are intended to represent realistic business situations and to suggest the wide range of problems to which waiting-line analysis may be applied.

NUMERICAL EXAMPLE #1   An insurance company has four claim adjusters in its branch office. People with claims against the company are found to arrive according to a Poisson distribution at an average rate of 20 per eight-hour day. The time that an adjuster spends with a claimant is found to be distributed exponentially with a mean of 40 minutes. Claimants are processed in the order of their appearance. The office manager would like to know 1) how many hours a week an adjuster spends with claimants, 2) how much time, on the average, a claimant spends waiting in the branch office, and 3) how many adjusters are needed to ensure that the waiting time averages between 5-10 minutes.

The Solution of Example #1   The initial situation must first be analyzed. The arrival rate averages 20 per eight-hour day, and the average service rate is calculated as 12 per eight-hour day per adjuster. There are 4 adjusters, so the utilization factor ($\frac{A}{MS}$) is $\frac{20}{12(4)} = 0.42$. This indicates an average waiting line ($\overline{w}$) of 0.078 (from Table 6-2) and, consequently, an average waiting time ($\overline{T}_w = \frac{\overline{w}}{A} = \frac{0.078}{20}$) of 0.0039 of an eight-hour day, or 1.87 minutes per arrival. It appears that the office manager is providing service to claimants beyond what may be required. This can be checked by determining the amount of time an adjuster spends with claimants during the day. T_o for the facility is 2.32, which appears to indicate excessive idle time, since $\frac{2.32}{4} = 58\%$ of each adjuster's time.

If the office manager reassigns one adjuster, what is the result? The average arrival and service rates are unchanged, but the number of channels is reduced to 3. The utilization factor increases to $\frac{20}{12(3)} = 0.55$. The average waiting line associated with this factor is 0.3573. The average waiting time for a claimant is then $\frac{0.3573}{20}$, or about 9 minutes. Each adjuster would now spend $\frac{1.35}{3}$, or 45% of the time, not seeing claimants. This situation seems to be more reasonable.

When the system is tested with only 2 adjusters, the average waiting time increases to 1 hour and 40 minutes. It thus appears that the office manager should assign three adjusters.

NUMERICAL EXAMPLE #2   There are four tool rooms serving a relatively large and active shop area. Each tool room is manned by one attendant. The average arrival rates and service rates are the same for each tool room and are as follows:

A = 10.9 arrivals per hour, following a Poisson distribution

S = 14.6 services per hour, with the duration of service times following an exponential distribution

Though the relationships between the average number of arrivals and the average service capacity of each tool room seem to indicate that a line should rarely exist, most of the time a line of some length has been observed. Further, there are times when there is no line and the attendant has nothing to do of any consequence. Management is concerned over this situation because of the lost production involved in having machines idle while machinists are waiting in line for tools and other equipment, and because there are times when tool room attendants are not performing any work.

Costs are given as follows:

C_1 = cost of waiting time = $5.15/hour

C_2 = cost of channel idle time = $2.10/hour

The Solution of Example #2   For the given situation, A/MS for each facility ($M = 1$) is $10.9/14.6$, or 0.75. Entering Tables 6-2 and 6-3 with $A/MS = 0.75$ and $M = 1$, it is observed that $\bar{w} = 2.25$ and $T_o = 0.25$. Then[2]

$C_1 (\bar{w})$ $= (5.15) (2.25) = \$11.58$

$C_2 (T_o)$ $= (2.10) (0.25) = \underline{\quad 0.53}$

$$\text{Waste cost} = \$12.11/\text{hour for each tool room}$$

$$\underline{\times \quad 4 \quad}$$

$$\text{Total waste cost} = \$48.44/\text{hour for the system}$$

The following possibilities may now be considered: 1) add attendants to the present tool rooms, or 2) combine the rooms physically, without increasing the number of attendants. The possible combinations are 1 & 3, 2 & 2, or all 4 together.

Analysis of the alternative solutions:

1a) Add one attendant to each tool room:

Now $M = 2$. Therefore $A/MS = 10.9/(2 \times 14.6) = 0.375$. Entering Tables 6-2 and 6-3 with the new M and A/MS figures, $\bar{w} = 0.13$ and $T_o = 1.25$. Hence,

$C_1 (\bar{w})$ $= (5.15) (0.13) = \$0.67$

$C_2 (T_o)$ $= (2.10) (1.25) = \underline{\quad 2.63}$

$$\text{New waste cost} = \$3.30 \text{ per tool room per hour}$$

$$\text{New system waste cost} = (4) (3.30) = \$13.20 \text{ per hour}$$

[2] The cost of waiting time = $C \times \bar{Tw} \times A = C \times \dfrac{\bar{w}}{A} \times A = C \times \bar{w}$.

This is a step in the right direction, so try adding two men to each tool room.

1b) Add two men to each tool room:

Now $M = 3$, and the new $A/MS = 10.9/(3 \times 14.6) = 0.25$. Entering Tables 6-2 and 6-3 as before with the new values of M and A/MS, $\overline{w} = 0.01$ and $T_o = 2.25$. Thus,

$$C_1\,(\overline{w}) \;\; = (5.15)\,(0.01) = \$\;.05$$

$$C_2\,(T_o) = (2.10)\,(2.25) = \underline{\;\;4.73\;\;}$$

Waste cost = \$4.78 per tool room per hour

New system waste cost = (4) (4.78) = 19.12 per hour

This is higher than was obtained for the addition of one man per tool room. Adding two men per tool room is clearly not advantageous, and adding more than two would increase costs still more.

2a) The possibility of combining one or more tool rooms will now be evaluated. Consider a combination of one single tool room and one triple facility. The waste cost per hour of the single operation is the same as in the original situation, namely \$12.11/hour. For the triple tool room, A/MS is still 0.75, since three similar operations have been combined, but now M = 3 instead of 1. Entering the tables with $A/MS = 0.75$ and $M = 3$, $\overline{w} = 1.70$ and $T_o = 0.75$. Thus,

$$C_1\,(\overline{w}) \;\; = (5.15)\,(1.70) = \$\;\;8.76$$

$$C_2\,(T_o) = (2.10)\,(0.75) = \underline{\;\;1.58\;\;}$$

New waste cost = \$10.34 for the triple crib

Hence, total hourly waste cost for the system = 10.34 + 12.11 = \$22.45. This solution results in a higher waste cost than the addition of one man to each crib.

2b) The next step is to evaluate combining the tool rooms in a two-two manner. This solution is obtained in a manner similar to the one-three combination, but using M = 2 for each of the new tool rooms. The total waste cost per hour for each facility is \$10.98. Hence, the total cost of the two-two system is \$10.98 $\times$ 2 = \$21.96 — about the same as the one-three system.

2c) Finally, it might be possible to combine all four cribs into one large crib. Now only one crib must be evaluated, in which A/MS is still 0.75, but M = 4. Entering the tables as before, $\overline{w} = 1.5$, and $T_o = 1.0$; hence:

$$C_1 \; (\overline{w}) \;\; = (5.15) \; (1.5) \;\; = \$7.73$$

$$C_2 \; (T_o) \;\; = (2.10) \; (1.0) \;\; = \;\; \underline{2.10}$$

$$\text{New waste cost} = \$9.83$$

The total waste cost of \$9.83 per hour is the lowest figure obtained. Note that this reduction was obtained by combining a number of small facilities into one large facility.

The manager must now choose among the several alternatives. Where a combination of tool rooms is not possible, the alternative of adding a man to each room still remains.

NUMERICAL EXAMPLE #3   Consider that the service window in an inventory storeroom has been found to have an average arrival rate of 10.7 persons per hour, and that the arrivals are Poisson distributed. The time required for performance of the service function has been found to be exponentially distributed. The facility has been operated for a time with one attendant.

The prevailing average service time is 3.6 minutes per arrival at the storeroom window. At peak periods during the day, as well as on unpredictable occasions, queues are forming at the window, causing delays in production and the loss of productive time for those who are waiting.

A methods department supervisor in the plant has estimated that it would be possible to study the storeroom layout, arrangements, handling of paperwork, etc. and possibly reduce the average service rate. From past experience he estimates that the average service time can be cut by at least a minute. He also estimates that such a study would cost about six hundred dollars in wages and overhead for study personnel. He further states that it will be 6-8 months before his overworked staff can get to this job.

The questions which may be answered are as follows:

1) How serious, in terms of cost, is the present situation?
2) How much may be lost in the 6-8 months' estimated time lapse before improvement can be expected from methods analysis?
3) How much would the service time have to be reduced in order to warrant the estimated cost of the study?
4) If an extra service attendant were hired on a temporary basis to be used until some more definite action can be taken, how would the storeroom situation be affected? Is it more economical to keep the extra attendant than have the study done in the next few months to eliminate the need? (It is assumed here that the service rate will be lowered by about the amount estimated if the study is made.)

The wage rate per hour for machinists, the personnel normally utilizing the storeroom window, is \$5.78/hour. The wage rate for the storeroom attendant is \$2.75/hour.

The Solution of Example #3   Consider the several questions posed earlier.

1) How serious is the present situation? Since there is only one attendant, this is a single-channel queuing situation involving an average arrival rate (A) of 10.7 per hour, and an average service rate (S) of 60/3.6 or 16.7 per hour. The A/S ratio is found to be 10.7/16.7, or 0.64.

$$\bar{w} = 1.14$$

$$T_o = 0.36$$

$$C_1 = \$5.78$$

$$C_2 = \$2.75$$

$$C_1 (\bar{w}) = \$6.59$$

$$C_2 (T_o) = \underline{0.99}$$

$$\text{Total} = \$7.58/\text{hour}$$

(Note: Waiting time cost = 85% of total waste cost.)

2) How much will be lost in 6 months? With the reduced service time after motion study,

$$S_2 = \frac{60}{2.6} = 23.1$$

$$\frac{A}{S_2} \text{ becomes } \frac{10.7}{23.1} = 0.464, \text{ or } 0.46$$

$$\bar{w} = 0.39$$

$$T_o = 0.54$$

$$C_1 (\bar{w}) = \$2.26$$

$$C_2 (T_o) = \underline{1.49}$$

$$\text{Total} = \$3.75/\text{hour (new waste cost)}$$

Each hour the study is not done, the waste cost = \$7.58 – \$3.75 = \$3.83 in potential savings. This amounts to about \$150/week.

3) What reduction in service rate would be needed to justify the study?

$$\frac{\$600.00 \text{ (cost of study)}}{2000 \text{ (hours)}} = \$0.30/\text{hour}$$

It is assumed that repayment is one year. Since waiting time can be expected to account for around 85% of waste cost, and since decreasing waiting time increases idle time and attendant costs, determine $\frac{A}{S}$ in order to save approximately \$0.36/hour on waiting-time costs. Thus, \$6.59 (present $\overline{w}$ costs) – \$0.36 = \$6.23 (the new cost allowable for $\overline{w}$) and \$6.23 ÷ \$5.78 = 1.08 (required $\overline{w}$). Enter Table 6-2: for $\overline{w}$ = 1.08, M = 1, read $\frac{A}{S}$ = 0.63.

$A = 10.7$ customers/hour

$$S = \frac{10.7}{0.63} = 17 \text{ customers/hour}$$

Therefore: $\dfrac{60 \text{ minutes/hour}}{17 \text{ customers/hour}} = 3.5$ minutes/customer.

To evaluate 3.5 minutes/customer average service time:

$\dfrac{A}{S} = 0.63$, and $\qquad\qquad \overline{w} = 1.08$ (as previously determined)

$$T_o = 0.37$$

$$C_1\ (\overline{w}) = \$6.24$$

$$C_2\ (T_o) = \underline{\quad 1.02 \quad}$$

$$\text{Total} = \$7.26$$

This results in savings of: \$7.58 – \$7.26 = \$0.32/hour. By reducing average service time from 3.6 minutes to 3.5 minutes, (a reduction of less than 3%), waste cost has been reduced by \$0.32/hour. A reduction in service time of only 0.1 minute/customer would thus pay for the cost of the study. Any reduction in the average service time greater than 0.1 minute would represent savings in the system.

4) Consider the temporary use of an additional service attendant.

$$\frac{A}{MS} = \frac{10.7}{2(16.7)} = 0.32, \text{ for } M = 2$$

$\overline{w} = 0.08;\ C_1\ (\overline{w}) = \$0.46$

$T_o = 1.36;\ C_2\ (T_o) = \underline{\quad 3.74 \quad}$

$\qquad\qquad\qquad\qquad \$4.20$ (waste cost/hour)

This represents a saving of \$3.38/hour contrasted with the present situation. Therefore, adding a temporary man is advantageous. Since estimated waste cost after the time study is less than waste cost after adding a man, the study should be undertaken as soon as possible.

6.8   SUMMARY

The procedures outlined in this chapter provide an approach to planning and controlling unstructured work activities in a wide range of business situations. This extends the conventional work-measurement techniques, which were developed in repetitive factory settings, to the work-planning problems inherent in the fast-growing service industries.

6.9   BIBLIOGRAPHY

Ackoff, R. L., and Sasieni, M. W. *Fundamentals of Operations Research*. New York: John Wiley & Sons, Inc., 1968.

Bowman, E. H., and Fetter, R. B. *Analysis for Production Management*, 3rd ed. Homewood, Ill.: Richard D. Irwin, Inc., 1967.

Churchman, C. West, Ackoff, R. L., and Arnoff, E. L. *Introduction to Operations Research*. New York: John Wiley & Sons, Inc., 1957.

Feller, W. *An Introduction to Probability Theory and Its Applications*, 2nd ed. New York: John Wiley & Sons, Inc., 1960.

Friedman, L., Sasieni, M. W., and Yaspan, A. *Operations Research*. New York: John Wiley & Sons, Inc., 1964.

Fry, T. C. *Probability and Its Engineering Uses*. New York: D. Van Nostrand Co., 1928.

Hillier, F. S., and Lieberman, G. J. *Introduction to Operations Research*, 2nd ed. San Francisco: Holden-Day, Inc., 1975.

Morse, P. M. *Queues, Inventories and Maintenance*. New York: John Wiley & Sons, Inc., 1958.

Palm, D. C. "The Assignment of Workers in Servicing Automatic Machines." *Journal of Industrial Engineering*, January-February 1958.

Wagner, H. M. *Principles of Operations Research*, 2nd ed. Englewood Cliffs, N. J.: Prentice-Hall, Inc., 1975.

PROBLEM SET

1. A barber shop has 5 chairs and 4 barbers. The customer arrivals follow a Poisson distribution, with an average of 12 per hour, and the service times are exponentially distributed with an average of 15 minutes for a haircut.

   a. Determine the utilization of the 4 barbers, the average number of customers in the shop, the average number of customers waiting for a haircut, and the average customer-waiting time.
   b. How will the addition of another barber affect each of the statistics in a?
   c. Two of the 4 barbers wish to take their vacations during the same week. What effect will this have?

2. A new service station on the turnpike will service only northbound cars. The manager estimates that customers will arrive every 4 minutes and will require 6 minutes to service. The arrivals are Poisson distributed, and the service times are exponentially distributed. How many pumps should be installed if the manager desires a utilization rate of 0.75? What percentage of the time will the pumps be idle? What is the likelihood that a customer will have to wait for service?

3. A discount store has 6 checkout lanes open. Shoppers arrive at the lanes in a Poisson fashion, one every minute, and the service times are exponentially distributed with a mean of three minutes.

   a. What are the chances that a customer will have to wait for service?
   b. What percentage of the time can each checkout clerk expect to be idle?

4. A computer programmer's task is to help engineers debug their computer programs. Engineers with programs to be corrected arrive according to a Poisson distribution with an average rate of one each hour, and on the average it takes 48 minutes to debug a program. The debugging times follow an exponential distribution.

   a. On the average, how many programs will be in a programmer's backlog of work?
   b. How much time per 8-hour workday can the programmer expect to have available to devote to new software system design?

5. An auto-rental agency has two employees at its airport counter. Customers arrive at an average rate of 18 per hour in a Poisson fashion. The service times are exponentially distributed, with a mean service rate of 15 per hour.

   a. What is the probability that a customer will have to wait for service?
   b. What is the expected waiting time?
   c. Each additional customer gives the agency $5 additional profit. If the average waiting time overall could be reduced 75%, two more customers per hour would be drawn from competing auto-rental agencies. Should additional employees be hired for $4 an hour?

6. The postmaster of a large metropolitan post office has decided to place two clerks in the lobby to answer typical Christmas season mailing questions from its customers. Last year this information booth was tested and the response was most favorable. The postmaster predicted that during the peak part of the day customers would arrive at the desk at an average rate of 27 per hour, following a Poisson distribution. Last year the time required to answer questions and make mailing suggestions was exponentially distributed with a mean of 4 minutes. If 2 clerks are placed in the lobby for 4 hours each day, the postmaster would like to know:

   a. What is the average time that each clerk will spend helping the customers?
   b. What are the chances that a customer will have to wait?

    c.   What will be the average waiting time?

    d.   How many clerks should be used to ensure that the waiting time averages less than 4 minutes?

    e.   Will the arrival pattern change as more clerks are added?

    f.   How many clerks would you recommend?

7. An appliance repair shop has two clerks working at its customer counter. One clerk handles only incoming appliances to be repaired; the other clerk handles only repaired appliances being picked up by customers. The service times for both incoming and outgoing appliances are exponentially distributed with an average time of 3 minutes. The arrival of customers with appliances to be repaired is Poisson distributed with a mean of 16 per hour. The arrival of customers to pick up repaired appliances is also Poisson distributed with an average of one every 4 minutes.

    a.   How would the average waiting time for both types of customers be changed if each clerk could handle either transaction?

    b.   What if this change could be made only by stretching the average service for both to 3.48 minutes?

8. Offloading and loading operations on a post office platform are affected by saturation problems since dock congestion can seriously slow down the throughput of the system. If a large number of mail sacks, carts, etc. are stacked around the facility, it may be extremely difficult and slow to service the arriving vehicles. In order to minimize the possibility of overload, special attention must be placed upon designating the size of the dock facility and selecting the appropriate number of dock spaces.

    A dock superintendent found that, on the average, collection vehicles were arriving in a Poisson pattern at a rate of 42 vehicles per hour. The mean time for one man to unload the vehicle and transport the contents away from the dock space was exponentially distributed with a mean of 5 minutes. The superintendent wished to determine the number of docks which should be reserved for collection vehicles such that the probability of an arriving vehicle waiting would be less than 0.25.

9. The results of a recent study covering the two windows at the Big Star post office are to be utilized in the planning of a new lobby facility. The two windows offer the same services and are considered to be independent of one another. Incoming customers choose the queue they enter at random, regardless of the queue length. The following characteristics were found:

    a.   Each window is fed by a separate queue.

    b.   Customer arrivals to the lobby are Poisson distributed with an average time of 0.66 minute between one arrival and the next.

    c.   Service time is the same at each window and is exponentially distributed with a mean of one minute per service.

    d.   Probability of the two-window system being idle is 0.0625.

    e.   Average number of customers waiting in both queues is 4.5.

    f.   Average time a customer spends in a queue before being served is 3.0 minutes.

    g.   Average number of customers in the system is 6.0.

The postmaster at Big Star has been anxious to have the new lobby facility designed such that the operation characteristics would be more attractive to the customers. Would a system consisting of a single queue feeding two lobby windows accomplish his objectives? Calculate the characteristics stated in a-g.

10. The manager of the break-bulk facility of the Dominion Trucking Company wants to determine the optimal crew size for unloading-platform operations, given that a recent study revealed that:

    a.   Trucks arrive according to a Poisson distribution at an average rate of 2.25 per hour.

b. The unloading time varies inversely with the number of workers in the crew.

c. The average unloading rate is one truck per man-hour, with exponentially distributed unloading times.

d. The dock crew wage equals $4.00 per hour per crew member.

e. The cost of an idle truck and driver waiting to be offloaded equals $30.00 per hour.

The manager employs the entire crew on the unloading operations of a single truck. Determine the optimal crew size on the basis of minimizing total waste cost.

APPENDIX 6-1
Tables of Waiting-Line Parameters[3]

Symbols:

M = Number of channels of service
n = Number of persons waiting and being serviced (number in system)
$\overline{n}$ = Average or expected number of persons in system
$\overline{w}$ = Average number of persons waiting (in addition to those being serviced)
P_o = Probability that the service facility is idle
T_o = Total idle service hours per hour of operation
P_n = Probability of n customers in the system
A/MS = Utilization factor (service density)

[3] For random arrivals and exponential service times.

TABLE 6-1 Table of $\bar{n}$

$\dfrac{A}{MS}$	$M = 1$	$M = 2$	$M = 3$	$M = 4$	$M = 5$
0.05	0.0526	0.1003	0.1500	0.2000	0.2500
0.10	0.1111	0.2020	0.3004	0.4001	0.5000
0.15	0.1765	0.3069	0.4520	0.6006	0.7502
0.20	0.2500	0.4167	0.6061	0.8024	1.0010
0.25	0.3333	0.5333	0.7647	1.0068	1.2534
0.30	0.4286	0.6602	0.9300	1.2149	1.5086
0.35	0.5385	0.8080	1.1051	1.4325	1.7696
0.40	0.6667	0.9532	1.2941	1.6605	2.0398
0.45	0.8182	1.1285	1.5022	1.9052	2.3243
0.50	1.0000	1.3333	1.7368	2.1739	2.6303
0.55	1.2222	1.5777	2.0073	2.4770	2.9682
0.60	1.5000	1.8743	2.3313	2.8295	3.3527
0.65	1.8571	2.2653	2.7282	3.3362	3.8050
0.70	2.3333	2.7298	3.2301	3.8258	4.3523
0.75	3.0000	3.4286	3.9528	4.5282	5.1353
0.80	4.0000	4.5172	4.9827	5.5848	6.2154
0.85	5.6667	6.1253	6.6806	7.2873	7.9542
0.90	9.0000	9.4709	10.0376	10.6866	11.3919
0.95	19.0000	19.3865	19.3825	20.2433	21.3876

$\dfrac{A}{MS}$	$M = 6$	$M = 7$	$M = 8$	$M = 9$	$M = 10$
0.05	0.3000	0.3500	0.4000	0.4500	0.5000
0.10	0.6000	0.7000	0.8000	0.9000	1.0000
0.15	0.9001	1.0500	1.2000	1.3500	1.5000
0.20	1.2004	1.4002	1.6001	1.8000	2.0000
0.25	1.5016	1.7508	2.0004	2.2502	2.5001
0.30	1.8048	2.1027	2.4015	2.7009	3.0005
0.35	2.1121	2.4575	2.8047	3.1530	3.5019
0.40	2.4266	2.8180	3.2123	3.6085	4.0059
0.45	2.7533	3.1887	3.6283	4.0709	4.5155
0.50	3.0991	3.5762	4.0590	4.5461	5.0361
0.55	3.4745	3.9907	4.5143	5.0434	5.5767
0.60	3.8949	4.4476	5.0093	5.5779	6.1520
0.65	4.3846	4.9712	5.5683	6.1736	6.7855
0.70	4.9840	5.6017	6.2314	6.8706	7.5174
0.75	5.7650	6.4114	7.0709	7.7411	8.4198
0.80	6.8711	7.5438	8.2306	8.9289	9.6367
0.85	8.6363	9.3329	10.0446	10.7684	11.5025
0.90	12.0611	12.7796	13.5138	14.2608	15.0186
0.95	22.1376	22.8756	23.6299	24.3974	25.1760

TABLE 6-2 Table of $\overline{w}$

$\frac{A}{MS}$	$M = 1$	$M = 2$	$M = 3$	$M = 4$	$M = 5$
0.05	0.0026	0.0003	0.0000	0.0000	0.0000
0.10	0.0111	0.0020	0.0004	0.0001	0.0000
0.15	0.0265	0.0069	0.0020	0.0006	0.0002
0.20	0.0500	0.0167	0.0061	0.0024	0.0010
0.25	0.0833	0.0333	0.0147	0.0068	0.0034
0.30	0.1286	0.0602	0.0300	0.0149	0.0086
0.35	0.1885	0.1080	0.0551	0.0325	0.0196
0.40	0.2667	0.1532	0.0941	0.0605	0.0398
0.45	0.3682	0.2285	0.1522	0.1052	0.0743
0.50	0.5000	0.3333	0.2368	0.1739	0.1303
0.55	0.6722	0.4777	0.3573	0.2770	0.2182
0.60	0.9000	0.6743	0.5313	0.4295	0.3527
0.65	1.2071	0.9653	0.7782	0.7362	0.5550
0.70	1.6333	1.3298	1.1301	1.0258	0.8523
0.75	2.2500	1.9286	1.7028	1.5282	1.3853
0.80	3.2000	2.9172	2.5827	2.3848	2.2154
0.85	4.8167	4.4253	4.1306	3.8873	3.7042
0.90	8.1000	7.6709	7.3376	7.0866	6.8919
0.95	18.0500	17.4865	17.1325	16.4433	16.6376

$\frac{A}{MS}$	$M = 6$	$M = 7$	$M = 8$	$M = 9$	$M = 10$
0.05	0.0000	0.0000	0.0000	0.0000	0.0000
0.10	0.0000	0.0000	0.0000	0.0000	0.0000
0.15	0.0000	0.0000	0.0000	0.0000	0.0000
0.20	0.0004	0.0002	0.0001	0.0000	0.0000
0.25	0.0016	0.0008	0.0004	0.0002	0.0001
0.30	0.0048	0.0027	0.0015	0.0009	0.0005
0.35	0.0121	0.0075	0.0047	0.0030	0.0019
0.40	0.0266	0.0180	0.0123	0.0085	0.0059
0.45	0.0533	0.0387	0.0283	0.0209	0.0155
0.50	0.0991	0.0762	0.0590	0.0460	0.0361
0.55	0.1745	0.1407	0.1143	0.0934	0.0767
0.60	0.2948	0.2476	0.2093	0.1779	0.1519
0.65	0.4846	0.4212	0.3683	0.3236	0.2855
0.70	0.7839	0.7017	0.6314	0.5705	0.5174
0.75	1.2650	1.1614	1.0709	0.9911	0.9198
0.80	2.0711	1.9438	1.8306	1.7289	1.6367
0.85	3.5363	3.3829	3.2446	3.1184	3.0026
0.90	6.6611	6.4796	6.3138	6.1608	6.0186
0.95	16.4376	16.2256	16.0299	15.8474	15.6760

TABLE 6-3 Table of T_o

$\frac{A}{MS}$	$M = 1$	$M = 2$	$M = 3$	$M = 4$	$M = 5$
0.05	0.9500	1.9000	2.8500	3.8000	4.7500
0.10	0.9000	1.8000	2.7000	3.6000	4.5000
0.15	0.8500	1.7000	2.5500	3.4000	4.2500
0.20	0.8000	1.6000	2.4000	3.2000	4.0000
0.25	0.7500	1.5000	2.2500	3.0000	3.7500
0.30	0.7000	1.4000	2.1000	2.8000	3.5000
0.35	0.6500	1.3000	1.9500	2.6000	3.2500
0.40	0.6000	1.2000	1.8000	2.4000	3.0000
0.45	0.5500	1.1000	1.6500	2.2000	2.7500
0.50	0.5000	1.0000	1.5000	2.0000	2.5000
0.55	0.4500	0.9000	1.3500	1.8000	2.2500
0.60	0.4000	0.8000	1.2000	1.6000	2.0000
0.65	0.3500	0.7000	1.0500	1.4000	1.7500
0.70	0.3000	0.6000	0.9000	1.2000	1.5000
0.75	0.2500	0.5000	0.7500	1.0000	1.2500
0.80	0.2000	0.4000	0.6000	0.8000	1.0000
0.85	0.1500	0.3000	0.4500	0.6000	0.7500
0.90	0.1000	0.2000	0.3000	0.4000	0.5000
0.95	0.0500	0.1000	0.1500	0.2000	0.2500

$\frac{A}{MS}$	$M = 6$	$M = 7$	$M = 8$	$M = 9$	$M = 10$
0.05	5.7000	6.6500	7.6000	8.5500	9.5000
0.10	5.4000	6.3000	7.2000	8.1000	9.0000
0.15	5.1000	5.9500	6.8000	7.6500	8.5000
0.20	4.8000	5.6000	6.4000	7.2000	8.0000
0.25	4.5000	5.2500	6.0000	6.7500	7.5000
0.30	4.2000	4.9000	5.6000	6.3000	7.0000
0.35	3.9000	4.5500	5.2000	5.8500	6.5000
0.40	3.6000	4.2000	4.8000	5.4000	6.0000
0.45	3.3000	3.8500	4.4000	4.9500	5.5000
0.50	3.0000	3.5000	4.0000	4.5000	5.0000
0.55	2.7000	3.1500	3.6000	4.0500	4.5000
0.60	2.4000	2.8000	3.2000	3.6000	4.0000
0.65	2.1000	2.4500	2.8000	3.1500	3.5000
0.70	1.8000	2.1000	2.4000	2.7000	3.0000
0.75	1.5000	1.7500	2.0000	2.2500	2.5000
0.80	1.2000	1.4000	1.6000	1.8000	2.0000
0.85	0.9000	1.0500	1.2000	1.3500	1.5000
0.90	0.6000	0.7000	0.8000	0.9000	1.0000
0.95	0.3000	0.3500	0.4000	0.4500	0.5000

TABLE 6-4 Table of P_o

$\frac{A}{MS}$	$M = 1$	$M = 2$	$M = 3$	$M = 4$	$M = 5$
0.05	0.9500	0.9048	0.8607	0.8187	0.7788
0.10	0.9000	0.8182	0.7407	0.6703	0.6065
0.15	0.8500	0.7391	0.6373	0.5487	0.4724
0.20	0.8000	0.6667	0.5479	0.4491	0.3678
0.25	0.7500	0.6000	0.4706	0.3673	0.2863
0.30	0.7000	0.5385	0.4035	0.3002	0.2228
0.35	0.6500	0.4815	0.3451	0.2449	0.1731
0.40	0.6000	0.4286	0.2941	0.1993	0.1343
0.45	0.5500	0.3793	0.2496	0.1616	0.1039
0.50	0.5000	0.3333	0.2105	0.1304	0.0801
0.55	0.4500	0.2903	0.1762	0.1046	0.0614
0.60	0.4000	0.2500	0.1460	0.0831	0.0466
0.65	0.3500	0.2121	0.1193	0.0651	0.0350
0.70	0.3000	0.1765	0.0957	0.0502	0.0259
0.75	0.2500	0.1429	0.0748	0.0377	0.0187
0.80	0.2000	0.1111	0.0562	0.0273	0.0130
0.85	0.1500	0.0811	0.0396	0.0186	0.0085
0.90	0.1000	0.0526	0.0249	0.0113	0.0050
0.95	0.0500	0.0256	0.0118	0.0051	0.0022

$\frac{A}{MS}$	$M = 6$	$M = 7$	$M = 8$	$M = 9$	$M = 10$
0.05	0.7408	0.7047	0.6703	0.6376	0.6065
0.10	0.5488	0.4966	0.4493	0.4066	0.3679
0.15	0.4066	0.3499	0.3012	0.2592	0.2231
0.20	0.3012	0.2466	0.2019	0.1653	0.1353
0.25	0.2231	0.1738	0.1353	0.1054	0.0821
0.30	0.1652	0.1224	0.0907	0.0672	0.0498
0.35	0.1222	0.0862	0.0608	0.0428	0.0302
0.40	0.0903	0.0606	0.0407	0.0273	0.0183
0.45	0.0666	0.0426	0.0272	0.0174	0.0111
0.50	0.0490	0.0298	0.0182	0.0110	0.0067
0.55	0.0358	0.0208	0.0121	0.0070	0.0040
0.60	0.0260	0.0144	0.0080	0.0044	0.0024
0.65	0.0187	0.0099	0.0052	0.0028	0.0015
0.70	0.0132	0.0067	0.0034	0.0017	0.0009
0.75	0.0091	0.0044	0.0021	0.0010	0.0005
0.80	0.0061	0.0028	0.0013	0.0006	0.0003
0.85	0.0038	0.0017	0.0008	0.0003	0.0001
0.90	0.0021	0.0009	0.0004	0.0002	0.0001
0.95	0.0009	0.0004	0.0002	0.0001	0.0000

TABLE 6-5 Values of P_n for n from 0-40, $M = 1$

n	.05	.10	.15	.20	.25	.30	.35	.40	.45	.50	.55	.60	.65	.70	.75	.80	.85	.90	.95	n
0	.95	.90	.85	.80	.75	.70	.65	.60	.55	.50	.45	.40	.35	.30	.25	.20	.15	.10	.05	0
1	.05	.09	.13	.16	.19	.21	.23	.24	.25	.25	.25	.24	.23	.21	.19	.16	.13	.09	.05	1
2		.01	.02	.03	.05	.06	.08	.10	.11	.13	.14	.14	.15	.15	.14	.13	.11	.08	.05	2
3				.01	.01	.02	.03	.04	.05	.06	.08	.09	.10	.10	.11	.10	.09	.07	.04	3
4						.01	.01	.02	.02	.03	.04	.05	.06	.07	.08	.08	.08	.07	.04	4
5									.01	.02	.02	.03	.04	.05	.06	.07	.07	.06	.04	5
6										.01	.01	.02	.03	.04	.04	.05	.06	.05	.04	6
7											.01	.01	.02	.02	.03	.04	.05	.05	.03	7
8												.01	.01	.02	.02	.03	.04	.04	.03	8
9													.01	.01	.02	.03	.03	.04	.03	9
10														.01	.01	.02	.03	.03	.03	10
11														.01	.01	.02	.03	.03	.03	11
12															.01	.01	.02	.03	.03	12
13															.01	.01	.02	.02	.03	13
14																.01	.01	.02	.02	14
15																.01	.01	.02	.02	15
16																	.01	.02	.02	16
17																	.01	.01	.02	17
18																	.01	.01	.02	18
19																		.01	.02	19
20																		.01	.02	20
21																			.02	21
22																			.02	22
23																			.02	23
24																			.01	24
25																			.01	25
26																			.01	26
27																			.01	27
28																			.01	28
29																			.01	29
30																			.01	30
31																			.01	31
32																			.01	32
33																			.01	33
34																			.01	34
35																			.01	35
36																			.01	36
37																			.01	37
38																			.01	38
39																			.01	39
40																			.01	40

Utilization factor (A/MS)

TABLE 6-6 Values of P_n for n from 0-40, $M = 2$

n									Utilization factor (A/MS)										
	.05	.10	.15	.20	.25	.30	.35	.40	.45	.50	.55	.60	.65	.70	.75	.80	.85	.90	.95
0	.90	.82	.74	.67	.60	.54	.48	.43	.38	.33	.29	.25	.21	.18	.14	.11	.08	.05	.03
1	.09	.16	.22	.27	.30	.32	.34	.34	.34	.33	.32	.30	.28	.25	.21	.18	.14	.09	.05
2		.02	.03	.05	.08	.10	.12	.14	.15	.17	.18	.18	.18	.17	.16	.14	.12	.09	.05
3			.01	.01	.02	.03	.04	.05	.07	.08	.10	.11	.12	.12	.12	.11	.10	.08	.04
4						.01	.01	.02	.03	.04	.05	.06	.08	.08	.09	.09	.08	.07	.04
5							.01	.01	.01	.02	.03	.04	.05	.06	.07	.07	.07	.06	.04
6								.01	.01	.01	.02	.02	.03	.04	.05	.06	.06	.06	.04
7										.01	.01	.01	.02	.03	.04	.05	.05	.05	.04
8												.01	.01	.02	.03	.04	.04	.05	.03
9												.01	.01	.01	.02	.03	.04	.04	.03
10													.01	.01	.02	.02	.03	.04	.03
11														.01	.01	.02	.03	.03	.03
12															.01	.01	.02	.03	.03
13															.01	.01	.02	.03	.03
14															.01	.01	.01	.02	.02
15																.01	.01	.02	.02
16																	.01	.02	.02
17																	.01	.02	.02
18																	.01	.01	.02
19																		.01	.02
20																		.01	.02
21																		.01	.01
22																			.01
23																			.01
24																			.01
25																			.01
26																			.01
27																			.01
28																			.01
29																			.01
30																			.01
31																			.01
32																			.01
33																			.01
34																			.01
35																			.01
36																			.01
37																			.01
38																			.01
39																			.01
40																			.01

TABLE 6-7 Values of P_n for n from 0-40, $M = 3$

n	.05	.10	.15	.20	.25	.30	.35	.40	.45	.50	.55	.60	.65	.70	.75	.80	.85	.90	.95	n
0	.86	.74	.64	.55	.47	.40	.35	.29	.25	.21	.18	.15	.12	.10	.07	.06	.04	.02	.01	0
1	.13	.22	.29	.33	.35	.36	.36	.35	.34	.32	.29	.26	.23	.20	.17	.13	.10	.07	.03	1
2	.01	.03	.06	.10	.13	.16	.19	.21	.23	.24	.24	.24	.23	.21	.19	.16	.13	.09	.05	2
3			.01	.02	.03	.05	.07	.08	.10	.12	.13	.14	.15	.15	.14	.13	.11	.08	.05	3
4					.01	.01	.02	.03	.05	.06	.07	.09	.10	.10	.11	.10	.09	.07	.04	4
5							.01	.01	.02	.03	.04	.05	.06	.07	.08	.08	.08	.07	.04	5
6								.01	.01	.01	.02	.03	.04	.05	.06	.07	.07	.06	.04	6
7										.01	.01	.02	.03	.04	.04	.05	.06	.05	.04	7
8											.01	.01	.02	.02	.03	.04	.05	.05	.04	8
9												.01	.01	.02	.03	.03	.05	.04	.03	9
10													.01	.01	.02	.03	.04	.04	.03	10
11														.01	.01	.02	.04	.04	.03	11
12														.01	.01	.02	.03	.03	.03	12
13															.01	.01	.03	.03	.03	13
14															.01	.01	.02	.03	.03	14
15																.01	.02	.02	.02	15
16																.01	.01	.02	.02	16
17																.01	.01	.02	.02	17
18																	.01	.02	.02	18
19																	.01	.02	.02	19
20																	.01	.01	.02	20
21																	.01	.01	.02	21
22																	.01	.01	.02	22
23																		.01	.01	23
24																		.01	.01	24
25																		.01	.01	25
26																		.01	.01	26
27																		.01	.01	27
28																		.01	.01	28
29																		.01	.01	29
30																			.01	30
31																			.01	31
32																			.01	32
33																			.01	33
34																			.01	34
35																			.01	35
36																			.01	36
37																			.01	37
38																			.01	38
39																			.01	39
40																			.01	40

Utilization factor (A/MS)

TABLE 6-8 Values of P_n for n from 0-40, M = 4

n	.05	.10	.15	.20	.25	.30	.35	.40	.45	.50	.55	.60	.65	.70	.75	.80	.85	.90	.95	n
0	.82	.67	.55	.45	.37	.30	.24	.20	.16	.13	.10	.08	.07	.05	.04	.03	.02	.01	.01	0
1	.16	.27	.33	.36	.37	.36	.34	.32	.29	.26	.23	.20	.17	.14	.11	.09	.06	.04	.02	1
2	.02	.05	.10	.14	.18	.22	.24	.26	.26	.26	.25	.24	.22	.20	.17	.14	.11	.07	.04	2
3		.01	.02	.04	.06	.09	.11	.14	.16	.17	.19	.19	.19	.18	.17	.15	.12	.09	.05	3
4				.01	.02	.03	.04	.05	.07	.09	.10	.11	.12	.13	.13	.12	.10	.08	.04	4
5						.01	.01	.02	.03	.04	.06	.07	.08	.09	.10	.10	.09	.07	.04	5
6								.01	.01	.02	.03	.04	.05	.06	.07	.08	.07	.06	.04	6
7									.01	.01	.02	.02	.03	.04	.05	.06	.06	.06	.04	7
8										.01	.01	.01	.02	.03	.04	.05	.05	.05	.04	8
9											.01	.01	.01	.02	.03	.04	.05	.05	.03	9
10												.01	.01	.02	.02	.03	.03	.04	.03	10
11													.01	.01	.02	.03	.03	.04	.03	11
12														.01	.01	.02	.03	.03	.03	12
13														.01	.01	.02	.02	.03	.03	13
14															.01	.01	.02	.03	.03	14
15															.01	.01	.02	.02	.03	15
16																.01	.01	.02	.02	16
17																.01	.01	.02	.02	17
18																	.01	.02	.02	18
19																	.01	.02	.02	19
20																	.01	.01	.02	20
21																	.01	.01	.02	21
22																	.01	.01	.02	22
23																	.01	.01	.02	23
24																		.01	.02	24
25																		.01	.02	25
26																		.01	.01	26
27																		.01	.01	27
28																		.01	.01	28
29																		.01	.01	29
30																		.01	.01	30
31																			.01	31
32																			.01	32
33																			.01	33
34																			.01	34
35																			.01	35
36																			.01	36
37																			.01	37
38																			.01	38
39																			.01	39
40																			.01	40

Utilization Factor (A/MS)

TABLE 6-9. Values of P_n for n from 0-40, $M = 5$

n									Utilization Factor (A/MS)											n
	.05	.10	.15	.20	.25	.30	.35	.40	.45	.50	.55	.60	.65	.70	.75	.80	.85	.90	.95	
0	.78	.61	.47	.37	.29	.22	.17	.13	.10	.08	.06	.05	.04	.03	.02	.01	.01	.00	.00	0
1	.19	.30	.35	.37	.36	.33	.30	.27	.23	.20	.17	.14	.11	.09	.07	.05	.04	.02	.01	1
2	.02	.08	.13	.18	.22	.25	.27	.27	.26	.25	.23	.21	.19	.16	.13	.10	.08	.05	.02	2
3		.01	.03	.06	.09	.13	.15	.18	.20	.21	.21	.21	.20	.19	.16	.14	.11	.08	.04	3
4			.01	.02	.03	.05	.07	.09	.11	.13	.15	.16	.16	.16	.15	.14	.12	.08	.05	4
5					.01	.01	.02	.04	.05	.07	.08	.09	.11	.11	.12	.11	.10	.08	.04	5
6							.01	.01	.02	.03	.04	.06	.07	.08	.09	.09	.08	.07	.04	6
7								.01	.01	.02	.02	.03	.04	.06	.06	.07	.07	.06	.04	7
8										.01	.01	.02	.03	.04	.05	.06	.06	.06	.04	8
9											.01	.01	.02	.03	.04	.05	.05	.05	.04	9
10												.01	.01	.02	.03	.04	.05	.05	.03	10
11													.01	.01	.02	.03	.04	.04	.03	11
12													.01	.01	.02	.02	.04	.04	.03	12
13														.01	.01	.02	.03	.03	.03	13
14															.01	.01	.03	.03	.03	14
15															.01	.01	.02	.03	.03	15
16																.01	.02	.02	.03	16
17																.01	.01	.02	.02	17
18																	.01	.02	.02	18
19																	.01	.02	.02	19
20																	.01	.02	.02	20
21																	.01	.01	.02	21
22																	.01	.01	.02	22
23																		.01	.02	23
24																		.01	.02	24
25																		.01	.01	25
26																		.01	.01	26
27																		.01	.01	27
28																		.01	.01	28
29																		.01	.01	29
30																		.01	.01	30
31																			.01	31
32																			.01	32
33																			.01	33
34																			.01	34
35																			.01	35
36																			.01	36
37																			.01	37
38																			.01	38
39																			.01	39
40																			.01	40

TABLE 6-10. Values of P_n for n from 0-40, $M = 6$

n	.05	.10	.15	.20	.25	.30	.35	.40	.45	.50	.55	.60	.65	.70	.75	.80	.85	.90	.95
0	.74	.55	.41	.30	.22	.17	.12	.09	.07	.05	.04	.03	.02	.01	.01	.01	.00	.00	.00
1	.22	.33	.37	.36	.33	.30	.26	.22	.18	.15	.12	.09	.07	.06	.04	.03	.02	.01	.01
2	.03	.10	.16	.22	.25	.27	.27	.26	.24	.22	.20	.17	.14	.12	.09	.07	.05	.03	.01
3		.02	.05	.09	.13	.16	.19	.21	.22	.22	.21	.20	.18	.16	.14	.11	.08	.06	.03
4			.01	.03	.05	.07	.10	.12	.15	.17	.18	.18	.18	.17	.16	.13	.11	.08	.04
5				.01	.01	.03	.04	.06	.08	.10	.12	.13	.14	.14	.14	.13	.11	.08	.05
6				.01	.01	.01	.01	.02	.04	.05	.06	.08	.09	.10	.11	.10	.09	.07	.04
7							.01	.01	.02	.02	.04	.05	.06	.07	.08	.08	.08	.07	.04
8						.01	.01	.01	.01	.01	.02	.03	.04	.05	.06	.07	.07	.06	.04
9							.01		.01	.01	.01	.02	.03	.03	.04	.05	.06	.05	.04
10										.01		.01	.02	.02	.03	.04	.05	.05	.04
11												.01	.01	.02	.02	.03	.04	.04	.03
12													.01	.01	.01	.02	.04	.04	.03
13														.01	.01	.02	.03	.03	.03
14															.01	.02	.03	.03	.03
15															.01	.01	.02	.02	.03
16															.01	.01	.02	.02	.02
17																.01	.02	.02	.02
18																.01	.01	.02	.02
19																.01	.01	.01	.02
20																	.01	.01	.02
21																	.01	.01	.02
22																	.01	.01	.02
23																	.01	.01	.02
24																	.01	.01	.02
25																		.01	.02
26																		.01	.02
27																		.01	.02
28																		.01	.01
29																		.01	.01
30																		.01	.01
31																			.01
32																			.01
33																			.01
34																			.01
35																			.01
36																			.01
37																			.01
38																			.01
39																			.01
40																			.01

Utilization Factor (A/MS)

TABLE 6-11 Values of P_n for n from 0-40, $M = 7$

Utilization Factor (A/MS)

n	.05	.10	.15	.20	.25	.30	.35	.40	.45	.50	.55	.60	.65	.70	.75	.80	.85	.90	.95	n
0	.70	.50	.35	.25	.17	.12	.09	.06	.04	.03	.02	.01	.01	.01	.00	.00	.00	.00	.00	0
1	.25	.35	.37	.35	.30	.26	.21	.17	.13	.10	.08	.06	.05	.03	.02	.02	.01	.01	.00	1
2	.04	.12	.19	.24	.27	.27	.26	.24	.21	.18	.15	.13	.10	.08	.06	.04	.03	.02	.01	2
3	.01	.03	.07	.11	.16	.19	.21	.22	.22	.21	.20	.18	.16	.13	.11	.08	.06	.04	.02	3
4		.01	.02	.04	.07	.10	.13	.16	.17	.19	.19	.19	.18	.16	.14	.12	.09	.06	.03	4
5				.01	.02	.04	.06	.09	.11	.13	.15	.16	.16	.16	.15	.13	.11	.08	.04	5
6					.01	.01	.03	.04	.06	.08	.09	.11	.12	.13	.13	.12	.11	.08	.05	6
7							.01	.02	.03	.04	.05	.07	.08	.09	.10	.10	.09	.07	.04	7
8								.01	.01	.02	.03	.04	.05	.06	.07	.08	.08	.06	.04	8
9									.01	.01	.02	.02	.03	.04	.05	.06	.06	.06	.04	9
10											.01	.01	.02	.03	.04	.05	.06	.05	.04	10
11												.01	.01	.02	.03	.04	.05	.05	.03	11
12												.01	.01	.02	.02	.03	.04	.04	.03	12
13													.01	.01	.02	.03	.03	.04	.03	13
14														.01	.01	.02	.03	.03	.03	14
15														.01	.01	.02	.03	.03	.03	15
16															.01	.01	.02	.03	.03	16
17															.01	.01	.02	.03	.03	17
18																.01	.02	.02	.02	18
19																.01	.01	.02	.02	19
20																.01	.01	.02	.02	20
21																	.01	.02	.02	21
22																	.01	.01	.02	22
23																	.01	.01	.02	23
24																	.01	.01	.02	24
25																		.01	.02	25
26																		.01	.02	26
27																		.01	.02	27
28																		.01	.01	28
29																		.01	.01	29
30																		.01	.01	30
31																		.01	.01	31
32																			.01	32
33																			.01	33
34																			.01	34
35																			.01	35
36																			.01	36
37																			.01	37
38																			.01	38
39																			.01	39
40																			.01	40

TABLE 6-12. Values of P_n for n from 0-40, $M = 8$

Utilization Factor (A/MS)

n	.05	.10	.15	.20	.25	.30	.35	.40	.45	.50	.55	.60	.65	.70	.75	.80	.85	.90	.95
0	.67	.45	.30	.20	.14	.09	.06	.04	.03	.02	.01	.01	.01	.00	.00	.00	.00	.00	.00
1	.27	.36	.36	.32	.27	.22	.17	.13	.10	.07	.05	.04	.03	.02	.01	.01	.01	.00	.00
2	.05	.14	.22	.26	.27	.26	.24	.21	.18	.15	.12	.09	.07	.05	.04	.03	.02	.01	.00
3	.01	.04	.09	.14	.18	.21	.22	.22	.21	.19	.17	.15	.12	.10	.08	.06	.04	.02	.01
4		.01	.03	.06	.09	.13	.16	.18	.19	.19	.19	.18	.16	.14	.12	.09	.07	.04	.02
5			.01	.02	.04	.06	.09	.11	.14	.16	.17	.17	.17	.16	.14	.12	.09	.06	.03
6					.01	.02	.04	.06	.08	.10	.12	.14	.14	.15	.14	.13	.10	.08	.04
7						.01	.02	.03	.04	.06	.08	.09	.11	.12	.12	.11	.10	.08	.04
8							.01	.01	.02	.03	.04	.06	.07	.08	.09	.09	.09	.07	.04
9									.01	.01	.02	.03	.05	.06	.07	.07	.07	.06	.04
10										.01	.01	.02	.03	.04	.05	.06	.06	.06	.04
11											.01	.01	.02	.03	.04	.05	.05	.05	.04
12											.01	.01	.01	.02	.03	.04	.04	.05	.03
13												.01	.01	.01	.02	.03	.04	.04	.03
14													.01	.01	.02	.03	.04	.04	.03
15														.01	.02	.02	.03	.03	.03
16															.01	.02	.03	.03	.03
17															.01	.01	.02	.03	.03
18																.01	.02	.02	.03
19																.01	.01	.02	.03
20																.01	.01	.02	.02
21																	.01	.02	.02
22																	.01	.01	.02
23																	.01	.01	.02
24																	.01	.01	.02
25																	.01	.01	.02
26																		.01	.02
27																		.01	.02
28																		.01	.02
29																		.01	.01
30																		.01	.01
31																		.01	.01
32																			.01
33																			.01
34																			.01
35																			.01
36																			.01
37																			.01
38																			.01
39																			.01
40																			.01

TABLE 6-13. Values of P_n for n from 0-40, M = 9

n									Utilization Factor (A/MS)										
	.05	.10	.15	.20	.25	.30	.35	.40	.45	.50	.55	.60	.65	.70	.75	.80	.85	.90	.95
0	.64	.41	.26	.17	.11	.07	.04	.03	.02	.01	.01	.00	.00	.00	.00	.00	.00	.00	.00
1	.29	.37	.35	.30	.24	.18	.13	.10	.07	.05	.03	.02	.02	.01	.01	.00	.00	.00	.00
2	.06	.16	.24	.27	.27	.24	.21	.18	.14	.11	.09	.06	.05	.03	.02	.02	.01	.01	.00
3	.01	.05	.11	.16	.20	.22	.22	.21	.19	.17	.14	.12	.09	.07	.05	.04	.02	.03	.01
4		.01	.04	.07	.11	.15	.18	.19	.19	.19	.18	.16	.13	.11	.09	.07	.05	.05	.01
5			.01	.03	.05	.08	.11	.14	.16	.17	.17	.17	.16	.14	.12	.10	.07	.06	.02
6				.01	.02	.04	.06	.08	.11	.13	.14	.15	.15	.15	.14	.12	.09	.08	.03
7					.01	.01	.03	.04	.06	.08	.10	.12	.13	.13	.13	.12	.10	.08	.04
8							.01	.02	.03	.05	.06	.08	.09	.10	.11	.11	.10	.07	.04
9								.01	.01	.02	.03	.05	.06	.07	.08	.09	.08	.06	.04
10									.01	.01	.02	.03	.04	.05	.06	.07	.07	.06	.04
11										.01	.01	.02	.03	.04	.05	.06	.06	.05	.04
12											.01	.01	.02	.03	.03	.04	.05	.04	.03
13												.01	.01	.02	.03	.04	.04	.04	.03
14													.01	.01	.02	.03	.04	.04	.03
15														.01	.01	.02	.03	.03	.03
16														.01	.01	.02	.03	.03	.03
17															.01	.01	.02	.03	.03
18															.01	.01	.02	.02	.02
19															.01	.01	.01	.02	.02
20																.01	.01	.02	.02
21																	.01	.02	.02
22																	.01	.01	.02
23																	.01	.01	.02
24																	.01	.01	.02
25																	.01	.01	.02
26																		.01	.01
27																		.01	.01
28																			.01
29																			.01
30																			.01
31																			.01
32																			.01
33																			.01
34																			.01
35																			.01
36																			.01
37																			.01
38																			.01
39																			.01
40																			.01

TABLE 6-14. Values of P_n for n from 0-40, $M = 10$

n										Utilization Factor (A/MS)										n
	.05	.10	.15	.20	.25	.30	.35	.40	.45	.50	.55	.60	.65	.70	.75	.80	.85	.90	.95	
0	.61	.37	.22	.14	.08	.05	.03	.02	.01	.01	.00	.00	.00	.00	.00	.00	.00	.00	.00	0
1	.30	.37	.33	.27	.21	.15	.11	.07	.05	.03	.02	.01	.01	.01	.00	.00	.00	.00	.00	1
2	.08	.18	.25	.27	.26	.22	.18	.15	.11	.08	.06	.04	.03	.02	.01	.01	.01	.00	.00	2
3	.01	.06	.13	.18	.21	.22	.22	.20	.17	.14	.11	.09	.07	.05	.03	.02	.02	.01	.00	3
4		.02	.05	.09	.13	.17	.19	.20	.19	.17	.15	.13	.11	.09	.07	.05	.03	.02	.01	4
5			.01	.04	.07	.10	.13	.16	.17	.17	.17	.16	.14	.12	.10	.08	.05	.03	.02	5
6				.01	.03	.05	.08	.10	.13	.15	.16	.16	.15	.14	.12	.10	.08	.05	.03	6
7					.01	.02	.04	.06	.08	.10	.12	.14	.14	.14	.13	.12	.09	.07	.03	7
8						.01	.02	.03	.05	.07	.08	.10	.11	.12	.12	.12	.10	.07	.04	8
9							.01	.01	.02	.04	.05	.07	.08	.10	.10	.10	.09	.07	.04	9
10									.01	.02	.03	.04	.05	.07	.08	.08	.09	.06	.04	10
11									.01	.01	.02	.02	.04	.05	.06	.07	.07	.05	.04	11
12										.01	.01	.01	.02	.03	.04	.05	.06	.05	.04	12
13											.01	.01	.01	.02	.03	.04	.05	.04	.04	13
14												.01	.01	.02	.02	.03	.04	.04	.03	14
15												.01	.01	.01	.02	.02	.04	.04	.03	15
16													.01	.01	.01	.02	.03	.03	.03	16
17													.01	.01	.01	.01	.03	.03	.03	17
18															.01	.01	.02	.03	.03	18
19															.01	.01	.02	.02	.03	19
20																.01	.02	.02	.02	20
21																	.01	.02	.02	21
22																	.01	.02	.02	22
23																	.01	.01	.02	23
24																	.01	.01	.02	24
25																	.01	.01	.02	25
26																	.01	.01	.02	26
27																	.01	.01	.02	27
28																		.01	.02	28
29																		.01	.02	29
30																		.01	.01	30
31																			.01	31
32																			.01	32
33																			.01	33
34																			.01	34
35																			.01	35
36																			.01	36
37																			.01	37
38																			.01	38
39																			.01	39
40																			.01	40

TABLE 6-15. Cumulative values of P_n for n from 0-40, M = 1

Utilization Factor (A/MS)

n	.05	.10	.15	.20	.25	.30	.35	.40	.45	.50	.55	.60	.65	.70	.75	.80	.85	.90	.95	n
0	.95	.90	.85	.80	.75	.70	.65	.60	.55	.50	.45	.40	.35	.30	.25	.20	.15	.10	.05	0
1	1.00	.99	.98	.96	.94	.91	.88	.84	.80	.75	.70	.64	.58	.51	.44	.36	.28	.19	.10	1
2		1.00	1.00	.99	.98	.97	.96	.94	.91	.87	.83	.78	.73	.66	.58	.49	.39	.27	.14	2
3			1.00	1.00	1.00	.99	.98	.97	.96	.94	.91	.87	.82	.76	.68	.59	.48	.34	.19	3
4					1.00	1.00	.99	.99	.98	.97	.95	.92	.88	.83	.76	.67	.56	.41	.23	4
5							1.00	1.00	.99	.98	.97	.95	.92	.88	.82	.74	.62	.47	.26	5
6								1.00	1.00	.99	.98	.97	.95	.92	.87	.79	.68	.52	.30	6
7									1.00	.99	.98	.98	.97	.94	.90	.83	.73	.57	.34	7
8										1.00	.99	.99	.98	.96	.92	.87	.77	.61	.37	8
9											1.00	.99	.99	.97	.94	.89	.80	.65	.40	9
10												1.00	.99	.98	.96	.91	.83	.69	.43	10
11													1.00	.99	.97	.93	.86	.72	.46	11
12														.99	.98	.95	.88	.75	.49	12
13														1.00	.98	.96	.90	.77	.51	13
14															.99	.96	.91	.79	.54	14
15															.99	.97	.93	.81	.56	15
16															.99	.98	.94	.83	.58	16
17															1.00	.98	.95	.85	.60	17
18																.99	.95	.86	.62	18
19																.99	.96	.88	.64	19
20																.99	.96	.89	.66	20
21																.99	.97	.90	.68	21
22																.99	.97	.91	.69	22
23																1.00	.98	.92	.71	23
24																	.98	.93	.72	24
25																	.98	.94	.74	25
26																	.99	.94	.75	26
27																	.99	.95	.76	27
28																	.99	.95	.77	28
29																	.99	.96	.79	29
30																	.99	.96	.80	30
31																	.99	.97	.81	31
32																	1.00	.97	.82	32
33																		.97	.83	33
34																		.97	.83	34
35																		.98	.84	35
36																		.98	.85	36
37																		.98	.86	37
38																		.98	.86	38
39																		.99	.87	39
40																		.99	.88	40

TABLE 6-16. Cumulative values of P_n for n from 0-40, $M = 2$

n	.05	.10	.15	.20	.25	.30	.35	.40	.45	.50	.55	.60	.65	.70	.75	.80	.85	.90	.95
0	.90	.82	.74	.67	.60	.54	.48	.43	.38	.33	.29	.25	.21	.18	.14	.11	.08	.05	.03
1	1.00	.98	.96	.93	.90	.86	.82	.77	.72	.67	.61	.55	.49	.42	.36	.29	.22	.15	.07
2		1.00	.99	.99	.98	.96	.94	.91	.87	.83	.79	.73	.67	.60	.52	.43	.34	.23	.12
3			1.00	1.00	.99	.99	.98	.96	.94	.92	.88	.84	.78	.72	.64	.54	.44	.31	.16
4					1.00	.99	.99	.99	.97	.96	.94	.90	.86	.80	.73	.64	.52	.38	.21
5						1.00	1.00	.99	.99	.98	.96	.94	.91	.86	.80	.71	.59	.44	.25
6								1.00	.99	.99	.98	.97	.94	.90	.85	.77	.65	.50	.28
7									1.00	.99	.99	.98	.96	.93	.89	.81	.71	.55	.32
8										1.00	.99	.99	.97	.95	.91	.85	.75	.59	.35
9											1.00	.99	.98	.97	.94	.88	.79	.63	.39
10												1.00	.99	.98	.95	.90	.82	.67	.42
11													.99	.98	.96	.92	.85	.70	.45
12													1.00	.99	.97	.94	.87	.73	.47
13														.99	.98	.95	.89	.76	.50
14														1.00	.98	.96	.91	.78	.52
15															.99	.97	.92	.80	.55
16															.99	.97	.93	.82	.57
17															.99	.98	.94	.84	.59
18															1.00	.98	.95	.86	.61
19																.99	.96	.87	.63
20																.99	.96	.88	.65
21																.99	.97	.90	.67
22																.99	.97	.91	.68
23																.99	.98	.92	.70
24																1.00	.98	.92	.72
25																	.98	.93	.73
26																	.99	.94	.74
27																	.99	.94	.76
28																	.99	.95	.77
29																	.99	.96	.78
30																	.99	.96	.79
31																	.99	.96	.80
32																	1.00	.97	.81
33																		.97	.82
34																		.97	.83
35																		.98	.84
36																		.98	.85
37																		.98	.85
38																		.98	.86
39																		.98	.87
40																		.99	.87

Utilization Factor (A/MS)

TABLE 6-17. Cumulative values of P_n for n from 0-40, $M = 3$

n	.05	.10	.15	.20	.25	.30	.35	.40	.45	.50	.55	.60	.65	.70	.75	.80	.85	.90	.95	n
0	.86	.74	.64	.55	.47	.40	.35	.29	.25	.21	.18	.15	.12	.10	.07	.06	.04	.02	.01	0
1	.99	.96	.92	.88	.82	.77	.71	.65	.59	.53	.47	.41	.35	.30	.24	.19	.14	.09	.05	1
2	1.00	1.00	.99	.98	.96	.93	.90	.86	.81	.76	.71	.65	.58	.51	.43	.35	.27	.18	.09	2
3			1.00	1.00	.99	.98	.96	.94	.92	.88	.84	.79	.73	.66	.57	.48	.38	.26	.14	3
4					1.00	.99	.99	.98	.96	.94	.91	.87	.82	.76	.68	.59	.47	.34	.18	4
5						1.00	1.00	.99	.98	.97	.95	.92	.88	.83	.76	.67	.55	.40	.22	5
6								1.00	.99	.99	.97	.95	.92	.88	.82	.73	.62	.46	.26	6
7									1.00	.99	.99	.97	.95	.92	.87	.79	.68	.52	.30	7
8										1.00	.99	.98	.97	.94	.90	.83	.72	.57	.33	8
9											1.00	.99	.98	.96	.92	.86	.77	.61	.37	9
10												.99	.99	.97	.94	.89	.80	.65	.40	10
11												1.00	.99	.98	.96	.91	.83	.68	.43	11
12													1.00	.99	.97	.93	.86	.72	.46	12
13														.99	.98	.94	.88	.74	.48	13
14														1.00	.98	.96	.90	.77	.51	14
15															.99	.96	.91	.79	.53	15
16															.99	.97	.92	.81	.56	16
17															.99	.98	.94	.83	.58	17
18															.99	.98	.95	.85	.60	18
19															.99	.99	.95	.86	.62	19
20															1.00	.99	.96	.88	.64	20
21																.99	.97	.89	.66	21
22																.99	.97	.90	.67	22
23																.99	.98	.91	.69	23
24																1.00	.98	.92	.71	24
25																	.99	.93	.72	25
26																	.99	.93	.74	26
27																	.99	.94	.75	27
28																	.99	.95	.76	28
29																	.99	.95	.77	29
30																	.99	.96	.78	30
31																	.99	.96	.80	31
32																	.99	.97	.81	32
33																	1.00	.97	.82	33
34																		.97	.82	34
35																		.97	.83	35
36																		.98	.84	36
37																		.98	.85	37
38																		.98	.86	38
39																		.98	.86	39
40																		.99	.87	40

Utilization Factor (A/MS)

TABLE 6-18. Cumulative values of P_n for n from 0-40, $M = 4$

n	.05	.10	.15	.20	.25	.30	.35	.40	.45	.50	.55	.60	.65	.70	.75	.80	.85	.90	.95	n
														Utilization Factor (A/MS)						
0	.82	.67	.55	.45	.37	.30	.24	.20	.16	.13	.10	.08	.07	.05	.04	.03	.02	.01	.01	0
1	.98	.94	.88	.81	.73	.66	.59	.52	.45	.39	.33	.28	.23	.19	.15	.11	.08	.05	.02	1
2	1.00	.99	.98	.95	.92	.88	.83	.77	.71	.65	.59	.52	.45	.39	.32	.25	.19	.12	.06	2
3		1.00	1.00	.99	.98	.96	.94	.91	.87	.83	.77	.71	.65	.57	.49	.40	.31	.21	.11	3
4				1.00	.99	.99	.98	.96	.94	.91	.88	.83	.77	.70	.62	.52	.41	.29	.15	4
5					1.00	1.00	.99	.99	.97	.96	.93	.90	.85	.79	.71	.62	.50	.36	.20	5
6							1.00	.99	.99	.98	.96	.94	.90	.85	.79	.69	.58	.43	.24	6
7								1.00	.99	.99	.98	.96	.94	.90	.84	.76	.64	.48	.27	7
8									1.00	.99	.99	.98	.96	.93	.88	.80	.69	.53	.31	8
9										1.00	.99	.99	.97	.95	.91	.84	.74	.58	.34	9
10											1.00	.99	.98	.96	.93	.87	.78	.62	.38	10
11												1.00	.99	.98	.95	.90	.81	.66	.41	11
12													.99	.98	.96	.92	.84	.69	.44	12
13													1.00	.99	.97	.94	.86	.73	.47	13
14														.99	.98	.95	.88	.75	.49	14
15														.99	.98	.96	.90	.78	.52	15
16														1.00	.99	.97	.92	.80	.54	16
17															.99	.97	.93	.82	.57	17
18															.99	.98	.94	.84	.59	18
19															.99	.98	.95	.85	.61	19
20															1.00	.99	.96	.87	.63	20
																.99	.96	.88	.65	21
																.99	.97	.89	.66	22
																.99	.97	.90	.68	23
																.99	.98	.91	.70	24
																1.00	.98	.92	.71	25
																	.98	.93	.73	26
																	.99	.94	.74	27
																	.99	.94	.75	28
																	.99	.95	.77	29
																	.99	.95	.78	30
																	.99	.96	.79	31
																	.99	.96	.80	32
																	.99	.97	.81	33
																	1.00	.97	.82	34
																		.97	.83	35
																		.98	.84	36
																		.98	.84	37
																		.98	.85	38
																		.98	.86	39
																		.98	.87	40

TABLE 6-19. Cumulative values of P_n for n from 0-40, $M = 5$

n	Utilization Factor (A/MS)																			n
	.05	.10	.15	.20	.25	.30	.35	.40	.45	.50	.55	.60	.65	.70	.75	.80	.85	.90	.95	
0	.78	.61	.47	.37	.29	.22	.17	.13	.10	.08	.06	.05	.04	.03	.02	.01	.01	.00	.00	0
1	.97	.91	.83	.74	.64	.56	.48	.40	.34	.28	.23	.19	.15	.12	.09	.06	.04	.03	.01	1
2	1.00	.99	.96	.92	.87	.81	.74	.67	.60	.53	.46	.40	.33	.28	.22	.17	.12	.08	.04	2
3		1.00	.99	.98	.96	.93	.90	.85	.80	.74	.67	.61	.53	.46	.38	.31	.23	.15	.08	3
4			1.00	1.00	.99	.98	.96	.94	.91	.87	.82	.76	.70	.62	.54	.45	.35	.24	.12	4
5					1.00	.99	.99	.98	.96	.93	.90	.86	.80	.74	.65	.56	.44	.31	.17	5
6						1.00	1.00	.99	.98	.97	.95	.91	.87	.81	.74	.65	.53	.38	.21	6
7								1.00	.99	.98	.97	.95	.92	.87	.81	.72	.60	.44	.25	7
8									1.00	.99	.98	.97	.95	.91	.85	.77	.66	.50	.29	8
9										1.00	.99	.98	.96	.94	.89	.82	.71	.55	.32	9
10											1.00	.99	.98	.96	.92	.85	.75	.59	.35	10
11												.99	.99	.97	.94	.88	.79	.64	.39	11
12												1.00	.99	.98	.95	.91	.82	.67	.42	12
13													1.00	.98	.97	.93	.85	.70	.45	13
14														.99	.97	.94	.87	.73	.47	14
15														.99	.98	.95	.89	.76	.50	15
16														.99	.99	.96	.91	.78	.53	16
17														1.00	.99	.97	.92	.81	.55	17
18															.99	.98	.93	.83	.57	18
19															.99	.98	.94	.84	.59	19
20															1.00	.98	.95	.86	.61	20
21																.99	.96	.87	.63	21
22																.99	.96	.89	.65	22
23																.99	.97	.90	.67	23
24																.99	.97	.91	.69	24
25																.99	.98	.92	.70	25
26																1.00	.98	.92	.72	26
27																	.98	.93	.73	27
28																	.99	.94	.74	28
29																	.99	.95	.76	29
30																	.99	.95	.77	30
31																	.99	.96	.78	31
32																	.99	.96	.79	32
33																	1.00	.96	.80	33
34																		.97	.81	34
35																		.97	.82	35
36																		.97	.83	36
37																		.98	.84	37
38																		.98	.85	38
39																		.98	.85	39
40																		.98	.86	40

TABLE 6-20. Cumulative values of P_n for n from 0-40, M = 6

n								Utilization Factor (A/MS)												n
	.95	.90	.85	.80	.75	.70	.65	.60	.55	.50	.45	.40	.35	.30	.25	.20	.15	.10	.05	
0	.00	.00	.00	.01	.01	.01	.02	.03	.04	.05	.07	.09	.12	.17	.22	.30	.41	.55	.74	0
1	.01	.01	.02	.04	.05	.07	.09	.12	.15	.20	.25	.31	.38	.46	.56	.66	.77	.88	.96	1
2	.02	.05	.07	.11	.14	.19	.23	.29	.35	.42	.49	.57	.65	.73	.81	.88	.94	.98	1.00	2
3	.05	.10	.16	.22	.28	.35	.42	.49	.56	.64	.71	.78	.84	.89	.93	.97	.99	1.00		3
4	.09	.18	.27	.35	.44	.52	.60	.67	.74	.80	.86	.90	.94	.96	.98	.99	1.00			4
5	.13	.26	.38	.48	.58	.66	.74	.80	.86	.90	.93	.96	.98	.99	1.00	1.00				5
6	.18	.33	.47	.59	.68	.76	.83	.88	.92	.95	.97	.98	.99	1.00						6
7	.22	.40	.55	.67	.76	.84	.89	.93	.96	.98	.99	.99	1.00							7
8	.26	.46	.62	.73	.82	.88	.93	.96	.98	.99	.99	.99								8
9	.29	.51	.67	.79	.87	.92	.95	.97	.99	.99	.99	1.00								9
10	.33	.56	.72	.83	.90	.94	.97	.98	.99	.99	1.00									10
11	.36	.61	.76	.86	.92	.96	.98	.99	1.00	1.00										11
12	.40	.65	.80	.89	.94	.97	.99	.99												12
13	.43	.68	.83	.91	.96	.98	.99	1.00												13
14	.45	.71	.86	.93	.97	.99	.99													14
15	.48	.74	.88	.94	.98	.99	.99													15
16	.51	.77	.90	.96	.98	.99	1.00													16
17	.53	.79	.91	.96	.99	.99														17
18	.56	.81	.92	.97	.99	1.00														18
19	.58	.83	.94	.98	.99															19
20	.60	.85	.95	.98	.99															20
21	.62	.86	.95	.99	1.00															21
22	.64	.88	.96	.99																22
23	.66	.89	.97	.99																23
24	.67	.90	.97	.99																24
25	.69	.91	.98	1.00																25
26	.71	.92	.98																	26
27	.72	.93	.98																	27
28	.73	.93	.98																	28
29	.75	.94	.99																	29
30	.76	.95	.99																	30
31	.77	.95	.99																	31
32	.78	.96	.99																	32
33	.79	.96	.99																	33
34	.80	.97	.99																	34
35	.81	.97	1.00																	35
36	.82	.97																		36
37	.83	.97																		37
38	.84	.98																		38
39	.85	.98																		39
40	.86	.98																		40

TABLE 6-21. Cumulative values of P_n for n from 0-40, $M = 7$

n										*Utilization Factor (A/MS)*									
	.05	.10	.15	.20	.25	.30	.35	.40	.45	.50	.55	.60	.65	.70	.75	.80	.85	.90	.95
0	.70	.50	.35	.25	.17	.12	.09	.06	.04	.03	.02	.01	.01	.01	.00	.00	.00	.00	.00
1	.95	.84	.72	.59	.48	.38	.30	.23	.18	.13	.10	.08	.05	.04	.03	.02	.01	.01	.00
2	.99	.97	.91	.83	.74	.65	.56	.47	.39	.32	.26	.20	.16	.12	.09	.06	.04	.03	.01
3	1.00	.99	.98	.95	.90	.84	.77	.69	.61	.53	.45	.38	.31	.25	.20	.15	.10	.06	.03
4		1.00	1.00	.99	.97	.94	.90	.85	.78	.72	.64	.57	.49	.41	.34	.26	.19	.12	.06
5				1.00	.99	.98	.96	.93	.89	.85	.79	.72	.65	.57	.48	.39	.30	.20	.10
6					1.00	.99	.99	.97	.95	.92	.88	.83	.77	.70	.61	.51	.40	.28	.15
7						1.00	1.00	.99	.98	.96	.94	.90	.85	.79	.71	.61	.49	.35	.19
8								1.00	.99	.98	.97	.94	.90	.85	.78	.69	.57	.42	.23
9									1.00	.99	.98	.96	.94	.90	.84	.75	.63	.48	.27
10										1.00	.99	.98	.96	.93	.88	.80	.69	.53	.30
11											.99	.99	.97	.95	.91	.84	.74	.57	.34
12											1.00	.99	.98	.96	.93	.87	.77	.62	.37
13												1.00	.99	.98	.95	.90	.81	.66	.40
14													.99	.98	.96	.92	.84	.69	.43
15													1.00	.99	.97	.93	.86	.72	.46
16														.99	.98	.95	.88	.75	.49
17														1.00	.98	.96	.90	.77	.51
18															.99	.97	.92	.80	.54
19															.99	.97	.93	.82	.56
20															.99	.98	.94	.84	.58
21															1.00	.98	.95	.85	.60
22																.99	.96	.87	.62
23																.99	.96	.88	.64
24																.99	.97	.89	.66
25																.99	.97	.90	.68
26																.99	.98	.91	.69
27																1.00	.98	.92	.71
28																	.98	.93	.72
29																	.99	.94	.74
30																	.99	.94	.75
31																	.99	.95	.76
32																	.99	.95	.77
33																	.99	.96	.79
34																	.99	.96	.80
35																	1.00	.97	.81
36																		.97	.82
37																		.97	.83
38																		.98	.83
39																		.98	.84
40																		.98	.85

TABLE 6-22. Cumulative values for P_n for n from 0-40, $M = 8$

n	Utilization Factor (A/MS)																		
	.05	.10	.15	.20	.25	.30	.35	.40	.45	.50	.55	.60	.65	.70	.75	.80	.85	.90	.95
0	.67	.45	.30	.20	.14	.09	.06	.04	.03	.02	.01	.01	.01	.00	.00	.00	.00	.00	.00
1	.94	.81	.66	.52	.41	.31	.23	.17	.13	.09	.07	.05	.03	.02	.01	.01	.01	.00	.00
2	.99	.95	.88	.78	.68	.57	.47	.38	.30	.24	.18	.14	.10	.08	.05	.04	.02	.01	.01
3	1.00	.99	.97	.92	.86	.78	.69	.60	.51	.43	.35	.29	.23	.17	.13	.09	.06	.04	.02
4		1.00	.99	.98	.95	.90	.85	.78	.70	.62	.54	.46	.39	.31	.25	.19	.13	.08	.04
5			1.00	.99	.98	.96	.93	.89	.84	.78	.71	.63	.55	.47	.39	.30	.22	.14	.07
6				1.00	1.00	.99	.97	.95	.92	.88	.83	.77	.69	.61	.52	.43	.33	.22	.11
7						1.00	.99	.98	.97	.94	.91	.86	.80	.73	.64	.54	.43	.30	.16
8						1.00	1.00	.99	.98	.97	.95	.92	.87	.81	.73	.63	.51	.37	.20
9							1.00	.99	.99	.99	.97	.95	.92	.87	.80	.71	.59	.43	.24
10								1.00	1.00	.99	.98	.97	.95	.91	.85	.77	.65	.49	.28
11											.99	.98	.96	.94	.89	.81	.70	.54	.31
12											1.00	.99	.98	.95	.92	.85	.75	.59	.35
13												1.00	.99	.97	.94	.88	.78	.63	.38
14													.99	.98	.95	.90	.82	.66	.41
15													1.00	.98	.96	.92	.84	.70	.44
16														.99	.97	.94	.87	.73	.47
17														.99	.98	.95	.89	.76	.49
18														1.00	.98	.96	.90	.78	.52
19															.99	.97	.92	.80	.54
20															.99	.97	.93	.82	.57
21															1.00	.98	.94	.84	.59
22																.98	.95	.86	.61
23																.99	.96	.87	.63
24																.99	.96	.88	.65
25																.99	.97	.89	.66
26																1.00	.97	.91	.68
27																	.98	.91	.70
28																	.98	.92	.71
29																	.99	.93	.73
30																	.99	.94	.74
31																	.99	.94	.75
32																	.99	.95	.77
33																	1.00	.95	.78
34																		.96	.79
35																		.96	.80
36																		.97	.81
37																		.97	.82
38																		.98	.83
39																		.98	.84
40																		.98	.84

TABLE 6-23. Cumulative value for P_n for n from 0-40, $M = 9$

Utilization Factor (A/MS)

n	.05	.10	.15	.20	.25	.30	.35	.40	.45	.50	.55	.60	.65	.70	.75	.80	.85	.90	.95	n
0	.64	.41	.26	.17	.11	.07	.04	.03	.02	.01	.01	.00	.00	.00	.00	.00	.00	.00	.00	0
1	.92	.77	.61	.46	.34	.25	.18	.13	.09	.06	.04	.03	.02	.01	.01	.00	.00	.00	.00	1
2	.99	.94	.85	.73	.61	.49	.39	.30	.23	.17	.13	.09	.07	.05	.03	.02	.01	.01	.00	2
3	1.00	.99	.95	.89	.81	.71	.61	.51	.42	.34	.27	.21	.16	.12	.08	.06	.04	.02	.01	3
4		1.00	.99	.96	.92	.86	.79	.71	.62	.53	.44	.36	.29	.23	.17	.13	.09	.05	.02	4
5			1.00	.99	.97	.94	.90	.84	.78	.70	.62	.53	.45	.37	.29	.22	.16	.10	.05	5
6				1.00	.99	.98	.96	.93	.88	.83	.76	.69	.60	.52	.43	.34	.25	.16	.08	6
7					1.00	.99	.98	.97	.94	.91	.86	.80	.73	.65	.56	.46	.35	.24	.12	7
8						1.00	.99	.99	.97	.95	.92	.88	.83	.76	.67	.57	.45	.32	.17	8
9							1.00	.99	.99	.98	.96	.93	.89	.83	.75	.65	.53	.38	.21	9
10								1.00	.99	.99	.98	.96	.93	.88	.81	.72	.60	.45	.25	10
11									1.00	.99	.99	.97	.95	.92	.86	.78	.66	.50	.28	11
12										1.00	.99	.98	.97	.94	.90	.82	.71	.55	.32	12
13											1.00	.99	.98	.96	.92	.86	.76	.60	.35	13
14												.99	.99	.97	.94	.89	.79	.64	.39	14
15												1.00	.99	.98	.96	.91	.82	.67	.42	15
16													1.00	.99	.97	.93	.85	.71	.45	16
17														.99	.98	.94	.87	.73	.47	17
18														1.00	.98	.95	.89	.76	.50	18
19															.99	.96	.91	.79	.53	19
20															.99	.97	.92	.81	.55	20
21															1.00	.98	.93	.83	.57	21
22																.98	.94	.84	.59	22
23																.98	.95	.86	.61	23
24																.99	.96	.87	.63	24
25																.99	.97	.89	.65	25
26																.99	.97	.90	.67	26
27																.99	.97	.91	.69	27
28																1.00	.98	.92	.70	28
29																	.98	.93	.72	29
30																	.98	.93	.73	30
31																	.99	.94	.74	31
32																	.99	.95	.76	32
33																	.99	.95	.77	33
34																	.99	.96	.78	34
35																	.99	.96	.79	35
36																	.99	.96	.80	36
37																	1.00	.97	.81	37
38																		.97	.82	38
39																		.98	.83	39
40																			.84	40

TABLE 6-24. Cumulative value for P_n for n from 0-40, $M = 10$

n									Utilization Factor (A/MS)										
	.05	.10	.15	.20	.25	.30	.35	.40	.45	.50	.55	.60	.65	.70	.75	.80	.85	.90	.95
0	.61	.37	.22	.14	.08	.05	.03	.02	.01	.01	.00	.00	.00	.00	.00	.00	.00	.00	.00
1	.91	.74	.56	.41	.29	.20	.14	.09	.06	.04	.03	.02	.01	.01	.00	.00	.00	.00	.00
2	.99	.92	.81	.68	.54	.42	.32	.24	.17	.12	.09	.06	.04	.03	.02	.01	.01	.00	.00
3	1.00	.98	.93	.86	.76	.65	.54	.43	.34	.26	.20	.15	.11	.08	.05	.03	.02	.01	.00
4		1.00	.98	.95	.89	.82	.73	.63	.53	.44	.35	.28	.22	.16	.12	.08	.05	.03	.01
5			1.00	.98	.96	.92	.86	.78	.70	.61	.52	.44	.36	.28	.22	.16	.11	.07	.03
6				1.00	.99	.97	.93	.89	.83	.76	.68	.59	.51	.42	.34	.26	.18	.12	.06
7					1.00	.99	.97	.95	.91	.86	.80	.73	.65	.56	.47	.37	.28	.18	.09
8						1.00	.99	.98	.96	.93	.89	.83	.76	.68	.59	.49	.38	.26	.13
9							1.00	.99	.98	.96	.94	.90	.85	.78	.69	.59	.47	.33	.17
10								1.00	.99	.98	.97	.94	.90	.84	.77	.67	.55	.40	.22
11									1.00	.99	.98	.96	.94	.89	.83	.74	.62	.46	.25
12										1.00	.99	.98	.96	.92	.87	.79	.67	.51	.29
13											.99	.99	.97	.95	.90	.83	.72	.56	.33
14											1.00	.99	.98	.96	.93	.87	.76	.61	.36
15												1.00	.99	.97	.95	.89	.80	.64	.39
16													.99	.98	.96	.91	.83	.68	.42
17													1.00	.99	.97	.93	.86	.71	.45
18														.99	.98	.95	.88	.74	.48
19														.99	.98	.96	.90	.77	.51
20														1.00	.99	.96	.91	.79	.53
21															.99	.97	.92	.81	.55
22															.99	.98	.94	.83	.58
23															1.00	.98	.95	.85	.60
24																.99	.95	.86	.62
25																.99	.96	.88	.64
26																.99	.97	.89	.65
27																.99	.97	.90	.67
28																1.00	.98	.91	.69
29																	.98	.92	.70
30																	.99	.93	.72
31																	.99	.93	.73
32																	.99	.94	.75
33																	.99	.95	.76
34																	.99	.95	.77
35																	.99	.96	.78
36																	.99	.96	.79
37																	1.00	.97	.80
38																		.97	.81
39																		.97	.82
40																			.83

APPENDIX 6-2
Curves of Waiting-Line Parameters[4]

6-1. $\overline{n}$ vs. A/MS, $M = 1\text{-}5$
6-2. $\overline{w}$ vs. A/MS, $M = 1\text{-}5$
6-3. T_O vs. A/MS, $M = 1\text{-}5$
6-4. P_O vs. A/MS, $M = 1\text{-}5$

Symbols:

M = Number of channels of service
n = Number of persons waiting and being serviced (number in system)
$\overline{n}$ = Average or expected number of persons in system
$\overline{w}$ = Average number of persons waiting (in addition to those being serviced)
P_O = Probability that the service facility is idle
T_O = Total idle service hours per hour of operation
P_n = Probability of n customers in the system
A/MS = Utilization factor (service density)

[4] For random arrivals and exponential service times.

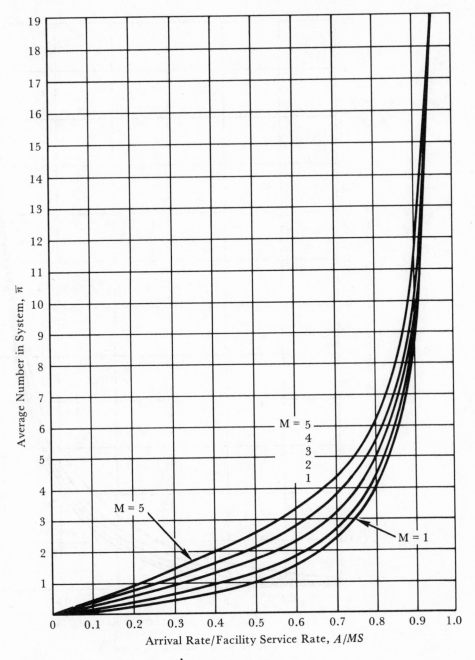

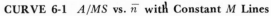

CURVE 6-1   *A/MS* vs. $\overline{n}$ with Constant *M* Lines

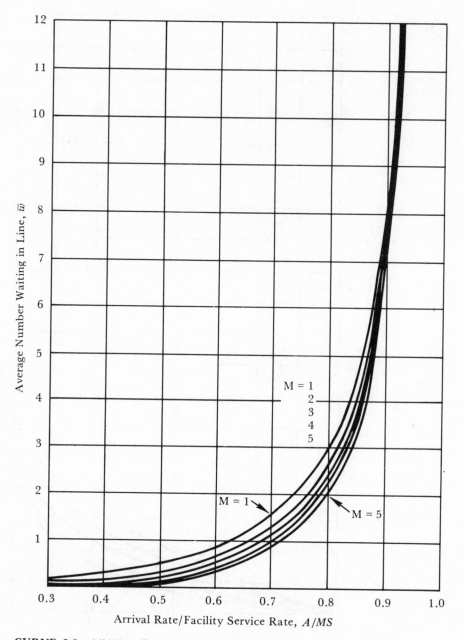

CURVE 6-2 A/MS vs. $\overline{w}$ **with Constant** M **Lines**

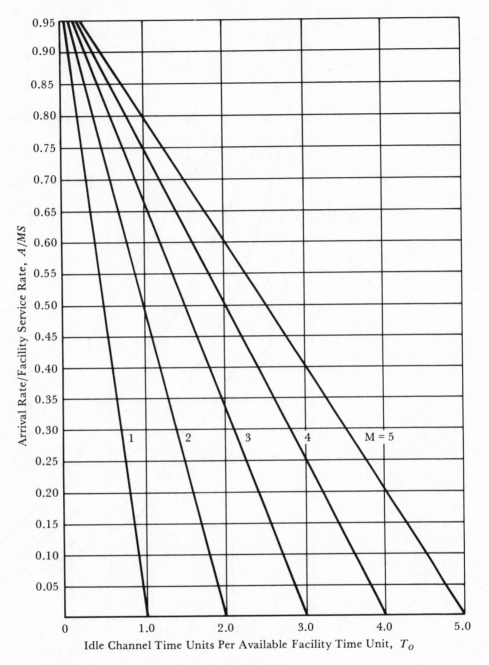

CURVE 6-3 *A/MS* vs. T_O **with Constant** *M* **Lines**

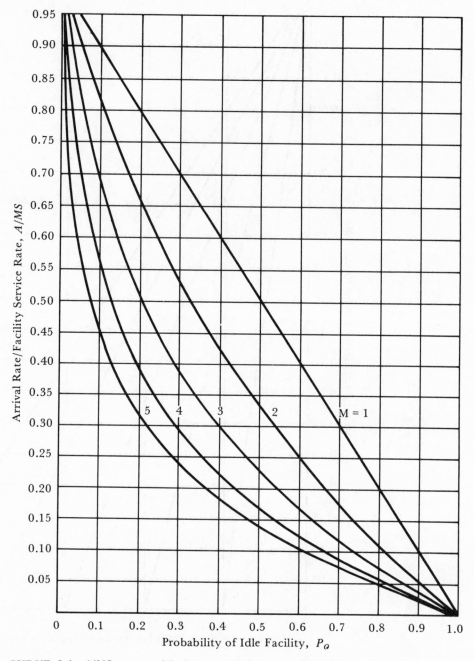

CURVE 6-4 A/MS vs. P_o with Constant M Lines

APPENDIX 6-3
Formulas for Waiting-Line Parameters

For the Single-Channel Situation:

$$T_O = P_O$$

$$P_O = 1 - \frac{A}{S}$$

$$P_n = \left(\frac{A}{S}\right)^n \left(1 - \frac{A}{S}\right) \text{ if } \frac{A}{S} < 1$$

$$\bar{n} = \sum_0^\infty nP_n = \frac{A/S}{1 - (A/S)}, \ \frac{A}{S} < 1$$

$$\bar{w} = \bar{n} - \left(\frac{A}{S}\right)$$

For the Multichannel Situation:

T_O: (defined by the authors to facilitate calculation of the cost of idle facility time)

$$M = 2, \ T_O = 2P_O + P_1$$

$$M = 3, \ T_O = 3P_O + 2P_1 + P_2$$

$$M = 4, \ T_O = 4P_O + 3P_1 + 2P_2 + P_3$$

$$M = 5, \ T_O = 5P_O + 4P_1 + 3P_2 + 2P_3 + P_4$$

$$P_O = \frac{1}{\dfrac{(A/S)^m}{m! \ (1 - A/mS)} + \sum_{n=0}^{m-1} \dfrac{(A/S)^n}{n!}}$$

$$P_n = P_O \left(\frac{A}{S}\right)^n \left(\frac{1}{n!}\right) \text{ for } n < m$$

$$P_n = P_O \left(\frac{A}{S}\right)^n \left(\frac{1}{m!m^{n-m}}\right) \text{ for } n \geqslant m$$

$$\bar{n} = \sum_0^\infty nP_n, \text{ or } \bar{n} = \frac{AS \left(\frac{A}{S}\right)^m P_O}{(m - 1)! \ (mS - A)^2} + \frac{A}{S}$$

$$\bar{w} = \bar{n} - \left(\frac{A}{S}\right)$$

$$\bar{T}_w = \bar{w}/A \text{ or } \bar{T}_n = \bar{n}/A \ \text{ (as appropriate)}$$

The Aggregate Planning Problem

7.1 INTRODUCTION

As explained earlier, inventories provide a means of storing capacity in periods of slack demand and assist in smoothing the impact of demand fluctuations on manpower levels. This chapter expands the options of the manager to include overtime, variable workweeks, subcontracting, and layoffs as viable approaches to managing fluctuating and unpredictable demand levels.

This problem is complicated in real business situations because of the numerous factors involved (the number of variables) and the uncertainty of the future (demand, productivity to be achieved, interest rates, etc.). In fact, there exists no single, rigorous analytical method for solving such problems in real-world situations. The task of the manager, then, is to search for the best manpower plan among the feasible and attainable operational plans which can be devised. What practical methods are available to assist the manager in achieving a series of satisfactory solutions to this open-ended problem? This question is the focus of this and the next chapter.

7.2 NATURE OF THE AGGREGATE PLANNING DECISION

Given a sales forecast, factory capacity, aggregate inventory levels, and the size of the work force, the manager of a manufacturing operation must decide at what rate of production he will operate his plant over a time frame of 3-18 months. The manager does not make this decision at budgeting time and then file it until a year-end review is made. The decision maker is rather in the position of continually reacting to a series of disequilibrium conditions caused by fluctuations in the incoming order rate.

In most firms this reaction need not be immediate as there is normally a buffer (an order backlog or finished-goods inventory) to absorb some fluctuations. Relying on these buffers is the only passive manner in which the decision maker can react to fluctuating order rates. All other options require active management decisions which tend to produce conflicts in trying to maintain a high customer-service level and a low inventory, a high customer-service level and a minimum idle time in the factory, and a low in-process inventory and minimum idle time.

In a study of 116 manufacturers of durables located in the Northeast, Shen reported that individual manufacturing units experienced more troublesome fluctuations than those shown in an aggregate indicator such as the Federal Reserve Board (FRB) manufacturing index.[1] Within a given business cycle, a firm would experience two or more cycles with amplitudes perhaps four times as great as the fluctuations in the FRB index during the general cycle. He also found that although a firm's output was adjusted to coincide with demand, the work-force level did not vary in proportion to the output change. From this evidence he concluded that manufacturing managements attempted to establish an equilibrium labor force and were slow to make work-force changes based on fluctuating demand. Once a change had been made, it was short-lived, and the work force quite rapidly returned to the equilibrium level when the demand shifted toward the expected norm.

Shen's study revealed a conscious bias on the part of the firms to meet fluctuations in orders through other buffer variables than the level of the work force. The strategy of changing the work force was the final option used only after the other options were tested and failed to produce satisfactory results.

DEFINING "THE MANAGER" AND "LABOR"

Before reviewing the possible courses of management action, it is necessary to be more specific concerning the identity of the decision maker who has been referred to thus far as the "manager." The manpower planning problem influences many facets of a firm's or profit center's performance, and decisions made strictly from the manufacturing manager's viewpoint might adversely affect the competitive marketing position of the firm and/or its financial stability. Thus, the focus for the decision *should* be that of the general manager, who is the integrating force for the various functions within the operation. The general manager is not necessarily expected to be involved in each problem situation, but should have established a broad set of guidelines

[1] T. Y. Shen, "Cyclical Behavior of Manufacturing Plants," *Journal of Industrial Economics*, April 1968, pp. 102-125.

within which the manufacturing manager is expected to meet manufacturing's shipment commitments to marketing, to control manufacturing costs within budget limits, and to maintain inventory investment levels consistent with an established policy. Within these guidelines the manufacturing manager is vested with the responsibility for making those adjustments in productive capacity which he deems necessary to solve particular manpower planning problems. His decisions to make major increases or decreases in the productive capacity are likely to be subject to review by the general manager. The terms "manager" or "decision maker" therefore refer to a manger responsible for manufacturing operations at the plant, division, or corporate level. It is assumed that all manpower planning decisions made by this manager may be reviewed and possibly altered by the general manager with final responsibility for integrating activities of the various business functions under his direction.

It is also necessary to provide a definition as to how the term "labor" is used in this text. The terms "labor force," "work force," "production employees," and other references to those engaged in production activities, are used interchangeably with "labor" throughout this text. These terms refer to the productive labor component of the work force, which includes that portion of the work force normally classified as direct labor and also certain other production employees within the work force who are normally classified as indirect labor, but whose numbers vary in direct proportion to changes in the firm's productive capacity.

THE MANAGER'S COURSES OF ACTION In resolving the manpower planning problem, the manager's broad courses of action in response to fluctuations in demand are to:

1) Make the labor-versus-inventory tradeoff.
2) Seek or farm out subcontract work.
3) Vary the load on the facility by altering the product mix.
4) Vary prices to counter-influence the demand pattern.
5) Increase or decrease the level of customer service.
6) Invest in equipment capable of large variations in output without requiring changes in the labor force.

As a qualification to the courses of management action discussed above, it should be pointed out that every alternative may not be open to the manager because the characteristics of his firm's business environment may bar him from considering various possible courses of action. An important example of this is the original equipment manufacturer (OEM) in the durable-goods industry. An OEM usually operates without a large finished-goods inventory, and the manufacturing schedule is based upon the backlog of booked orders; therefore, the alternative of absorbing demand increases via reductions in inventory is not available. The competitiveness of many OEM market segments mitigates against a general policy by OEMs of absorbing order increases into the backlog (which would lengthen delivery times), because their customers may turn to alternate suppliers and this loss of market share may be permanent. Therefore, OEMs must generally have the flexibility to expand (and contract) their productive capacity in response to the demand variations, either by adding to their labor force or by subcontracting production overflows during periods of peak orders. The remainder of this discussion is based on the assumption that a manufacturer can absorb some demand fluctuations without capacity adjustment, either by allowing the order backlog to vary in the case of the OEMs or by allowing the finished-goods inventory to fluctuate in those cases where manufacturers maintain sizable inventories.

LABOR VS. INVENTORY (OR BACKLOG) TRADEOFF   In making adjustments for the erratic inflow of orders over time, the manager has three "pure" strategies which involve a manpower-versus-inventory or manpower-versus-backlog tradeoff.

Alter the Work Force   The manager may attempt to match the production rate to the incoming order rate by hiring or laying off production employees. Although not ideal for the production employees, it could be useful for a firm such as a cannery, which adds a large force of college students on summer vacation to reach peak production during the harvest season. In most instances expansion of the work force requires training costs and a temporary lowering of average productivity. A reduction in the work force frequently results in lower worker morale and intensifies any management/labor conflicts. This leads to lower productivity, and the potential cost savings of the work-force reduction are not realized as the remaining employees retard their output to protect themselves against a similar fate.

Alter the Work Hours   The manager may try to maintain a constant work force and adjust the production rate to the incoming order rate by working undertime or overtime. The fluctuations in product demand are absorbed by working overtime to meet the peak demand and by working shorter workweeks in response to slack periods. Short-run changes in work-force size are avoided by varying the hours worked per week. This strategy is better than continual adjustments in the work force and thus may eliminate certain "frictional" costs and result in higher morale and productivity. The lowering in frictional costs cannot be achieved without encountering other problems. There is an upper limit to the number of hours an employee is willing to work in a week and there is a drop in productivity during prolonged periods of overtime work.

In periods of slack demand the firm faces the difficult task of dealing effectively with the costs of worker idle time. Limited use of shortened workweeks for all employees is possible and generally preferable by the management to an equivalent work-force reduction. Union contracts are now seeking to limit the manager's flexibility in using this option, as discussed later.

Alter the Inventory Level   The manager may try to maintain a constant work force and a constant production rate and allow inventories to fluctuate. This appears to be the textbook way to operate a consumer durables firm with an established product and a low risk of product obsolescence. For most firms this "pure" strategy creates a large buildup in inventory as a company enters a period of slack demand, requiring large and usually expensive storage facilities and the commitment of a substantial sum of working capital during a period of mixed expectations; it also exposes the firm to a major risk of obsolescence. Should the slack period be protracted due to generally soft economic or industry conditions, this third strategy would necessarily be modified or abandoned. Conversely, in a period of increased demand with concomitant changes in inventory or backlog, the result of employing this strategy would be an increase in order backlog, longer lead times, poorer customer service, possible lost sales, and potential entry of new competitors, both foreign and domestic.

SUB-CONTRACTING The manager may attempt to subcontract a portion of the peak demand to avoid undesirable variations in work-force levels while maintaining market share. Using subcontracting as an alternative, the firm should have smaller and more manageable shifts in inventory and work-force levels. Subcontracting is not without associated costs. Since subcontracted items generally cost more than items made in-house, the firm will earn a lower margin on these products unless it can pass along the higher cost. With spot subcontracting, the manager may have less control over timely deliveries and product quality. The best strategy is to select a subcontractor who has been a dependable supplier to the firm and is a known quantity with a vested interest in doing a good job. A survey of union agreements reported that 1 in 5 has a provision limiting the use of subcontracting.[2]

PRODUCT MIX The product mix is another variable whose manipulation provides an option in the manpower planning decision. In periods of peak demand, the work force would concentrate on those items having a lower labor content. This is a special case of the third "pure" strategy discussed earlier with interesting possibilities, which requires both a sophisticated control system and a high degree of success in forecasting the demand for individual product groups.

CUSTOMER SERVICE This term, as used here, refers to both the capacity to meet present shipping commitments and the ability to meet future customer demands within a suitable time period. When firms are operating their facilities at or very near their productive capacity, any increase in the customer order rate usually results in an increased order backlog (or decreased finished-goods inventory level). The manager can elect either to allow the backlog (or the finished-goods inventory) to absorb both increases and decreases in demand, or he can alter the productive-capacity level of the firm. For increased order levels the manager must make a tradeoff between the costs of increasing capacity versus the possibility of losing market share as a result of poor customer service.

---

[2] W. L. Tillery, "Layoff and Recall Provisions in Major Agreements," *Monthly Labor Review*, July 1971, pp. 41-46.

Given a decreasing order rate, the manager must tradeoff the disruption and costs of the layoff against the cost of increasing the finished-goods inventory (or decreasing the backlog).

Since fluctuating demand is the principal culprit in the manpower planning problem, one alternative is to exert some influence on the demand pattern. The airline and telephone companies are well known examples of service companies who have attempted to divert some of their business from the day hours to nights and weekends by offering substantial rate reductions. In manufacturing, the demand lacks such regularity, and the decision maker may lack the authority to adjust prices. An increase in prices to deflate a backlog or a price decrease to sell off excessive inventory are feasible solutions to the manpower planning problem, but the difficulty of implementation restricts the usefulness of price adjustments as alternatives.

7.3   RECENT DEVELOPMENTS IN THE ORGANIZED LABOR AREA

A substantial portion of all unionized manufacturing employees work under union contracts which provide for unemployment benefits, paid for by the employer, which supplement state Unemployment Insurance (UI). These unemployment plans are generally called Supplemental Unemployment Benefit (SUB) plans. The employer contributes a fixed amount per employee-hour to create a benefit fund. When the level of the fund reaches a value specified in the contract, the employer stops contributing until there is a layoff and the amount of the fund, including interest, falls below the specified value. An eligible worker may receive more than 90% of his normal take-home pay while on layoff, for up to 26 weeks. The unions have also attempted to eliminate short weeks or "work sharing" as management options in dealing with the manpower planning problem.

The supplemental benefits for layoffs accrue to the junior employees, while the elimination of short work weeks benefits the senior members since they can attain income continuity. Since short-week benefits are paid from the SUB fund, there is some question whether this clause serves as a deterrent to work sharing or as an incentive to the management, which can recover funds that would otherwise not be recoverable. The SUB plans have created an unusual attitude on the part of union members toward layoffs. Some contracts have a "reverse seniority" clause which gives the members an option to elect to be laid off, based on seniority.[3] The senior employees choose to be laid off at slightly reduced pay while newer employees who have not been employed long enough to receive SUB or UI, remain employed and build seniority. Productivity drops as the less skilled employees produce fewer goods at higher unit costs, and the potential benefits of the layoff to the company are only partially realized.

[3] Tillery, *Monthly Labor Review*, July 1971.

The uncertainties and conflicts arising from a reduction in the work force increase the complexities of the decision to add new personnel. In the future, additions to a firm's work force may be considered as similar to capital budgeting decisions, resulting from the push of unions to make labor a fixed cost.

The changing character of union wage settlements has also had an impact on decisions to adjust the level of the work force. These settlements have featured increasing fringe benefits, some of which become quasi-fixed costs to the firm, independent of the level of hours worked. A high level of fixed benefits relative to the overtime rate tends to induce the substitution of overtime hours for additions to the work force. To expand employment, some national economists have suggested that a change in the ratio of overtime pay to regular pay from 1.5 to 2 is required.

7.4   SUMMARY OF TRENDS

For the manufacturing sector in the U.S. to continue to grow at a rapid pace, manufacturing firms must do a better job of manpower planning. The following general trends of the 1960s give support to this position:

1) Product lines proliferated as firms sought the dollars of an increasingly selective and demanding set of consumers. More product variations meant more production setups and threatened efficient utilization of workers.
2) Trade unions made significant gains toward making labor a fixed cost. Contracts containing supplemental unemployment benefits, short-week benefits, and guaranteed annual wage provisions increased significantly.

The foregoing observations emphasize the economic benefits to be derived from an improvement in the manpower planning process.

7.5   THE AGGREGATE PLANNING PROBLEM – AN ILLUSTRATION

The crux of the manpower planning problem is the development of production-inventory plans to serve as the framework for managerial decisions on aggregate production levels and employment levels. Management, in general, and operations managers, in particular, are called upon to obtain the best utilization of organizational resources in meeting an anticipated dynamic demand pattern. Toward this end, managers have found that a process, generally known as master scheduling, provides a quantitative approach for evaluating alternative production-inventory plans in terms of product availability and cost considerations.

The planning of productive efforts on an aggregate basis can be defined as providing a schedule of production activity for an entire operating system. The diagram in Figure 7-1 represents an operating system which combines materials, labor, and other resources in an organized way with the objective of producing some particular goods or services. Regardless of the variety of goods or services which may flow from the system, a common unit of activity is selected as a base for allocating productive resources. The unit might be the physical dimensions of the goods or services — such as pounds, gallons, or pieces — or the productive inputs — such as equivalent machine hours, actual or standard man-hours, or raw materials. One dimension is chosen to represent all goods or services which have been forecast as the aggregate output for a planning period of from 6-18 months. Based on information about the system's operational transformation processes — such as productivity, material requirements, and equipment capacity — the manager adopts a production-inventory plan which will provide the quantity of planned aggregate output.

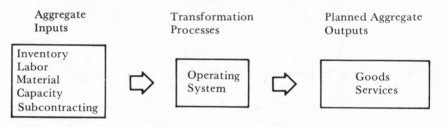

FIGURE 7-1 Input — Output Flow

The suitability of a production-inventory plan can be measured in terms of its capability for satisfactorily supplying needed goods or services and the extent to which it provides for maximizing profits or alternately minimizing costs. In most cases the two measures of success represent opposing forces, and a balance between the two must be brought about by management. For example, inventories allow an organization to achieve a smooth workflow, obtain reasonable capacity utilization, and provide acceptable service to consumer demands. All of these functions provide a service to either an organizational subsystem or to a customer; yet, maintaining these inventories may tie up 30% of an organization's invested capital. Management therefore plans and controls the accumulation of inventories to ensure that a desirable balance between inventory availability and inventory carrying cost is maintained for a given planning period.

Employment levels must also be planned and controlled. A work force is selected, trained, and paid to produce quality goods or services. Based on anticipated levels of activity and costs, employment levels are established for a planning period. If the management's expectations of future demand are not realized, should the work force be laid off or be asked to work shorter hours? Although employee morale and productivity and community good will would be enhanced by a stable employment policy, no organization can afford for very long the luxury of maintaining idle workers during a slack season.

7.6   DEVELOPING A MASTER PLAN[4]

As a basis for illustrating the nature of the master-scheduling problem, the development of alternative programs of action, and the selection of a suitable plan, consider the twelve-month forecast of demand (in terms of production units) shown in Figure 7-2.

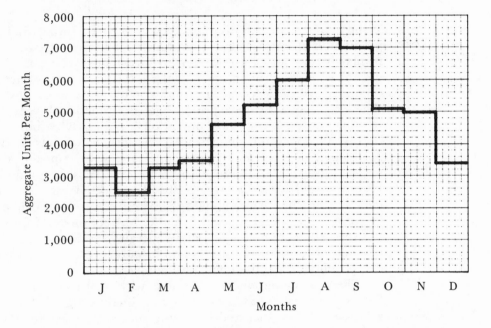

FIGURE 7-2   Twelve-Month Forecast of Aggregate Production Requirements

FORECASTING   Forecasting is the first step in the master-scheduling process. As noted earlier, future production requirements transformed into aggregate common units, serves as a base for developing alternative production programs. Different kinds of variation in the production requirements can be accounted for by forecasting methodology. Trends in the average requirements represent long-run growth or decay forces, and period-to-period variations in the requirements reflect recurrent seasonal and cyclical forces.

One kind of variation in a requirements pattern — random variations — cannot be accounted for by forecasting. Although the methods of forecasting provide an effective mechanism for establishing the probable trend and seasonal variations, random variations cannot be predicted. Consequently, management must maintain inventory accumulations to absorb random fluctuations. These inventories were called buffer stocks in Chapters 3 and 4. Service operations which cannot maintain inventories must absorb random fluctuations through the maintenance of excess capacity (including labor), or the use of overtime or part-time workers or subcontracting.

[4] This illustration was developed by using the master-scheduling problem approach and analysis procedures found in Elwood S. Buffa's books, *Production-Inventory Systems: Planning and Control* and *Operations Management*.

Given that a reliable forecast of production requirements (including trend and seasonal components) can be developed, how should a manager determine the best combination of resources for meeting the changing pattern of requirements? Which alternative programs of action are feasible and which program will be the least costly to a particular manufacturing company?

STRATEGIES AND COSTS   Two extreme or limiting strategies for structuring and evaluating production-inventory plans are available. First, a manager may choose to match fluctuating production requirements by increasing or decreasing the level of production activities. Increases in production can be generated by using direct and indirect overtime hours, by using part-time employees, by hiring additional full-time employees, by subcontracting certain production operations, and/or by adding a second- or third-shift operation. In a similar manner reductions in the level of production activity may be accomplished with opposite actions. The second fundamental strategy is to provide finished-goods inventories which are sufficient in size to absorb expected variations in requirements over the planning period. These inventories, called seasonal inventories, are held in excess of the buffer stocks of finished goods. Between these two fundamental strategies a manager can develop any number of alternative production-inventory plans to meet the forecast production requirements of Figure 7-2.

The cost components associated with a given plan are considered only when they are *incremental costs*. Incremental costs, such as those in Table 7-1, are incurred by virtue of a particular program of action and can vary widely with any proposed list of alternative programs. Production-related costs which do not vary with alternative programs are not relevant to the master-scheduling decision and are not considered as incremental costs. The manager estimates the incremental costs of changing the production activity from its existing level and of maintaining seasonal inventories of finished goods; he then adopts the production-inventory plan with the least total incremental costs. Within this plan more specific management decisions concerning the detailed schedules of individual products or services must be made.

INCREMENTAL COST ANALYSIS   The twelve-month forecast of aggregate production requirements and the buffer stocks held to absorb random fluctuations are listed in Table 7-2 along with the production days available in each month. From these data the cumulative data in Table 7-3 are developed. Columns 1 and 2 are obtained by an addition process, using the data from Table 7-2, Columns 1 and 2. Since a beginning buffer stock is available, this fact must be accounted for by subtracting its value from each of the values in Column 2, Table 7-3, thereby providing the data in Column 3. Then by adding for each month the cumulative requirements (Column 3, Table 7-3) to the buffer-stock requirements (Column 4, Table 7-3), the cumulative maximum production requirements in Column 5, Table 7-3 are found.

The cumulative maximum production requirements and the cumulative production days are plotted as shown in Figure 7-3. This

TABLE 7-1 Incremental Costs

Components of a Production-Inventory Plan	Types of Costs Incurred
Direct and indirect overtime hours	Loss of productivity, payroll costs 1.5—2 times greater than regular time
Direct and indirect undertime	Loss of productivity and morale
Part-time employees	Hourly rates, added supervisory responsibility
Hiring new employees	Recruiting, testing, training
Firing or laying off employees	Unemployment benefits, severance pay, community relations
Subcontracting	Unit costs are usually greater
Second and/or third shifts	Supervision, shift premiums, overhead
Seasonal inventory	Handling, storage, obsolescence, pilferage, capital investment
Production-capacity changes	Reorganizing facilities, starting up and shutting down equipment, rebalancing work force

TABLE 7-2 Forecast of Aggregate Production Requirements and Buffer Stocks

Month	(1) Available Production Days	(2) Units of Forecast Production Requirements	(3) Buffer Stock Requirements[1]
January	22	3300	1800
February	18	2520	1500
March	22	3300	1800
April	22	3520	2000
May	22	4620	2200
June	21	5250	2300
July	12	6000	2400
August	21	7350	2500
September	20	7000	2500
October	23	5060	2300
November	20	5000	2200
December	18	3420	1800

[1] January 1 beginning buffer-stock inventory is given at 2000 units.

graph shows the cumulative requirements which must be satisfied by any production-inventory plan considered in the master-scheduling process. As noted earlier, the evaluation of an alternative production-inventory plan is made on an incremental cost basis. Before deciding which of the alternative plans is best in terms of total incremental costs, additional information about the company's production operations and

TABLE 7-3 Development of Cumulative Data

Month	(1) Cumulative Production Days	(2) Cumulative Units of Production Requirements	(3) Cumulative Requirements less Beginning Buffer Stock of 2000 Units	(4) Buffer Stock Requirements	(5) Cumulative Maximum Production Requirements
January	22	3,300	1,300	1800	3,100
February	40	5,820	3,820	1500	5,320
March	62	9,120	7,120	1800	8,920
April	84	12,640	10,640	2000	12,640
May	106	17,260	15,260	2200	17,460
June	127	22,510	20,510	2300	22,810
July	139	28,510	26,510	2400	28,910
August	160	35,860	33,860	2500	36,360
September	180	42,860	40,860	2500	43,360
October	203	47,920	45,920	2300	48,220
November	223	52,920	50,920	2200	53,120
December	241	56,340	54,340	1800	56,140

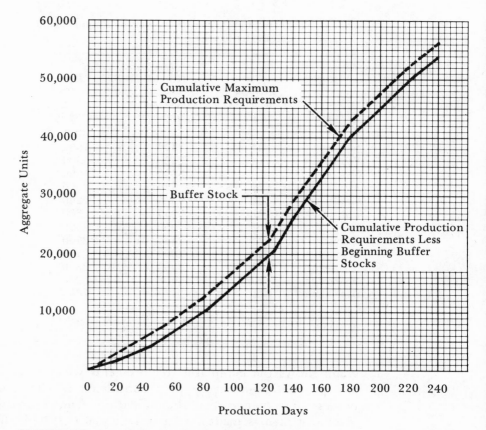

FIGURE 7-3 Cumulative Production Requirements

associated costs must be gathered. The following data are relevant to this example:

1) Maximum regular-time production capacity is given as 340 units per day.
2) Maximum combined regular-time and overtime production capacity is estimated to be 400 units per day.
3) The use of overtime capacity adds $20 to the production costs of a unit.
4) Seasonal inventory carrying costs are given as $40 per unit per year.
5) Subcontracting capacity may be utilized when the production rate exceeds 400 units per day.
6) Subcontracting adds $35 to the production costs of a unit.
7) Daily regular-time production rates may be changed monthly with an added change cost of $100/unit. This incremental cost includes the employment or separation costs which are incurred as management changes the level of productive activity. For a one-unit increase in the daily production rate, management must recruit, select, and train two men at a cost of $50 per man. A production decrease of one unit per day requires the separation of two men at a cost of $50 per man.

To illustrate the process of evaluating a plan, three possible alternatives will be examined. Each plan, stated in terms of the daily production rate, is shown in Figure 7-4. Plan 1 incorporates a constant daily production rate over the twelve-month planning period. This plan should result in high seasonal inventory carrying costs; however, it should minimize the overtime, production-rate change, and subcontracting costs. Plan 2 incorporates a daily production rate which follows the cumulative maximum-requirements curve, and it should result in low or no seasonal inventory carrying costs and high overtime, production-rate change, and subcontracting costs. Plan 3 is a production-inventory alternative that incorporates features of Plans 1 and 2.

These plans can also be drawn on a cumulative maximum-requirements graph. In Figure 7-5 each of the alternative production-inventory plans is represented. The seasonal inventory accumulated by a plan at any point in time is represented by a vertical line between a production-inventory plan curve and the cumulative maximum-requirements curve.

Plans 1 and 3 call for a substantial accumulation of seasonal inventory. Since the incremental inventory costs are stated in dollars per unit per year, the average seasonal inventory maintained under each plan must be calculated. The procedure for performing this calculation is illustrated in Table 7-4.

Using the information on the company's operations and costs, the incremental costs of seasonal inventories, overtime hours, production-rate changes, and subcontracting for each of the proposed plans are computed. The calculations of the incremental costs for Plan 3 are

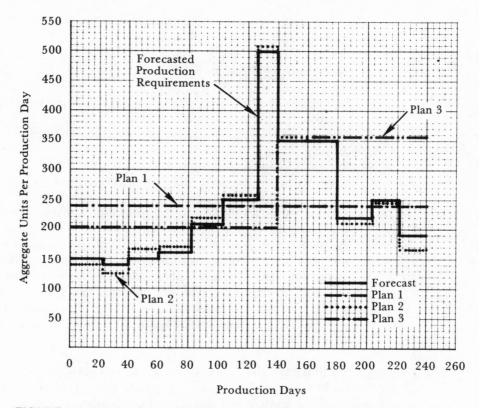

**FIGURE 7-4 Forecast Production Requirements, Plan 1, Plan 2, and Plan 3 —
All Based on Available Production Days**

illustrated in Table 7-5. The incremental costs for Plans 1 and 2 may be computed in a comparable way.

Table 7-6 shows the incremental cost components and totals for three alternative production-inventory plans. On the basis of least cost, a manager would favor Plan 2. However, Plan 2 requires large and frequent changes in the work force. If the labor market or company work force was sensitive to a fluctuating employment policy such as in Plan 2, a manager would most likely choose the level production strategy of Plan 1.

7.7   CONCLUSIONS

The procedures described do not generate alternative proposals to meet a forecast pattern of production requirements, but they make it possible to visualize some of the incremental cost effects of proposed production-inventory plans. The manager or staff specialist must supply the list of feasible alternative plans to be evaluated. For a complex problem hundreds of alternative plans may have to be evaluated before a satisfactory program is developed.

Key planning decisions regarding the levels and uses of productive resources are regularly made with only the tools of managerial experience, judgment, and intuition. When realistic cost data can be developed, however, key decisions for the planning and scheduling of

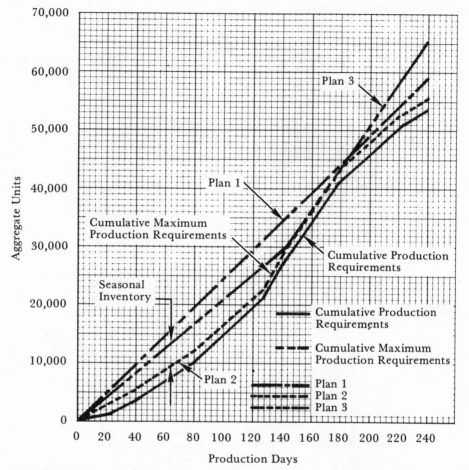

FIGURE 7-5 Cumulative Requirements and Production — Inventory Plans

aggregate production rates and employment levels can be made more effectively through an organized process of master scheduling. The degree of sophistication employed in the process may vary from largely intuitive to the use of simulation or mathematical programming techniques.

The next chapter treats the ways by which the process of generating and evaluating alternative strategies may be improved.

7.8   BIBLIOGRAPHY

Buffa, Elwood S. *Operations Management.* New York: John Wiley & Sons, Inc., 1968.

Buffa, Elwood S., and Taubert, William H. *Production-Inventory Systems: Planning and Control.* Homewood, Ill.: Richard D. Irwin, Inc., 1972.

Burack, Elmer H. *Manpower Planning and Programming.* Boston: Allyn & Bacon, Inc., 1972.

Holt, Charles C., Modigliani, Franco, Muth, John F., and Simon, Herbert A. *Planning Production, Inventories, and Work Force.* Englewood Cliffs, N.J.: Prentice-Hall, Inc., 1960.

Johnson, Lynwood A., and Montgomery, Douglas C. *OR in Production Planning, Scheduling, and Inventory Control.* New York: John Wiley & Sons, Inc., 1974.

TABLE 7-4 Average Seasonal Inventory Calculation for Plan 3

Month	(1) Available Production Days	(2) Planned Production Rate per Day	(3) Production Output per Month	(4) Cumulative Production Output per Month	(5) Cumulative Maximum Production Requirements	(6) Seasonal Inventory Column (4) − Column (5)
January	22	208	4576	4,576	3,100	1476
February	18	208	3744	8,320	5,320	3000
March	22	208	4576	12,896	8,920	3976
April	22	208	4576	17,472	12,640	4832
May	22	208	4576	22,048	17,460	4588
June	21	208	4368	26,416	22,810	3606
July	12	208	2496	28,912	28,910	2
August	21	355	7455	36,367	36,360	7
September	20	355	7100	43,467	43,360	107
October	23	355	8165	51,632	48,220	3412
November	20	355	7100	58,732	53,120	5612
December	18	355	6390	65,122	56,140	8982
Totals	241					39,600

$$\text{Average seasonal inventory} = \frac{\text{Seasonal inventory total}}{\text{Number of months}} = \frac{39,600}{12} = 3,300$$

TABLE 7-5 Calculation of Incremental Costs Components for Plan 3

Month	(1) Available Production Days	(2) Planned Production Rate (units/day)	(3) Magnitude of Production-Rate Change (units/day)	(4) Units/Day Produced by Overtime Activity = Planned Prod. Rate − Regular-Time Prod. (not to exceed overtime capacity)	(5) Units/Month Produced by Overtime Activity	(6) Units/Day Produced by Subcontracting = Planned Production Rate − [Regular-Time + Overtime Capacity]	(7) Units/Month Produced by Subcontracting Capacity
J	22	208	0	0	0	0	0
F	18	208	0	0	0	0	0
M	22	208	0	0	0	0	0
A	22	208	0	0	0	0	0
M	22	208	0	0	0	0	0
J	21	208	0	0	0	0	0
J	12	208	0	0	0	0	0
A	21	355	132	15	315	0	0
S	20	355	0	15	300	0	0
O	23	355	0	15	345	0	0
N	20	355	0	15	300	0	0
D	18	355	0	15	270	0	0
Totals			132		1,530	0	0

Production-level change cost = Column 3 total × dollars/unit   =   132 units × $100/unit = $ 13,200

Overtime costs   = Column 5 total × dollars/unit   = 1,530 units × $ 20/unit = $ 30,600

Seasonal inventory costs   = Average seasonal inventory × dollars/unit = 3,300 units × $ 40/unit = $132,000
(See Table 7-4)

Subcontracting costs   = Column 7 total × dollars/unit   =   0

Total incremental costs $175,800

TABLE 7-6 Incremental Cost Comparisons for Plans 1, 2, and 3

	Plan 1	Plan 2	Plan 3
Production-level changes	$ 0	$ 47,300	$ 13,200
Overtime	$ 0	$ 24,700	$ 30,600
Seasonal inventory	$153,690	$ 413	$132,000
Subcontracting	$ 0	$ 45,780	$ 0
Totals	$153,690	$118,193	$175,800

Approaches To The Aggregate Planning Problem

8.1 INTRODUCTION

The literature in the management science field offers a number of quantitative methods that could be used to compute aggregate workforce and production-rate decisions for most manufacturing firms. These quantitative methods would yield optimal decisions within the limited framework of their specific restrictive assumptions. Most of these methods are taught in industrial management, industrial engineering, graduate business, or operations research curricula, and are regularly discussed at technical society meetings. Despite this wide understanding and the substantial economic benefits to be derived from optimal decisions, reports of successful applications of these quantitative methods to the manpower planning problem remain scarce after more than a decade since reports of the first applications were published.

Why are these methods not being widely utilized to determine optimal manpower planning decisions? The reason cited most often is that the management decision maker considers the manpower planning problem to be too complex to be approximated by continuous linear or quadratic relationships, as required by most of the optimizing methods. Other logical reasons why quantitative methods have not been generally adopted by operating managers include:

1) Managers may not view the aggregate production planning decision in toto, but may focus their attention on short-term segmented

production and inventory decisions and on long-term company objectives.

2) The quantitative methods tend to support more frequent changes in the level of the work force than the managements find palatable.

3) Poor intermediate-range forecasting systems exist throughout most manufacturing industries.

While the first two reasons represent organizational or attitudinal impedances to the use of mathematical methods, the third presents a difficult operational reality. The availability of a manpower forecast is absolutely essential to manpower planning. The results of one study showed that although 72% of the sample of manufacturing firms forecast all or part of their manpower requirements, only 11% used their forecasts to make production planning decisions.[1] This evidence supports the conclusion that the manpower planning decision was not thought of as a coordinated decision.

If a company made a manpower forecast, why was it not utilized for production planning decisions? First, the majority of the forecasts (72%) were made at intervals of one year or longer and were of limited use in manpower planning. Second, many firms (50%) had been preparing manpower forecasts for less than five years, and these were used more for technical- and special-skill recruiting by the personnel department than for any other purpose. Finally, many firms found their forecasts to be grossly inaccurate and felt better quantitative methods were required.

Managers thus lack an accepted quantitative approach to the manpower planning problem. The existing optimization approaches are too restrictive in their model formulations and generally require excessive computation. The management science research efforts in the manpower planning area continue to be concentrated on the formulation or modeling of these problems in terms of well-known mathematical optimization techniques. Only a few reported studies have focused on either the development of nonoptimizing heuristic approaches to such problems or the application of digital computer simulation methodology for the modeling of the industrial environment. Progress in these latter areas may be beneficial in reducing the perceived "applications gap" that exists between the published management science approaches and actual industrial applications.

8.2 A SURVEY OF CURRENT AGGREGATE PLANNING PRACTICES

A survey[2] was conducted to establish a baseline of current industry practices within the area of manpower planning and aggregate produc-

---

[1] H. G. Heneman, et al., *Manpower Planning and Forecasting in the Firm: An Exploratory Probe.* National Technical Information Service Publications (Washington, 1968).

[2] Winston T. Shearon, *A Study of the Aggregate Production Planning Problem,* a dissertation submitted in partial fulfillment of the requirements for the degree of Doctor of Business Administration, The Colgate Darden Graduate School of Business Administration, University of Virginia, August, 1974.

tion scheduling policies. The survey was intended to provide both quantitative and qualitative data which could form a basis for model building and analysis in the area of manpower planning. For these purposes the questionnaire was directed toward plant-level production controllers or plant managers. The respondents represented a broad variety of corporations from among the largest in the country to a few small companies with fewer than 200 employees.

Of the 100 subjects polled, 48 submitted positive responses. The reasons given by five firms declining by letter to respond to the questionnaire were of considerable interest. These firms were all prominent among the 500 largest industrial companies in the U.S. In each case the survey addressee had passed the survey on to a corporate-level manager of manufacturing or manpower planning and development. These recipients stated that the diverse nature of their operations would prohibit a single answer to many of the questions, and most of their divisions (and probably all plants) would lack the information to respond from the vantage point intended by the survey. These statements support an earlier view that the manpower planning problem is not considered to be a single problem in a large corporation, but rather is segmented and coped with independently in the decentralized operating units.

SURVEY RESPONSES[3]   The survey provided a measure of the breadth in size of the operations among the reporting firms. A fairly broad range of plant sizes (from 100 employees to 6,000 employees per plant) were represented in the results. Some of the survey firms doubtless felt that a range of plant sizes made response to the question infeasible.

Thirty-six of the 48 respondents reported their manufacturing employees were represented by a union. The 3-to-1 split between union and nonunion plants offered some assurance that the survey reached a broad sample of industrial settings.

Nineteen of the 36 firms reporting union representation (more than 50%) had supplemental unemployment benefit (SUB) clauses. These data emphasized the growing effort by organized labor to make manpower adjustments an expensive alternative for solving the aggregate production planning problem. Additionally, 14 of the 36 firms with union contracts stated that their union agreement had a restrictive subcontracting clause.

Decisions regarding work-force changes were reported to be made at the plant level by the plant manager or his staff. By attempting to optimize his plant's performance review, the plant manager might trade off poor customer service which would not be reflected in his personal performance review. The plant manager does not view the problem from the broader corporate or divisional vantage point, but rather approaches the decision process from his narrower point of view.

Forty-four of the 48 firms reported that manufacturing employment had risen, dropped, or fluctuated by more than 5% during the past five years. The 11-to-1 response indicated overwhelmingly that employment levels had changed within the respondent firms.

---

[3] The detailed survey responses are given in Appendix 8-1.

Forty-two of the 48 firms reported they attempt to maintain a level pattern of production and a constant-size work force. Managers thus make their manpower planning decisions within the strictures of a policy of labor stability. The data indicate that most firms attempt to maintain a constant-size work force regardless of the demand pattern for their products.

The firms reported they operate in a labor market that may be best described as tight (11 firms), moderate (34 firms), or abundant (3 firms). The finding that less than 25% of the respondents' plants were in "tight" labor markets discounted scarce labor supply as a principal justification for the many firms electing to maintain constant-size work forces.

Demand increases are met first through overtime and are followed, when required, by manpower additions. The passive actions concerning the inventory and backlog are thus utilized with less frequency than are the aggressive actions of overtime and manpower adjustments. Under conditions of increasing demand these passive actions could prove more economic if the demand subsequently declined. Pressure on operations management to meet increased demand with increased productive capacity is great, however. This is explained by data reported later which show that meeting customer demand schedules is the most important measure of operations management performance.

The survey data show that when faced with falling demand, management responds first through passive activities. Reducing the backlog and building inventories allows plant management to ride out a temporary downturn without layoffs which damage morale, productivity, and union/management relations. Plant management is seen to be more likely to reduce the work force than to reduce the workweek hours. If the downturn persists, the company will be faced with a small backlog and a large inventory, and the eventual layoff situation will be more severe. The low ranking of price cutting followed the earlier finding that manpower decisions are typically made at the plant level. The product price is rarely within the plant manager's sphere of authority. The most logical microeconomic response to a decreased demand must therefore be made apart from the manpower planning decision.

Meeting delivery schedules outranks all other criteria and explains why managers react to demand increases with agressive rather than passive action. The additional direct and indirect costs incurred for overtime and manpower training were rated as less significant measures of performance than meeting schedules. The low ranking of inventory turnover as a performance measure supports the management uses of inventory as an alternative to work-force reductions when demand sags.

The last-place rating for even-tempered union relations can be interpreted to imply that few managers are actually rewarded on that measure. In the long run, however, superior performance at meeting schedules and controlling costs is highly dependent upon successful handling of the union on a daily basis. The majority of responses (about three-fourths) indicated that potential management/union conflicts would not dissuade management from an economic course.

To summarize the survey results, work-force levels in a typical firm are planned on a three-month horizon, and plans are reviewed monthly for the purpose of adjustment. The decision maker usually has sales forecasts which are considered accurate to ±10%. When faced with a slackening demand, the alternative of work sharing via 32-hour work-weeks would not normally be selected.

If overtime is required to meet expanded demand, the firm would follow a 48-hour week (when required) for 9-12 weeks before increasing the size of the work force. The expansion of the workweek to 56 or more hours is not considered feasible by the typical firm.

When manpower is added, the normal training period before an employee reaches the standard rate is 5-6 weeks. Internal promotion of employees to higher job grades requires a similar training period. Employees recalled from layoff status are expected to resume the standard production rate within two weeks, and workers who are bumped down to a lower labor-skill position when there is a general layoff also usually achieve the standard rate in two weeks or less.

The typical firm does not know the cost of laying off an employee, although many indicated qualitatively that this is an expensive item. Of the 13 firms who supplied a quantitative response, the majority placed their costs within the $500-$1,000 bracket. The data suggest that the decision makers consider work-force reductions to be very expensive and seek to avoid them by alternative feasible actions.

CONCLUSIONS A number of important findings have been drawn from the survey reported in this chapter. The more significant findings were:

1) Plant managers and their staffs make manpower planning decisions. These managers are responsible for operational decisions but not for marketing decisions; hence, they must solve problems arising from demand fluctuations without the ability to influence demand through marketing efforts.

2) A majority of firms attempt to maintain a constant-size work force whether their demand pattern is uniform, seasonal, cyclical, or constant growth. In more than half of the union agreements the firms were committed to pay supplemental benefits to employees who were layed off. With union pressure to maintain steady employment increasing the economic consequences of altering work-force levels, managers will find their options to respond to demand variations increasingly restricted and expensive.

3) The survey provided significant results concerning the ranking of decision alternatives. If demand increases beyond normal capacity, the most likely management reaction is to work overtime for 2-3 months before adding to the work force. The tenuous nature of demand increases and the pressure to meet customer demands make this policy the most feasible approach. Managers' initial response to declining demand is to build inventory and reduce the order backlog. These passive actions avoid union/management conflicts but increase the exposure to risks of obsolete inventory or an inadequate backlog to support efficient production.

4) The results concerning the criteria for evaluating operations management provided insight into the factors influencing the choices of management actions discussed in the preceding paragraphs. The most important criterion is the ability to meet customer demand schedules. The logical response in an increasing demand situation is to work overtime even though per-unit costs are increased. When the situation reverses and demand falls below capacity, the most important criteria of meeting schedules and controlling direct costs and indirect costs are all met satisfactorily while building inventory or reducing the backlog. The relatively low-perceived importance of inventory turnover makes this policy the most reasonable for a manager. A particular point to reemphasize is that operations managers are evaluated on multiple criteria, and the formal structuring of a general decision framework is complicated by the lack of a single measure of performance.

8.3   THE MANPOWER DECISION FRAMEWORK: THE INDICATORS

The results of the Shearon survey have been used to construct a decision framework for the general manpower planning problem.

For the decision-maker to function rationally in resolving the manpower planning problem, he must have available indicators which can serve as measures of the demand/capacity conditions over both the short and the long term. The short-range indicator should refer to the situation in the short-range planning period, i.e., the *next* week or the *next* month for which a production-level decision must be made. The appropriate indicator for this short-range view is the product required to service demand in that period. When production capacity differs from the short-term product requirement, then some adjustment of the production-capacity level may be necessary. Before deciding upon a particular adjustment, however, the decision maker should look beyond the short-term imbalance and consider the future impact of an adjustment of productive capacity. For assessment of long-term demand/capacity relationships, the decision maker needs a forecast of product requirements. A sales forecast for the next 3-6 months might serve in many firms as such a projection of future requirements. An indicator which compares the projected sales rate to the current production-capacity rate could function as the long-term measure.

In the durable-goods industry a better indicator of future demand during the next 3-6 months would be the backlog of orders already booked but possibly not yet released to production. When combined with information concerning special sales campaigns or product seasonability, the size of the order backlog gives the decision maker a valid measurement of future productive-capacity requirements.

The manager thus operates within a decision framework in which he must consider separate indicators to reflect demand/capacity relationships over two different time frames. These two time frames are 1) the current month (or week) for which a production level decision must be made, and 2) the planning period beyond the current month (or week) for which the backlog serves as a useful forecast of future demand conditions. The latter period could vary from a single month to a year, depending upon a particular firm's competitive environment.

The Current Period Ratio (CPR) for the short-term time frame is defined as:

$$CPR = \frac{\text{Demand for current period production}}{\text{Current period productive capacity}}$$

When demand and capacity for the current period are equal, this indicator would be 1. A CPR approximately equal to 1 would indicate no need for management action without further study of the second parameter, the Planning Period Ratio (PPR).

The PPR measures the long-run time frame and is defined as follows:

$$PPR = \frac{\text{Average monthly order backlog and additional anticipated orders in planning period}}{\text{Monthly productive capacity}}$$

The norm for the PPR would also be a ratio approximately equal to one. For example, a firm that looked ahead for three months beyond the current month would normally expect to have a forecast average load equal to the monthly productive capacity. If the ratio differed from the norm, it might indicate a need either to take some action within the current production period to add manpower (when PPR is greater than 1) or, conversely, to reduce productive capacity (when PPR is less than 1).

The CPR and PPR indicators are familiar in one form or another to almost all plant managers and their staffs as necessary inputs to the manpower planning process. The plant decision maker would usually be more concerned with an imbalance indicated by CPR than with one indicated by PPR because CPR measures the extent of the immediate problem which he faces. Although potential future imbalance indicated by PPR could not be discounted by the decision maker, he would, nonetheless, concentrate his energies on developing a solution to the more immediate demand/capacity matching problem. The manpower decision framework in this chapter allows a decision maker to consider CPR and PPR simultaneously in his decision process.

8.4   THE MANPOWER DECISION FRAMEWORK

In Table 8-1, a 3 × 3 matrix has been drawn to represent nine possible joint combinations of CPR and PPR. The rows correspond to the alternative conditions of PPR — less than, approximately equal to, or

TABLE 8-1. The Manpower Decision Matrix

Planning Period Ratio (PPR)	Current Period Ratio (CPR)		
	<1	$\simeq 1$	>1
<1	CPR = Low PPR = Low State I	CPR = Normal PPR = Low State II	CPR = High PPR = Low State III
$\simeq$	CPR = Low PPR = Normal State IV	CPR = Normal PPR = Normal State V	CPR = High PPR = Normal State VI
>1	CPR = Low PPR = High State VII	CPR = Normal PPR = High State VIII	CPR = High PPR = High State IX

greater than a preferred or ideal level of unity. The columns correspond to the possible conditions that the current demand/capacity ratio (CPR) could indicate — less than, approximately equal to, or greater than unity. The term "approximately equal" is intended to indicate that small deviations (for example, 5%) from the norm will be allowed in the CPR and PPR ratios. With this nine-position matrix, a manpower planning problem can be categorized as being one of nine distinct subproblems. The ability to separate this problem into manageable subproblems should improve the understanding of the particular situation within each subunit.

The remainder of the chapter focuses sequentially on each of the nine problem states. Feasible courses of action for each state are evaluated, and a "best" set of actions is selected for each state.

STATE I:
CPR = LOW,
PPR = LOW

In State I the manager faces an overcapacity situation in both the short and long terms. The alternative of building up a finished-goods inventory in order to ride out the downturn usually represents a high-risk policy, as inventory financing costs and the conversion of liquid financial resources into less liquid inventory could seriously damage the financial position of the firm. If the manager had available any significant flexibility in altering the degree of subcontracting activity, he could consider "bringing inside" some items now subcontracted to suppliers.

Union pressure against work-sharing (working short weeks) often prevents this option from being more than an interim measure. Even if this option were available to a manager as a viable alternative, he would still probably not choose to pursue it if demand/capacity conditions were as defined in State I. This is because productivity drops when short weeks are instituted, as the imminent threat of a layoff encourages a slowdown to preserve some jobs. Also, the employee fringe benefit costs are approximately 30% of the employees' total compensation. These costs do not vary with the hours worked. Hence, the ratio of indirect to direct costs would increase more under a short-workweek policy than under a policy in which a layoff was used to reduce productive capacity. Therefore a manager should generally respond to State I with a layoff decision. The extent of the layoff should be a cutback to the maximum employee level needed to produce either the current demand or the projected demand (monthly backlog).

STATE II:
CPR = NORMAL,
PPR = LOW

In State II the short-range demand/capacity relationship is balanced, but the projections show a serious drop in the demand over the long-run planning horizon. Intracorporate pressure to meet the current demand schedules (usually from marketing management) often prevents the manager from taking any actions that might reduce current output. The manager might consider the possibility of bringing inside any subcontracts which may expire in the near future or which could be easily terminated. A manager might cut back on the number of recently hired trainees (if any) who are not entitled to layoff and unemployment benefits. The personnel cutback should be to a level that would adjust future capacity to a point perhaps midway between the current demand and the projected future demand levels.

STATE III:
CPR = HIGH,
PPR = LOW

In State III the short-range demand is greater than the productive capacity, but the projected long-run demand reflects a potentially serious overcapacity situation. The importance of meeting demand schedules presents the manager with the difficult trade off of working overtime in the current period and then laying off some employees in the next period or leveling the demand pattern somewhat by delaying the production of some current orders until the later period. In those cases where a general manager was the decision maker, he might select the latter alternative to trade off a lowering in customer service for a more stable work force. In most situations, however, manufacturing managers are the decisionmakers, and they are most likely to elect the alternative of overtime in the current period followed by a layoff the next period. Thus, some production leveling would occur if current demand exceeded current capacity by more than the normal 20% additional capacity that could be gained through a 48-hour workweek.

STATE IV:
CPR = LOW,
PPR = NORMAL

The projected demand/capacity ratio in State IV is balanced over the long-term planning horizon, but the short-term demand is significantly less than the available productive capacity. The plant manager must, in this case, trade off the risk and cost of building inventory against the disruption and union pressures resulting from a shortened workweek.

The plant manager assumes only a small risk when inventory is manufactured against an order backlog since his performance measurement usually does not emphasize inventory turnover. Consequently, the decision to build inventory appears very logical. Following this alternative, however, does not actually solve the problem but merely shifts it into the next time frame. If the future demand turns out to be less than expected, then the inventory of finished goods becomes an undesirable permanent investment. A more satisfactory policy would be to mix inventory and short-workweek policies to more nearly balance demand

and capacity. A reasonable policy might be to work no more than two shortened weeks in any month and no more than four in any quarter.

STATE V:
CPR=NORMAL,
PPR = NORMAL

Both short- and long-range demand/capacity ratios are balanced in State V, so no management decision is required.

STATE VI:
CPR = HIGH,
PPR = NORMAL

State VI short-term demand is considerably greater than the productive capacity. Over the longer planning horizon, however, demand and capacity appear to be balanced. The need is for immediate action to meet the current demand. The addition of manpower, however, is not feasible since the new personnel would not be required after the current production period. The manager may choose to meet as much of the excess current demand as possible with overtime. Alternatively, he may restrict the overtime and shift some of these requirements to the next period. In State III the manager faced a somewhat similar situation of excess current demand and was assumed to respond with limited overtime to meet schedules even though the demand projections indicated a layoff would be required in the following period. The situation is similar here as the manager would face the same pressure to meet the schedules, but in State VI he would respond with more overtime per employee than in State III. An upper limit on overtime is assumed to be 40% greater than the standard workweek, or 56 hours per week. There is little, if any, justification for shifting any of the current period demand into the following period because it would still require overtime to produce.

STATE VII:
CPR = LOW,
PPR = HIGH

In State VII short-term demand is less than the available capacity, but future demand is projected to be substantially greater than the present production limit. The manager's logical response to this state would be to produce at the normal productive capacity level and build ahead some of the items in the backlog. In addition to this response, the manager must also face the question of whether to hire additional employees in the current period or to wait a month before deciding on manpower adjustments. The high cost of training and subsequently laying off a trained employee would probably influence the manager to follow a wait-and-see policy with respect to additional hirings. For these reasons the decision to run the production facility at its present capacity in order both to meet current demand and to build up a modest inventory would be the most rational decision for State VII.

STATE VIII:
CPR=NORMAL,
PPR = HIGH

The short-term capacity in State VIII matches the current demand requirements, but future projections indicate that demand will exceed capacity over the longer-term planning interval. The preferred response in State VII of producing at present capacity and waiting a month before deciding if additional manpower was required should not be followed in this situation. Producing at current capacity would not provide any inventory buffer for the following period, and overtime would be needed in great amounts in later periods in order to meet increased demand.

The opposite reaction to the wait-and-see policy would be to hire (or in some cases, recall from layoff) sufficient workers to balance future capacity with future demand. Since most firms responding to the survey indicated that new hires took five or more weeks to train, the manager might possibly decide to hire enough new employees in the current month to be able to meet the future demand requirements of the period when the new people achieve the standard skill levels. The uncertain nature of future demand projections, however, gives a degree of risk to this decision. If the projections were overly optimistic, then the training and subsequent discharging of the new employees would be both expensive and unnecessary. A moderate approach midway between the wait-and-see and the hire-to-meet-future-capacity decisions would be to hire about one-half the additional manpower. This policy would offer less risk if projections of future demand are too high. Furthermore, if sales increase, there would probably be sufficient additional capacity to meet demand with moderate overtime until more workers could be trained.

STATE IX:
CPR = HIGH,
PPR = HIGH

In State IX both the current demand and the projected demand exceed the firm's productive capacity. The manager's response to this situation must reflect both the desire to satisfy the current period's demand and the need for increases in the permanent work force, as indicated by the larger order backlog. The current period's requirements might be satisfied by extending the workweek to the extent possible. There is, in fact, no other alternative action open to the manager if he is to meet the demands on time.

For the plant to be able to meet the projected demand requirements without great amounts of overtime in future months, new employees must be hired within the current month. The question arises whether to hire the full staff required to meet future demand or to hire an increment, as in State VIII. The higher current demand is interpreted as a positive leading indicator that the high future demand projections are likely to be fulfilled. Therefore hiring the full complement of additional employees would probably be the most effective decision.

8.5   SUMMARY

The preceding discussion developed a Manpower Decision Framework (MDF) in which the manpower planning problem can be subdivided into nine subproblems. The subproblems correspond to different states defined by demand/capacity ratios. The determination of the "best" decision, given a set of ratios which fall very near the borderline between matrix cells, would be based on management's judgment and not strictly on general decisions specified for that cell. For each subproblem, the preceding discussion focused on the "best" decision the manager could make, given the various union, marketing, and cost pressures impinging upon the situation. A summary of these actions has been compiled in Table 8-2.

TABLE 8-2 Summary of Manpower Planning Decisions

CPR = Low PPR = Low State I	CPR = Normal PPR = Low State II	CPR = High PPR = Low State III
Layoff	No action	Limited overtime
CPR = Low PPR = Normal State IV	CPR = Normal PPR = Normal State V	CPR = High PPR = Normal State VI
Short weeks, build inventory	No action	Overtime
CPR = Low PPR = High State VII	CPR = Normal PPR = High State VIII	CPR = High PPR = High State IX
Build inventory	Limited hiring	Overtime, hire new personnel

The organization of the manpower planning problem into the MDF provides a basis for improved communications between decision makers and planning specialists. A research study which presents the results of simulation studies of the MDF is presented with the case studies at the end of this section. The MDF achieved relevant cost levels very close to the optimal solution to a well-known published manpower planning problem. The MDF approach required significantly fewer changes in manpower levels and thus provided more acceptable production-inventory patterns.

8.6   BIBLIOGRAPHY

Conrath, David W., and Hamilton, William F. "The Economics of Manpower Pooling." *Management Science*, October 1971.

Lundgren, Earl F., and Schneider, James V. "A Marginal Cost Model for the Hiring-Overtime Decision." *Management Science*, February 1971.

Rothstein, Marvin. "Scheduling Manpower by Mathematical Programming." *Industrial Engineering*, April 1972.

Shearon, Winston T. *A Study of the Aggregate Production Planning Problem*, a dissertation submitted in partial fulfillment of the requirements for the degree of Doctor of Business Administration, The Colgate Darden Graduate School of Business Administration, University of Virginia, August, 1974.

Sobel, Matthew J. "Employment Smoothing (Capital Accumulation) with Production for Stochastic Demand." *Management Science*, January 1970.

Warner, D. Michael, and Prawda, Juan. "A Mathematical Programming Model for Scheduling Nursing Personnel In A Hospital." *Management Science*, December 1972, Part I.

Weber, Wesley L. "Manpower Planning in Hierarchial Organizations: A Computer Simulation Approach." *Management Science*, November 1971.

APPENDIX 8-1
Responses to the Survey of Current
Aggregate Planning Practices

The employment levels in the respondents' plants were reported as follows:[4]

Plant Employment	Number of Responses
50-150	4
151-350	13
351-500	5
501-750	4
751-1250	8
>1250	11

Decisions concerning work-force additions or reductions were reported to be made at various levels in the organization as shown:

Decision Level	Number of Responses
Plant	36
Division	8
Group	1
Corporate	3

The manager generally responsible for altering the work force level was reported as follows:

Decision Maker	Number of Responses[5]
Plant manager	21
Plant staff	17
Division director of manufacturing	13
Division general manager	5
Corporate general manager	1

The variations in employment level were attributed to the following factors:

4	Expansion into new products (including mergers)
5	Technological changes in manufacturing
27	Changes in the rate of demand for products
12	General condition of the economy

The pattern of monthly demand for the firms' products was described as follows:

12	Uniform throughout the year
12	Cyclical (with erratic fluctuations)
13	Seasonal
11	Steady growth

[4] Some of the table entries do not add to 48 since not all of the respondents answered each part of each question.
[5] Totals more than 48 due to multiple responses by 9 respondents.

APPENDIX 8-1 (continued)

The cross-classification of intent to stabilize the work force versus the nature of the product demand is presented below:

Product Demand	Stable Work Force	Volatile Work Force
Uniform	12	—
Seasonal	10	3
Cyclical	12	—
Steady growth	8	3

The normal time horizon for planning production work-force levels was reported as follows:

Horizon	Number of Firms
1 month	6
3 months	20
6 months	12
9 months	1
12 months	6

The production plan was reported to be reviewed monthly (27), weekly (20), and daily (1).

The number of 56-hour overtime weeks that would be used to meet an increased demand before new manpower was added was given as follows:

Usage of 56-Hour Week	Number of Responses
Zero weeks	16
1-2 weeks	5
3-4 weeks	10
5-8 weeks	10
9-12 weeks	6
12-20 weeks	1

The number of 48-hour overtime weeks which would be used was stated as follows:

Usage of 48-Hour Week	Number of Responses
Zero weeks	3
1-2 weeks	3
3-4 weeks	5
5-8 weeks	8
9-12 weeks	18
12-26 weeks	8
26-52 weeks	3

APPENDIX 8-1 (continued)

The number of 32-hour weeks that would be used to meet a decreased demand before there would be a general layoff was reported as follows:

Usage of 32-Hour Week	Number of Responses
Zero weeks	30
1-2 weeks	3
3-4 weeks	3
5-8 weeks	9
9-12 weeks	3

The typical training period for entry-level positions to achieve standard performance was stated as follows:

Training Period	Number of Responses
1-2 weeks	14
3-4 weeks	18
5-8 weeks	12
9-12 weeks	4

The typical training period for employees promoted to a higher skill level was given as follows:

Training Period	Number of Responses
1-2 weeks	8
3-4 weeks	17
5-8 weeks	8
9-12 weeks	7
13-26 weeks	7

The typical training period for employees bumped down as a result of a reduction in force was described as follows:

Training Period	Number of Responses
Zero weeks	15
1-2 weeks	23
3-4 weeks	10

The costs associated with training a new employee as a percent of total wages paid during the training period were reported as follows:

Training Costs as Percent of Wages	Number of Responses
0-24%	5
25-49%	14
50-74%	13
75-100%	4
>100%	3
Unknown	9

APPENDIX 8-1 (continued)

The estimated cost of laying off a trained employee was stated as follows:

Layoff Costs	Number of Responses
Unknown	35
$100-$200	2
$201-$500	1
$501-$1,000	8
>$1,000	2

When the incoming order rate increases, several options are available to management. The data below summarize the options in order of preference of the respondents.

Management Decision	Response Ranking of Each Activity						Summary Ranking[6]
	1	2	3	4	5	6	
Increase manpower level	6	24	12	4	2	0	2
Work overtime	32	12	4	0	0	0	1
Allow backlog to increase	2	5	10	22	8	1	4
Reduce inventory	8	2	14	12	9	3	3
Raise prices	0	0	0	4	10	34	6
Subcontract out	0	5	8	6	19	10	5

The following actions were reported as preferred when the incoming order rate *decreases:*

Management Decision	Response Ranking of Each Decision						Summary Ranking[6]
	1	2	3	4	5	6	
Layoff	3	15	14	10	6	0	3
Short weeks	1	7	14	16	4	6	4
Build inventory	7	20	11	5	2	3	2
Cut prices	0	2	3	6	8	29	6
Reduce backlog	37	3	3	3	2	0	1
Seek subcontracts	0	1	3	8	26	10	5

The criteria on which manufacturing managers are evaluated were ranked by the survey participants as follows:

Evaluation Criteria	Ranking of Criteria					Summary Ranking
	1	2	3	4	5	
Meeting schedules	23	5	11	0	0	1
Controlling direct costs	13	27	6	2	0	2
Indirect costs	3	11	27	7	0	3
Inventory turnover	0	2	4	26	16	4
Union relations	0	3	0	13	32	5

[6] Rankings were made by placing first those items with the greatest quantity of first-place rankings, second those items with the largest cumulative first- and second-place rankings. Third-, fourth-, fifth- and sixth-place rankings were made with this cumulative measure.

SIMULATION MODELING OF THE MANPOWER DECISION FRAMEWORK

INTRODUCTION

In Chapter 8 the Manpower Decision Framework (MDF) approach to manpower planning outlined a set of reasoned management responses for various states of balance (or unbalance) between demand and capacity. This framework was developed on the hypothesis that each heuristic management decision was the "best" response, given any one of nine mutually exclusive and exhaustive problem states. For each state, the individual heuristic response should provide a satisfying solution to a particular problem. It is more difficult to argue "a priori," however, that a combined set of decision rules will produce feasible management decisions in an actual or simulated environment. This study presents the significant features of a digital computer simulation model which was developed to provide an experimental tool to investigate the feasibility and performance of the MDF.

ENVIRONMENT TO BE MODELED

The following major assumptions were drawn principally from the survey responses presented in Chapter 8.

1) *Decision maker.* The plant manger in a multiplant firm or the manufacturing manager in a firm having only a single production facility was assumed to have responsibility for the manpower planning decision.
2) *Decision variables.* The decision maker has the responsibility for and control over the work-force size, the length of the workweek, and the inventory levels. He uses these controls to maintain a balance between product demand and factory capacity.
3) *Planning horizon and review period.* The decision maker plans over a three-month horizon for the purposes of adjusting the control variables.
4) *Plant capacity.* The physical plant capacity was assumed to be fixed, and the model did not allow for capital investment to expand

capacity. The physical plant capacity is thus a constraint for the manpower planning decision maker. Available production capacity was a function of the work-force size, not to exceed physical plant capacity.

5) *Productivity of labor force.* The labor productivity was assumed to vary with the length of the workweek and the presence of new hires in the work force, as shown in Table 1.

TABLE 1 Labor Productivity Assumptions
        in Simulation Model

Length of Workweek	Work-Force Productivity (% of Standard)
0-40 hours	100%
41-48 hours	95%
49-56 hours	85%

Training Period for New Hires	Productivity of New Hires (% of Standard)
Weeks 1-4	30%
Weeks 5-8	70%
After 8 weeks	100%

6) *Plant labor-force size.* The maximum size of the labor force would be 1000 production employees. This was larger than the median plant size of 500 found in the survey but was not considered a serious departure from the survey results, and it allowed more range for experimentation.

7) *Measures of performance.* The decision maker was evaluated, first, on the ability to meet schedules and second, on success in controlling production costs. Inventory turnover and carrying costs were less important factors in the decision-maker evaluation.

8) *Production-level adjustment costs.* In reviewing the cost assumption for adjusting production levels, two insights are useful: 1) The simulation model selected the monthly levels independently of the cost assumption; the role of the cost factors was to record the resulting effect of these decisions. 2) These adjustment costs are assumed to be linear in nature; however, the model would function with any type of cost model subject to some reprogramming. These costs were assumed as follows:

   a) *Inventory carrying costs and shortage cost.* This cost function was a piecewise linear function as shown in Figure 1. The monthly carrying cost for finished-goods inventory was assumed to be 1.50% of the manufacturing cost of inventory on hand at the end of each month. On an annual basis the cost would be approximately 18% of the average inventory. This carrying cost is within the range of 15-25% per annum, often cited as a typical carrying cost for most manufacturing companies.

Monthly Inventory Costs

Net Inventory

FIGURE 1 Graph of Inventory Carrying Costs

The cost of not meeting the monthly demand, and thereby effectively creating a negative inventory of finished goods, was assumed to be 6% of the value of unsatisfied demand in each month of the simulation.[1] A precise specification of the inventory-shortage cost has long been a point of controversy in both the theory and practice of inventory management, and the value assumed for this simulation was not intended to shed light on that controversy. The survey of Chapter 8 indicated that meeting schedules was the most important measure (among those listed) of a manager's performance. The simulation model thus assumes the shortage cost would be four times the inventory carrying costs.

b) *Manpower adjustment costs.* This cost function was assumed to be a linear step function as shown in Figure 2. The cost of laying off an employee was assumed to be $400, which is within the range of responses to the survey in Chapter 8. The cost of rehiring the same employee on layoff was assumed to be $25, but the cost to hire a new employee was set at $75 per new employee.

Cost of Manpower Adjustments

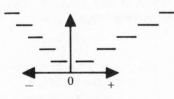

Manpower Levels

FIGURE 2 Graph of Manpower Adjustments Costs

c) *Cost of extending or shortening the workweek.* The normal workweek was assumed to be 40 hours in length. The direct costs of extending the workweek beyond 40 hours were the overtime wages of 150% of base wages for those hours between 41-48 hours per week and 200% of base wages for those hours

---

[1] Customer orders not completed within the proper month were assumed to be filled first in the following month without assuming any attrition.

between 49-56 hours per week. The maximum allowed length of the workweek was 56 hours. The shortening of the workweek to less than 40 hours was limited to a minimum workweek of 32 hours. The frequency of this management decision option was also limited to no more than two weeks in a month. Manufacturing productivity was assumed to remain at the same level as for a standard 40-hour workweek. Therefore no explicit costs were assumed when the workweek was shortened.

9) *Other model parameters.* The survey reported in Chapter 8 did not provide information sufficient to estimate all the parameters required for the simulation model. It was necessary to estimate these remaining parameters from a composite of survey results, case research, industry statistics, and available literature. These parameters were as follows:

a) Sales per manufacturing employee in durable-goods industries: $30,000 per year.

b) Average hourly wage in durable-goods industry: $4.00 per hour.

c) Attrition of furloughed employees form pool available for recalls: 20% per month.

FUNCTIONING OF THE COMPUTER SIMULATION MODEL

The computer model was designed to simulate the monthly manpower and inventory adjustment decision process of a plant manger as he attempted to strike a balance between production capactiy and product demand. A condensed flow chart of the eight major steps in the simulation model is presented in Figure 3. Each step in the program is discussed briefly below.

STEP I. INPUT BASIC MODEL PARAMETERS   These items were described earlier in this chapter as parameters of the model environment. These parameters were fixed for all model experiments and are summarized as follows:

1) Inventory carrying cost — 1.5% per month of inventory value.

2) Inventory-shortage cost — 6% per month of the value of past-due orders.

3) Production employee wages — $4.00 per hour.

4) Overtime wages for workweek hours 41-48 — 150% of base wages.

5) Overtime wages for workweek hours 49-56 — 200% of base wages.

6) Overtime productivity for workweek hours 41-48 — 95% of straight-time productivity.

7) Overtime productivity for workweek hours 49-56 — 85% of straight-time productivity.

8) Hiring cost — $75 per employee.

9) Productivity of new hires — 1st month, 30% of standard; 2nd month, 70% of standard; 3rd month, 100% of standard.

10) Layoff costs — $400 per employee.

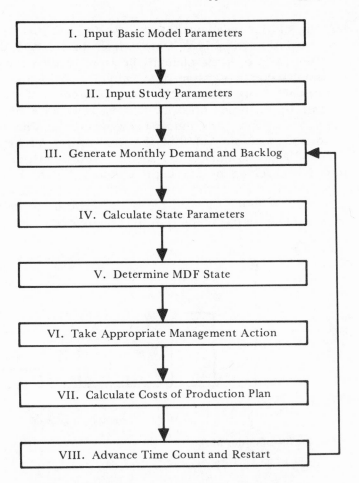

FIGURE 3 Basic Flow Chart of Simulation Model

11) Rehiring costs — $25 per employee.
12) Attrition of employees from layoff pool — 20% per month.
13) Plant sales per production employee — $30,000 per year.

STEP II. **INPUT** **STUDY** **PARAM-** **ETERS**	The study parameters (discussed later) for each experiment are entered in this step. The parameters include the market demand curve, the planning horizon, the accuracy of the forecast, the initial inventory level, the initial work-force size, and the number of months to be simulated.
STEP III. **GENERATE** **MONTHLY** **DEMAND** **AND** **BACKLOG**	The decision maker must estimate the quantity of products likely to be shipped in the initial month and must forecast the probable level of demand during the balance of the planning horizon. In the durable-goods industry, almost all firms book orders a month or more in advance of the promised shipment date. At the beginning of each month, then, the decision maker should know the shipment requirements for that month with a high degree of certainty. The order backlog presents an incomplete pattern of the demand over the remain-

ing months of the planning horizon. A decision maker can use the backlog, however, as a base from which to forecast the probable monthly demands over the planning horizon. In the simulation model the decision maker was assumed to employ a naive forecasting technique to convert the order backlog into a monthly forecast of shipments over the planning horizon. For example, in a situation where plans were made on a three-month planning horizon, the order backlog might normally contain 100% of the final orders for the first month and only 20% of the final orders for the third month of the planning horizon. This backlog profile is presented in Figure 4. The decision maker would then divide the actual monthly order levels in the backlog by the respective percentages in the backlog profile to extrapolate the probable demand for each month in the planning horizon.

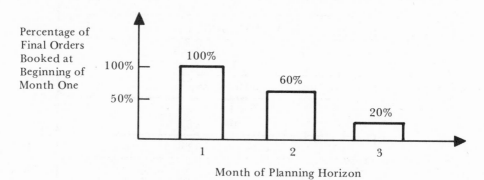

FIGURE 4 Profile of Order Backlog

The backlog profile represents the total information available to the decision maker concerning future demand patterns. As the simulation advances from one time period to the next, incremental shipment demands are generated for each month in the planning horizon. These new demands are added to the existing order backlog for each month, and the decision maker must again interpret the order backlog to initiate the manpower planning decision process.

STEP IV. CALCULATE STATE PARAMETERS   In the discussion of the MDF in Chapter 8 two indicators were required to identify the particular system state; these were referred to as CPR and PPR. The CPR represented the ratio of current demand to present capacity, and PPR represented the ratio of the average demand during the planning horizon to the planned capacity. The specification of the numerator of these ratios presented a complex problem. In the case of CPR the numerator should have reflected not only the current demand but also the past-due orders, the level of finished-goods inventory on hand, and possibly the demand level expected in the next one or two periods. Various expressions for CPR were evaluated, and the results are presented later in this chapter. An example of one such expression for CPR is:

$$CPR = \frac{\text{Current month's demand} + \dfrac{\text{Backorders}}{3} - \dfrac{\text{Inventory}}{3}}{\text{Present capacity}}$$

In the above expression the current month's demand is adjusted by increasing current demand by one-third the total of past-due orders and by decreasing current demand by one-third of the current inventory level. The effect of this expression is to smooth adjustments to the production level in order to satisfy past-due orders and to reduce finished-goods inventory.

The PPR indicator is defined as follows:

$$PPR = \left[\frac{\dfrac{1}{N-1} \displaystyle\sum_{i=2}^{N} D_i}{\text{Planned capacity}} \right]$$

where D_i = demand in ith month of planning horizon, and N = number of months in planning horizon.

The monthly demands during the remaining months of the planning horizon are averaged, and this average level of future demand is compared against planned future capacity in the calculation of PPR.

STEP V.
DETERMINE
MDF STATE

After calculating CPR and PPR, the simulation selected one of the nine system states shown in Figure 8-2. As was pointed out in Chapter 8, it would be very unlikely for CPR or PPR to be exactly equal to 1.0, which would represent a perfect state of balance for each parameter. Limits around 1.0 which represented a range of "balanced conditions" were specified for each parameter. This range was arbitrarily set at 1.0 ± 0.05 for CPR. The range of balanced conditions for PPR were allowed to vary between 0.95 and 1.025. With values for CPR and PPR given, the appropriate system state could be selected from Table 2.

TABLE 2 Framework for Determination of Simulation Problem State

	CPR < 0.95	0.95 ≤ CPR ≤ 1.05	CPR > 1.05
PPR < 0.95	I	II	III
0.95 ≤ PPR ≤ 1.025	IV	V	VI
PPR > 1.025	VII	VIII	IX

Sensitivity testing for improved limits for CPR and PPR was not performed because the specifications of CPR and PPR were thought to be a more productive line of inquiry. The limits were set to be very close to the nominal value in each case on the assumption that this would test the reactive capability of the model.

**STEP VI.
TAKE
APPRO-
PRIATE
MANAGE-
MENT
ACTION**

After determining the system state, the management actions proposed in Chapter 8 were implemented, with some further definition. Briefly, these actions were:

State I: Reduce capacity through layoffs to the greater of the numerators of CPR and PPR.

State II: Produce at capacity, but cut back all employees on training programs.

State III: Meet excess current demand through overtime only.

State IV: Work a shortened workweek; no more than two 32-hour weeks in any month.

State V: Produce at normal capacity.

State VI: Meet excess demands through overtime.

State VII: Produce at normal capacity and build inventory.

State VIII: Produce at normal capacity and hire new employees in anticipation of increased sales.

State IX: Meet excess current demand through overtime; hire new employees in anticipation of increased sales.

**STEP VII.
CALCULATE
COSTS OF
PRODUC-
TION PLAN**

As noted in assumption 8 of Environment to be Modeled, cost calculations measured past performace but did not influence the simulated decision processes.

**STEP VIII.
ADVANCE
TIME
COUNT AND
RESTART**

The cost calculations completed the simulation cycle, and then the index which counted the simulated months was advanced by one. The cycle was repeated, beginning again at Step III until the desired number of simulated operational periods had been completed.

VERIFICATION AND VALIDATION OF THE MODEL

Before beginning the experimentation with the programmed model, it was necessary to establish, via testing, some degree of confidence in the computer program and in the basic model. Fishman and Kiviat have divided this initial testing phase of a computer simulation study into two categories. "1) *Verification* insures that a simulation model behaves as an experimenter intends. 2) *Validation* tests the agreement between the behavior of the simulation model and a real system."[2]

Verification of the simulation model was effected through comparisons of simulated program results with hand-calculated simulated data. All potential computer program paths were evaluated in this

---

[2] G. S. Fishman and P. J. Kiviat, *Digital Computer Simulation: Statistical Considerations* (Santa Monica, Cal: Rand Corporation (RM-5387) 1967.

phase, and the debugging process was continued until the simulated computer results replicated the hand calculations.

The process of validation posed a different obstacle since direct access to a real system was not available. The most feasible alternative was to use published information concerning an actual system. The paint factory cost model developed by Holt, Modigliani, Muth, and Simon (HMMS) offered a well-documented study of a real system which could serve as the baseline for validating the proposed MDF methodology.[3] The HMMS model employs linear and quadratic approximations of the cost structure of an actual paint factory studied by HMMS. By applying the HMMS Linear Decision Rule (LDR), this model can be solved to produce a set of mathematically optimal decisions with respect to the cost model. These aggregate production-rate and work-force level decisions are assumed to be made on a monthly basis, given a forecast for an N-month horizon.

These decision rules provide mathematically optimal decisions for any demand pattern, given the cost employed. For the purpose of making direct comparisons of the performance of the MDF approach and the LDR method, the demand pattern presented in the original publication of the paint factory investigation was selected for the initial testing of the MDF simulation model.[4] Taubert presented the detailed numerical results for the HMMS cost model used in this chapter in his comparative study of the Search Decision Rule (SDR) and the Linear Decision Rule (LDR).[5]

Before the MDF model could be applied to the paint factory data, the state parameters CPR and PPR needed to be specified in detail. The parameter CPR, which represents the ratio of current demand to capacity, was defined as:

$$CPR = \frac{D_1 + \text{Backorders} + (320 - \text{Inventory})}{\text{Capacity}}$$

where D_1 = the demand for the current period.

This specification of CPR adjusts the current month's demand (D_1) by the total backorders (if any) and by the difference between the ideal inventory level of 320 units (per HMMS) and the actual inventory level. This was considered to be a naive definition of CPR because it did not attempt to smooth out the adjustments for backorders or nonideal inventory levels, nor did it anticipate demand fluctuations during the planning horizon. This basic statement for CPR was considered to be

[3] C. Holt, F. Modigliani, J. Muth, and H. Simon, *Planning Production, Inventories, and Work Forces* (Englewood Cliffs, N.J.: Prentice-Hall, Inc., 1969).

[4] C. Holt, F. Modigliani, and H. Simon, "A Linear Decision Rule for Production and Employment Scheduling," *Management Science*, vol. 2, no. 1, (1955), pp. 1-30.

[5] W. H. Taubert, "The Search Decision Rule Approach to Operations Planning," unpublished doctor's dissertation (Los Angeles: University of California, 1968).

the logical starting point for any investigation of model behavior. The PPR parameter was defined as

$$\text{PPR} = \left[\frac{\dfrac{1}{6} \sum\limits_{i=2}^{7} D_i}{\text{Capacity}} \right]$$

where D_1 = the expected demand in month i of the planning horizon.

This specification of PPR assumed an available forecast over the six-month period subsequent to the current month. The demands for these months were averaged to reflect the future demand trend with the PPR parameter.

The monthly results of the MDF simulation model are compared in Table 3 with the optimal results of the LDR methodology. The total cost of the MDF production simulation was $766,090, or 4.3% higher than the LDR optimal solution. From the breakdown of total costs presented in Table 4, it can be observed that the MDF approach used fewer employees but incurred higher overtime costs, inventory carrying costs, and layoff and hiring costs than did the optimal LDR solution. The higher costs for the MDF solution can be attributed to the less frequent and larger incremental changes in the labor-force size. The MDF method altered employment levels 6 times in the 24-month period in contrast to the 23 level changes dictated by the LDR in the same 24-month period. From the standpoint of costs, the quadratic hiring/layoff cost equation placed a heavy penalty on large manpower changes. The less frequent manpower changes would be more acceptable to both management and labor, however, than would the LDR policy, which changed the manpower levels each month. The less frequent manpower changes are an important positive feature of the MDF's performance in this test case. The higher overtime and inventory carrying costs resulted primarily from the nonoptimal manpower adjustments, and the quadratic cost model has exaggerated the differences between the performance of the MDF and LDR solutions. For example, the inventory levels in the MDF solution were only 17.6% higher than the inventory levels specified by the LDR solution, but the inventory costs of the MDF solution were 126.1% higher.

On balance, the simulated MDF performance was considered to provide a satisfactory solution to the paint factory aggregate planning problem. The relatively small 4.3% increase in total costs was an acceptable tradeoff for the much less frequent manpower adjustments. Hence, the MDF model was judged to have passed the test of validity and was ready for further simulation studies.

MDF SIMULATION STUDIES

After completion of the validation testing of the computer simulation model, a set of simulation studies were undertaken to further explore

TABLE 3 A Comparison of LDR and MDF Operation on the Paint Factory Problem

Month	Monthly Sales (gallons)	Production (gallons)		Work Force (men)		Inventory (gallons)		Monthly Cost (dollars)	
		LDR	MDF	LDR	MDF	LDR	MDF	LDR	MDF
0				81	81	263	263		
1	430	468	486	78	81	301	319	29,348	29,953
2	447	442	450	75	75	296	322	27,797	30,246
3	440	416	450	72	75	272	332	26,294	27,943
4	316	381	378	69	63	338	394	24,094	33,149
5	397	377	340	67	63	318	337	23,504	22,139
6	375	368	378	66	63	311	340	22,879	23,471
7	292	360	340	65	63	379	388	22,614	22,496
8	458	382	402	65	67	303	332	23,485	25,729
9	400	377	402	66	67	280	334	23,367	24,705
10	350	366	402	67	67	296	386	22,846	25,048
11	284	365	402	69	67	377	504	23,408	27,482
12	400	404	402	72	67	381	506	25,750	27,543
13	483	447	402	75	67	345	425	28,266	25,599
14	509	477	492	79	82	313	408	30,180	45,420
15	500	495	492	83	82	307	400	31,310	30,842
16	475	511	492	87	82	343	417	32,422	31,090
17	500	543	492	91	82	386	409	34,858	30,967
18	600	595	558	96	93	380	367	38,119	42,283
19	700	641	612	100	102	321	279	40,849	43,110
20	700	661	673	103	102	282	252	41,848	42,649
21	725	659	673	105	102	216	200	41,945	43,456
22	600	627	612	106	102	244	212	39,074	38,715
23	432	605	550	107	102	417	330	38,134	34,288
24	615	653	612	109	102	455	327	41,785	37,767
Totals		11,621	11,550	1,972	1,918	7,861	9,262	734,176	766,090

TABLE 4 LDR and MDF Cost Comparison on the Paint Factory Problem

Cost Element	LDR	MDF
Straight-time labor	$670,395	$652,120
Overtime	46,097	60,617
Hiring and layoff	11,804	40,057
Inventory, backorder, and setup	5,880	13,296
Total cost	$734,176	$766,090

the performance of the MDF methodology. Two issues were of major interest:

1) Would the heuristic MDF methodology perform in a satisfactory manner over a range of test conditions?
2) Could the cost performance of the MDF methodology be improved

through the development of alternative rules for state parameter CPR?

The development of alternative rules for CPR and the specifications of the simulation test conditions are described, along with the results of the 288 simulation runs which were executed.

DEVELOP-ING RULES FOR THE STATE PA-RAMETERS The rules for the state parameters CPR and PPR that were used for the MDF simulation of the paint factory model were selected as the basic format from which to construct new rules for further testing. The basic rules for CPR and PPR were

$$\text{CPR} = \frac{D_1 + \text{Backorders} + (\text{Ideal inventory} - \text{Actual inventory})}{\text{Capacity}}$$

$$\text{PPR} = \frac{\dfrac{1}{N-1} \displaystyle\sum_{i=2}^{N} D_i}{\text{Capacity}}$$

where D_i = projected demand in month i (i = 1,2,3, . . ., N), N = number of months in the planning horizon, and ideal inventory = zero units for this investigation.

The scope of the research design discussed in the following paragraphs was limited to investigating four alternative rules for state parameter CPR. CPR was assumed to be more critical to the MDF model performance because the decisions which are actually implemented incorporate this parameter in their derivation. The PPR state parameter had a more passive role in the MDF decision-making process, and any efforts to improve the MDF performance through changes in the statement of PPR were assumed to be less fruitful in this exploratory investigation.

Four modified versions of CPR were developed and tested over the various model conditions. These modifications are presented below and designated as Rules 1-4.

Rule 1

$$\text{CPR} = \frac{D_1 + \text{BO} - \text{INV} + \text{SMDH} \times \left[\dfrac{\displaystyle\sum_{i=2}^{N} D_i}{N-1} - \text{Capacity} \right]}{\text{Plant capacity}}$$

where D_i = projected demand in month i, BO = backorders, INV = inventory, N = number of months in the planning horizon, and SMDH = smoothing constant ($0 \leqslant \text{SMDH} \leqslant 1$).

In Rule 1 a new term has been added to the original definition of CPR to incorporate a measure of the possible difference between average demand over the planning horizon and plant capacity. If future average demand requirements were projected to be in excess of plant capacity, this formulation would detect that signal in the current month and could build some inventory or add manpower to smooth the transition from one production level to a higher one. The smoothing constant (SMDH) determines how much of the imbalance between demand and capacity to include in the calculation of CPR. In the experimental studies duscussed in this chapter, SMDH assumed only the three levels of 0.0, 0.333, and 0.5. At the first level, where SMDH = 0.0, CPR would be indentical with the basic statement for CPR.

Rule 2

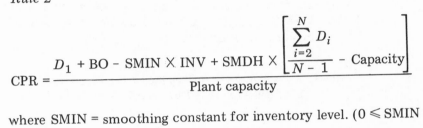

$$CPR = \frac{D_1 + BO - SMIN \times INV + SMDH \times \left[\dfrac{\sum\limits_{i=2}^{N} D_i}{N - 1} - Capacity \right]}{\text{Plant capacity}}$$

where SMIN = smoothing constant for inventory level. ($0 \leqslant SMIN \leqslant 1$).

Rule 2 differs from Rule 1 because of the smoothing constant which has been added to smooth out adjustments for excess inventory. For the purposes of this investigation, SMIN was assigned the constant value of 0.333. Rule 2 would therefore gradually reduce excess inventory balances systematically over a number of periods.

Rule 3

$$CPR = \frac{D_1 + SMBO \times BO - SMIN \times INV + SMDH \times \left[\dfrac{\sum\limits_{i=2}^{N} D_i}{N - 1} - Capacity \right]}{\text{Plant capacity}}$$

where SMBO = smoothing constant for backorder level ($0 \leqslant SMBO \leqslant 1$).

Rule 3 was developed by modifying Rule 2 to include the option of smoothing out the adjustments made by the MDF simulation to reduce backorders. Managers would normally attempt to manufacture enough product to satisfy the backorders and the current demand because of an assumed high cost of stockouts. For the purposes of this study, SMBO was assigned the constant value of 0.333. Rule 3 would therefore gradually reduce backorder levels over several successive periods.

Rule 4

$$\text{CPR} = \frac{\displaystyle\sum_{i=1}^{3} \frac{D_i}{3} + \text{SMBH} \times \text{BO} - \text{SMIN} \times \text{INV} + \text{SMDH} \times \left[\frac{\displaystyle\sum_{i=2}^{N} D_i}{N-1} - \text{Capacity} \right]}{\text{Plant capacity}}$$

In creating Rule 4, the first term of Rule 3, which had been the current period's demand, was replaced with a measurement of the average demand for the next three demand periods. The objective was to smooth out MDF responses to short-term fluctuations in demand.

A summary of the significant characteristics of the four rules has been presented in Table 5. Each rule was evaluated at three different levels of SMDH: therefore twelve distinct measures of CPR were employed in the simulation testing.

TABLE 5   A Comparison of the Significant Features of the
Four Rules for State Parameter CPR

	Current Demand Measure	SMBO	SMIN	SMDH
Rule 1	D_1	1	1	0, 0.333, 0.5
Rule 2	D_1	1	0.333	0, 0.333, 0.5
Rule 3	D_1	0.333	0.333	0, 0.333, 0.5
Rule 4	$\displaystyle\sum_{i=1}^{3} \frac{D_i}{3}$	0.333	0.333	0, 0.333, 0.5

SIMULATION MODEL TEST CONDITIONS   A set of model parameters was proposed earlier as descriptive of a "typical" firm in the durable-goods industry. These model parameters remained unchanged throughout the simulation experiments with one important exception. One parameter, the number of months in the planning horizon, was varied in a series of simulation tests. The survey reported in Chapter 8 revealed that the "typical" firm was most likely to plan aggregate production over a three-month planning horizon. A large percentage of the firms surveyed, however, planned on either a one-month or a six-month horizon. The costs of manpower planning decisions were expected to be very sensitive to the length of the planning horizon with a lowering of costs as the horizon was extended. There existed the possibility that a proposed rule for indicator CPR would produce the least cost decisions for one length of planning horizon but not perform as well if given other planning horizons. The planning horizon (PH) was thus selected as one of the simulation model test factors.

Planning horizon levels of two, four, and seven months were selected for simulation testing and were designated as PH_1, PH_2, and PH_3, respectively. The backlog profiles for PH_1, PH_2, and PH_3, are shown in Table 6. The figures in each cell of the matrix represent the percentage of the potential orders for Month 1 that would be booked at the beginning of Month 1. For example, given planning horizon PH_2, an order backlog of ten units for Month 4 would represent 20 percent of the total orders for fifty units that would eventually be shipped in Month 4. The backlog profile provided a forecasting mechanism for converting the order backlog into a monthly sales forecast over the planning horizon.

TABLE 6 Backlog Profiles for Planning Horizons

Planning Horizon	Decision Point	Month 1	Month 2	Month 3	Month 4	Month 5	Month 6	Month 7
PH_1 = 2		100%	20%	—	—	—	—	—
PH_2 = 4		100%	100%	50%	20%	—	—	—
PH_3 = 7		100%	100%	100%	90%	45%	20%	5%

The product demand pattern (DP) was selected as the externally generated simulation experiment factor. Four hypothetical deterministic demand patterns were selected for testing and are presented in Figure 5. The demand patterns for DP_1 and DP_2 are representative of long-term business and economic cycles which have significant impacts on the manpower requirements of the durable-goods industry. The demand patterns of DP_3 and DP_4 reflect the large shifts in demand within a year which compound the manpower planning problems for durable-goods manufacturers.

A characteristic of each demand pattern was the overall smoothness of the month-to-month demand patterns. A second set of demand patterns (DP_{1R}, DP_{2R}, DP_{3R}, and DP_{4R}, which had irregular month-to-month variations) were derived by imposing a uniform random variate on the original four smooth demand patterns. In the irregular demand patterns the monthly demands varied randomly within the range of ±20% of the respective original monthly demands. The derived demand patterns were deterministic, however, and the decision maker was assumed to have complete knowledge of the demand over his planning horizon. The large irregular variations in some month-to-month demand trends of DP_{1R}, DP_{2R}, DP_{3R}, and DP_{4R} provided additional testing grounds for the state parameter rules.

The combination of the eight demand patterns and the three planning horizons produced 24 simulation test conditions. The four

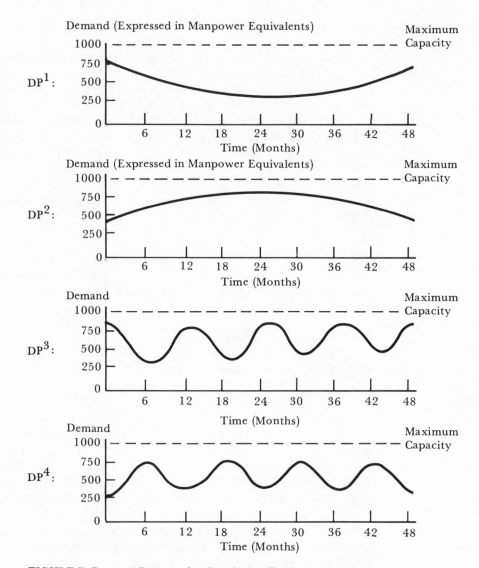

FIGURE 5 Demand Patterns for Simulation Tests

proposed rules for the state parameters and the three levels of the smoothing constant SMDH combined with the 24 simulation test conditions to yield 288 distinct simulation experiments of the MDF.

SIMULATION
TESTING

The total cost of the manpower planning decisions as defined in Chapter 8 was selected as the measure of relative merit for the simulation results for each state parameter rule. All simulation experiments were conducted under deterministic conditions, and the variations in the total costs between any two experiments were attributable strictly to the differences in the test conditions. Traditional methods of evaluating nonstochastic data were followed in evaluating the experimental results.

For each of the 288 experimental conditions, the operations of the hypothetical firm were simulated for 48 months. The MDF model produced decisions for 48 monthly production planning problems for each test case. The manpower planning costs for these 288 experiments have been recorded in Table 7. Each entry represents the sum of the costs incurred for the 48 decision periods per experiment.

EVALUATION OF SIMULATION RESULTS

The analysis of the simulation data investigated the sensitivity of the MDF performace to the demand patterns and planning horizons, evaluated the relative overall performance of the rules for the state parameters, and analyzed the impact of the individual terms which were added to the basic format of the state parameter CPR.

DEMAND PATTERNS   Each of the eight demand patterns was an experimental factor in 36 simulation experiments. The costs of the 36 experiments for each demand pattern were summed to create a macromeasure of the overall performance of the MDF simulation for the individual demand patterns, and these summary data were entered in Table 8. Inspection of Table 8 shows that the total cost for demands DP_{1R}, DP_{2R}, DP_{3R}, and DP_{4R} was $203.8 million, which was 74% greater than the corresponding total cost of $117.0 million for demands DP_1, DP_2, DP_3, and DP_4. The impact of this cost differential on a "typical" firm is difficult to grasp from these aggregate figures. When these data are translated to the scale of a single firm, the costs for the "typical" firm reacting to the irregular DP_{iR} demand patterns would be 6.6% of the total annual manufacturing labor costs, whereas the costs for the smooth DP_i demand patterns would be only 3.7% of annual manufacturing labor costs. As would be expected, these results indicated that manpower planning costs of a firm should be lower for the demand patterns with smaller month-to-month variations. How could the manufacturing manager capitalize on this result if he had no influence over the basic demand patterns? One approach would be to smooth his responses to demand perturbations and thereby possibly reduce the costs. This is the basic methodology of the MDF approach, and the various state parameter rules were created with this end in view.

PLANNING HORIZON   The manpower planning costs for a firm should normally decrease if the decision maker could extend the planning horizon farther into the future. The results of the MDF simulation experiments were consistent with this norm. As shown in Table 8, the total costs for the 96 experiments using planning horizon PH_1 (two months) were $135.0 million. These costs were reduced to $85.2 million when planning horizon PH_3 (seven months) was employed for the same 96 test situations; a reduction in costs of 37%. The MDF methodology successfully took advantage of the additional information available with a longer planning horizon to produce decisions which effectively lowered the total costs.

TABLE 7 Manpower Planning Costs for 288 Simulation Experiments[1]

Rule	SMDH	DP₁			DP₂			DP₃			DP₄			Total
		PH_1	PH_2	PH_3	PH_1	PH_2	PH_3	PH_1	PH_2	PH_3	PH_1	PH_2	PH_3	
1	0.0	$ 703.0	$ 613.8	$ 385.5	$ 651.5	$ 599.5	$ 440.1	$1,200.8	$1,118.6	$1,116.2	$1,151.2	$1,057.8	$ 926.1	$ 9,964.1
	0.33	702.2	585.7	394.7	645.2	603.8	478.5	1,128.0	918.7	986.9	992.7	871.9	971.6	9,279.9
	0.50	701.4	590.1	411.6	682.5	609.4	486.1	1,071.0	874.5	1,270.9	1,120.9	833.8	782.9	9,434.7
2	0.0	733.9	630.7	414.1	802.0	652.9	439.8	1,218.5	1,073.0	841.3	1,192.2	932.6	727.8	9,658.3
	0.33	713.4	583.4	376.1	634.0	594.1	420.9	1,023.3	907.1	624.0	994.1	800.7	528.2	8,199.3
	0.50	711.4	573.2	401.7	637.3	594.7	461.8	1,033.8	819.6	673.1	932.3	751.7	708.4	8,299.0
3	0.0	821.4	738.9	414.3	690.2	778.0	439.8	1,177.7	970.1	836.0	1,105.2	884.3	727.7	9,583.6
	0.333	776.2	649.4	376.9	728.7	678.7	429.7	1,213.0	794.5	642.0	1,129.7	808.8	541.6	9,075.0
	0.50	741.2	609.3	424.7	775.8	616.9	477.6	1,280.0	841.7	686.4	1,166.9	829.7	624.8	8,769.2
4	0.0	731.4	600.9	419.3	746.6	658.2	424.5	1,399.0	982.6	677.2	1,363.5	876.0	635.7	9,514.9
	0.333	722.3	663.2	556.3	801.6	696.1	516.9	1,646.0	1,424.3	868.5	1,686.4	1,208.0	834.2	11,623.8
	0.50	755.2	720.2	580.6	809.5	722.2	643.1	1,804.6	1,535.6	1,272.3	1,923.2	1,572.6	1,272.8	13,611.9

[1] All cost figures are in thousands of dollars.

TABLE 7 (continued)

Rule	SMDH	DP$_{1R}$			DP$_{2R}$			DP$_{3R}$			DP$_{4R}$			Total
		PH$_1$	PH$_2$	PH$_3$	PH$_1$	PH$_2$	PH$_3$	PH$_1$	PH$_2$	PH$_3$	PH$_1$	PH$_2$	PH$_3$	
1	0.0	$1,239.5	$1,325.8	$1,250.2	$1,230.7	$ 923.4	$1,064.8	$1,919.8	$1,746.8	$1,839.0	$1,337.5	$1,373.7	$1,329.6	$16,580.5
	0.333	1,136.5	897.5	979.9	941.4	677.9	914.8	1,666.9	1,307.6	1,461.4	1,118.7	1,037.1	1,085.7	13,225.4
	0.50	1,786.2	927.9	896.3	1,756.5	843.7	1,009.4	2,177.9	1,336.2	1,357.3	1,983.7	1,124.1	1,097.2	16,294.4
2	0.0	1,187.0	1,219.4	1,173.7	1,266.2	1,066.8	1,056.1	1,920.9	1,684.4	1,779.5	1,128.9	1,204.9	1,379.7	16,067.5
	0.333	1,152.9	977.7	943.5	980.8	710.6	731.7	1,807.0	1,356.8	1,095.2	1,080.8	904.9	949.9	12,691.8
	0.50	1,661.6	768.9	671.7	1,553.0	714.2	497.2	2,059.9	1,155.9	754.5	1,736.5	646.8	506.4	12,726.6
3	0.0	1,185.0	1,219.4	1,081.9	1,266.3	1,065.9	1,056.1	2,007.3	1,684.4	1,779.5	1,138.0	1,204.9	1,380.0	16,068.6
	0.333	1,269.9	980.4	917.6	935.9	731.9	775.5	2,017.3	1,393.9	871.5	1,086.1	897.6	829.2	12,706.8
	0.50	1,421.1	836.9	749.2	1,486.6	598.6	548.6	2,297.4	1,236.8	1,890.3	1,660.2	844.7	660.3	14,228.7
4	0.0	2,131.9	1,024.7	725.0	2,037.4	1,060.2	684.4	2,878.9	1,509.2	1,134.8	2,275.8	1,102.5	733.7	17,298.5
	0.333	1,514.0	1,543.3	1,131.9	2,872.0	1,845.4	1,225.8	3,577.0	2,349.3	1,623.0	3,289.8	2,008.0	1,269.3	24,248.8
	0.50	2,290.6	2,208.2	1,643.0	3,025.5	2,492.7	1,649.9	4,050.1	3,100.8	2,580.7	3,490.3	2,629.3	1,889.8	31,680.9

TABLE 8 Total Manpower Planning
Costs for Planning Horizon
and Demand Factors[1]

	DP_i	DP_{iR}	Total
PH_1	\$ 47.371	\$ 87.662	\$135.033
PH_2	39.052	61.502	100.554
PH_3	30.591	54.656	85.247
Total	\$117.014	\$203.820	

[1] All cost figures are in millions of dollars.

OVERALL EFFECTIVE- NESS OF THE RULES

As summarized in Table 9, Rule 2 produced the lowest costs for the aggregate of 72 simulation experiments over which it was operative. The remaining rankings, in order of rising costs, were Rule 3 second, Rule 1 third, and Rule 4 a distant fourth. Rule 1 was originally defined as a baseline decision rule, and the objective was to seek new forms of CPR which were variations of Rule 1 and which would produce lower costs than Rule 1. Rules 2 and 3 have achieved this objective in the aggregate for the conditions simulated by the MDF model.

TABLE 9 Aggregate Performance of State
Parameter Rules[1]

	Rank	DP_i	DP_{iR}	Total
Rule 1	3	\$28,787.7	\$46,102.3	\$ 74,890.0
Rule 2	1	26,157.6	41,485.9	67,643.5
Rule 3	2	27,427.8	43,004.0	70,431.8
Rule 4	4	34,750.6	73,228.2	105,978.8

[1] All cost figures are in thousands of dollars.

It is important to note that the rankings of the four rules are the same for both the smooth demand patterns and the irregular demand patterns. However, when the data were disaggregated, in Table 10, to inspect the performance of the rules over the eight individual demand patterns, an interesting finding arose. Rule 2 produced least-cost results for demands DP_3, DP_4, DP_{3R}, and DP_{4R}, which represented the various seasonal demand patterns and required greater month-to-month adjustments in the firm's productive capacity. For demands DP_1 and DP_2, which were the smooth long-term cyclic demands, Rule 1 produced the lowest overall costs with Rule 2 a close second. The costs generated by applying Rule 3 were the lowest costs for the irregular long-term cyclic demands, DP_{1R} and DP_{2R}, with Rule 2 again a close second. Therefore, depending upon the traditional demand patterns of a firm, a researcher might want to investigate

TABLE 10 Cost Performance for Each Rule by Demand
Pattern[1]

Rule	DP_1	DP_2	DP_3	DP_4
1	$5,088.0	$5,196.2	$ 9,685.6	$ 8,708.9
2	5,137.9	5,237.5	8,213.7	7,568.0
3	5,552.3	5,615.4	8,441.4	7,818.7
4	5,749.4	6,018.7	11,610.0	11,372.4

Rule	DP_{1R}	DP_{2R}	DP_{3R}	DP_{4R}
1	$10,439.8	$ 9,362.6	$14,812.9	$11,487.3
2	9,756.4	8,576.6	13,614.1	9,538.8
3	9,661.4	8,463.3	15,178.3	9,701.0
4	14,842.6	16,893.3	22,803.8	13,110.8

[1] All cost figures are in thousands of dollars.

variations of Rule 2, Rule 3, and/or Rule 1 in attempting to apply the MDF methodology.

The simulation parameter SMDH has not yet been discussed in this overview of the MDF simulation results because SMDH was so closely related to the rules for the state parameter CPR. The matrix in Table 11 was formed to present a view of the interaction between the rules and SMDH. The lowest cost figure for each column in the matrix has been circled to highlight the least-cost rule. In five of the six columns the results for Rule 2 have been circled as being the least cost. In addition, Rule 3 ranked second, Rule 1 third, and Rule 4 fourth for those five columns. These rankings were unchanged from the earlier rankings of the aggregate results. However, in the first column of the matrix, when SMDH = 0 and the demand patterns have the smooth month-to-month transitions, Rule 4 yielded the lowest costs. This important observation implies that there may be some merit in further evaluation of the other forms of Rule 4 where demand is smooth.

A second important observation from Table 11 is that, with the exception of Rule 4, the remaining rules produced their lowest total costs for each set of demands when SMDH = 0.333. There the addition of the term

$$\text{SMDH} \times \left[\frac{\sum_{i=2}^{N} D_i}{N - 1} - \text{Capacity} \right]$$

to Rule 1, Rule 2, and Rule 3 had a positive impact in reducing costs for the simulated conditions with the best results achieved when SMDH = 0.333.

Thus far, this discussion has compared the performance of the rules

TABLE 11   Interactions between Rules, SMDH, and DP[1]

| | DP_1, DP_2, DP_3, DP_4 | | |
Rule	SMDH = 0	SMDH = 0.33	SMDH = 0.50
1	$9,964.1	$ 9,279.9	$ 9,434.7
2	9,658.3	⟨8,199.3⟩	⟨8,299.0⟩
3	9,583.6	8,769.2	9,075.0
4	⟨9,514.9⟩	11,623.8	13,611.9

| | DP_{1R}, DP_{2R}, DP_{3R}, DP_{4R} | | |
Rule	SMDH = 0	SMDH = 0.33	SMDH = 0.50
1	$16,580.5	$16,296.4	$13,225.4
2	⟨16,067.3⟩	⟨12,691.8⟩	⟨12,726.6⟩
3	16,068.8	12,706.8	14,228.7
4	17,298.5	24,248.8	31,680.9

[1] All cost figures are in thousands of dollars.

in terms of the total costs over a large number of experiments. A second approach follows in which the rules have been ranked, based on the peak performance for each of the 24 combinations of demand patterns (eight levels) and planning horizons (three levels). The least cost or peak performance for each of these 24 conditions has been selected from the respective columns of Table 7. These results were then recorded in a matrix format as shown in Table 12. Rule 2 yielded a least-cost result in 18 of the 24 experiments with Rules 1 and 3 sharing equally in the remaining 6 experiments. Rule 4 failed to produce a least-cost solution for any of the 24 experimental situations.

An investigation of a possible interaction between the planning horizons and the rules produced Table 13. As shown by the data in this table, Rule 2 yielded the least-cost solutions for all planning horizons. For PH_1, the shortest planning horizon, Rule 1 ranked second and produced lower costs than did third-ranked Rule 3. Rule 3 reversed positions with Rule 1, however, for the longer planning horizons, PH_2 and PH_3. This was interpreted to imply that the simpler decision rules could be as effective as the more sophisticated ones, given the limited data of a short planning period.

TABLE 12 Matrix Record of Peak Rule Performance

	SMDH = 0.0	SMDH = 0.33	SMDH = 0.5	Total
Rule 1	0	2	1	3
Rule 2	0	8	10	18
Rule 3	0	2	1	3
Rule 4	0	0	0	0
Totals	0	12	12	24

TABLE 13 Rule by Planning Horizon Interactions[1]

	PH_1	PH_2	PH_3
Rule 1	$29,045.3	$22,799.3	$22,936.7
Rule 2	28,161.7	21,325.0	18,156.3
Rule 3	29,375.0	21,895.7	19,161.2
Rule 4	48,452.6	34,533.5	24,992.7

[1] All cost figures are in thousands of dollars.

TERMS ADDED TO THE BASIC RULE FOR CPR

Rule 1: Rule 1 differed from the basic statement of CPR by the addition of the term:

$$SMDH \times \left[\frac{\sum_{i=2}^{N} D_i}{N-1} - \text{Capacity} \right]$$

described earlier. The impact of this modification can be evaluated by comparing the performance for the 24 simulation tests using Rule 1 when $SMDH_2 = 0.0$ with the results over these same conditions for $SMDH_2 = 0.33$ and $SMDH_3 = 0.50$. The total costs for these three sets of experiments have been summarized in Table 14 along with similar data for Rules 2, 3, and 4.

TABLE 14 Rule by SMDH Interaction[1]

	SMDH = 0.0	SMDH = 0.333	SMDH = 0.50
Rule 1	$26,544.6	$22,505.3	$25,731.1
Rule 2	25,725.6	20,891.1	21,025.6
Rule 3	25,652.4	21,476.0	23,303.7
Rule 4	26,813.4	35,872.6	45,292.8

[1] All cost figures are in thousands of dollars.

For the case when $SMDH_1 = 0$, the total costs for 24 experiments with Rule 1 were $26,544 thousand. These costs were reduced by 3.1% when $SMDH_3 = 0.50$ and by 15.6% when $SMDH_2 = 0.33$. These results were positive indications that the addition of this term which incorporated a forward-looking feature into CPR, had been an effective improvement over the basic statement of CPR.

Rule 2:   Rule 2 differed from Rule 1 because of the addition of the parameter SMIN to smooth out the adjustments to excess inventory. For the purposes of this study, SMIN was assigned the value of 0.33 for all testing of Rule 2. By inspection of Table 14, the simulation test performance of Rule 2 was found to be better (lower costs) than those of Rule 1 for all levels of SMDH. The addition of the inventory smoothing feature to the state indicator CPR tended to reduce costs.

Rule 3:   Rule 3 was developed by modifying Rule 2 to include the option of smoothing out the manager's response to the presence of backorders. The normal pressures on a manufacturing manager would influence him to attempt to satisfy all past-due orders plus the current demand in any given month. The term, SMBO × Backorders, was included in Rule 3 with SMBO assigned the value 0.333 for all MDF simulation test conditions using Rule 3.

The results for Rule 3, as recorded in Table 14, were only marginally (0.2%) better than those for Rule 2 for $SMDH_1 = 0$, and they were considerably poorer for $SMDH_2 = 0.333$ and $SMDH_3 = 0.50$. The conclusion drawn from these observations was that the smoothing of response to backorders was not likely to be as fruitful a branch for future research as was the smoothing of inventory adjustments because the high cost of backorders makes smoothing their adjustments less feasible.

Rule 4:   The term D_1 in Rule 3 was replaced by

$$\sum_{i=1}^{3} \frac{D_i}{3}$$

to create Rule 4. The objective had been to smooth out the MDF simulation responses to short-term fluctuations in the demand. As noted earlier, Rule 4 was consistently the poorest performer among the four rules.

PAINT FACTORY MODEL REVISITED

The paint factory study of Holt, Modigliani, Muth, and Simon was introduced as the reference data for validation testing of the MDF simulation methodology. After completion of the simulation evaluation of the various rules for state indicator CPR, the focus of the investigation again returned to the paint factory model as a test ground for Rule 2, which had proven superior in the simulation experimentation. This second simulation of the paint factory using the MDF methodology served as an additional evaluation of the merits of Rule 2 and the MDF approach to manpower planning.

The monthly results of the MDF simulation of the paint factory operations, using Rule 2 with SMDH = 0.333, are presented in Table 15. The total cost of this simulated production plan for the paint factory was $740,367, which exceeded the LDR's optimal cost solution by $6,189, or 0.8%, as shown in Table 16. In the validation testing, the MDF with the basic rule produced manpower planning costs of $766,090, which were $31,914, or 4.3% greater than the optimal LDR solution. The use of Rule 2 reduced the difference between the MDF's performance and the optimal LDR solution by 81%. This represented persuasive evidence that the research effort described in this chapter has yielded significant results which constitute an important step in the exploratory development and evaluation of the MDF.

From the breakdown of total cost presented in Table 16, it is observed that the MDF Rule 2 approach used less total manpower than the LDR solution. But the MDF Rule 2 solution relied more heavily on overtime to meet short-term demand fluctuations and spent more for manpower adjustments than the LDR optimal solution. The higher overtime and manpower adjustment costs of the MDF Rule 2 solution are attributed to the less frequent and larger manpower adjustments which were an importnat attribute of the MDF methodology. The LDF solution adjusted manpower levels for 23 of the 24 months under study. The MDF methodology made six adjustments in the manpower levels, using the basic rule, and eight adjustments, using Rule 2.

The quadratic cost model placed a severe penalty on the less frequent but larger manpower adjustments of the two MDF solutions. These MDF solutions were also heavily penalized by the quadratic cost model for their use of overtime to smooth the manpower levels. However, the less frequent manpower changes of both MDF solutions would be an acceptable tradeoff to a manager for the slightly higher costs of either MDF solution. The utility of the MDF approach is therefore in the development of feasible production-planning decisions which, although nonoptimal, provide a practical solution to actual situations.

CONCLUSIONS

The set of MDF simulation experiments reported in this study were undertaken to explore two issues:

1) Would the MDF methodology be a feasible heuristic approach to aggregate production planning problems?
2) Could alternative formats for CPR improve the cost performance of the MDF methodology?

TABLE 15 A Comparison of LDR and MDF Rule 2 Operation of the Paint Factory Problem

Month	Monthly Sales (gallons)	Production (gallons)		Work Force (men)		Inventory (gallons)		Monthly Cost (dollars)	
		LDR	Rule 2	LDR	Rule 2	LDR	Rule 2	LDR	Rule 2
0						263	263		
1	430	468	450	81	81	301	283	29,348	30,015
2	447	442	434	78	75	296	270	27,797	29,179
3	440	434	416	75	69	272	264	26,294	26,917
4	316	382	340	72	69	337	288	24,094	23,584
5	397	377	378	69	63	317	269	23,504	23,371
6	375	368	378	67	63	311	272	22,879	23,346
7	292	360	340	66	63	379	320	22,614	21,185
8	458	382	402	65	63	303	264	23,485	25,921
9	400	377	402	65	67	280	266	23,367	24,875
10	350	366	361	66	67	296	277	23,846	22,661
11	284	365	361	67	67	377	354	23,408	22,603
12	400	404	402	69	67	381	356	25,750	29,947
13	483	447	456	72	76	345	329	28,266	31,115
14	509	477	490	75	83	313	318	30,180	30,545
15	500	495	498	79	83	307	316	31,310	30,546
16	475	511	498	83	83	343	339	32,422	30,576
17	500	543	552	87	92	386	391	34,858	39,498
18	600	595	612	91	102	380	403	38,119	44,576
19	700	641	673	96	102	321	376	40,849	42,527
20	700	661	673	100	102	282	349	41,848	42,337
21	725	659	612	103	102	216	235	41,945	38,161
22	600	627	612	105	102	244	248	39,074	38,006
23	432	605	550	106	102	417	365	38,134	34,506
24	615	653	550	107	102	455	301	41,785	34,370
				109					
Totals	11,620		11,466	1,972	1,931	7,859	7,717	734,176	740,367

TABLE 16 Cost Comparison for Secont Paint
Factory Simulation

Cost Element	LDR	MDF (Rule 2)
Straight-time labor	$670,395	$656,520
Overtime	46,097	51,374
Hiring and layoff	11,804	27,971
Inventory, backorder, and setup	5,880	4,482
Total cost	$734,176	$740,367
		100.8%

The feasibility of the MDF methodology was dependent upon the practical utility of the decisions, the costs of these decisions, and the overall model behavior. As demonstrated in the two MDF simulations of the paint factory, the MDF approach produced manpower schedules which would be much more acceptable to the average manufacturing manager. The total costs for either MDF production plan represented only very modest increases above LDR's minimum cost solution and should have been an acceptable tradeoff to any manager in search of more labor-force stability.

The judgment of the feasibility of the MDF approach was also dependent on the consistent cost behavior of the MDF solutions over the 288 test conditions. One property of the MDF simulation results was a decrease in the costs as the planning horizon was extended. This behavior was consistent with the expectation that a feasible approach should produce better (lower-cost) solutions when given additional reliable information about future demand patterns. A second property of the MDF results was that changes in the basic demand patterns produced changes in costs which were qualitatively consistent with the prior expectations.

The second issue involved the investigation of alternative formats of the state parameter CPR for the purpose of improving the cost performance of the MDF methodology. Four rules were devised as trial improvements on the basic state parameter format for CPR which considered only the current demand and the inventory and backorder levels in setting production levels. The proposed improvements smoothed adjustments for excess inventory or high backorder levels over several future periods and also incorporated a measure of future demand projections into the current period's decision process. Each of the new formats produced a cost improvement for one or more sets of experimental conditions. Rule 2, which smoothed inventory adjustments and anticipated future demand-versus-capacity inbalances, was rated superior in overall performance. When this superior rule for CPR was utilized in the application of the MDF methodology to the classic paint factory model of HMMS, the costs showed a marked improvement over the earlier trial with the basic rule, and were within 1% of the optimal cost found by applying HMMS's Linear Decision Rule. The conclusion is thus drawn that the exploration of alternative state parameter formats has produced significant improvements in the MDF performance.

IV

WORKFLOW PLANNING
AND CONTROL

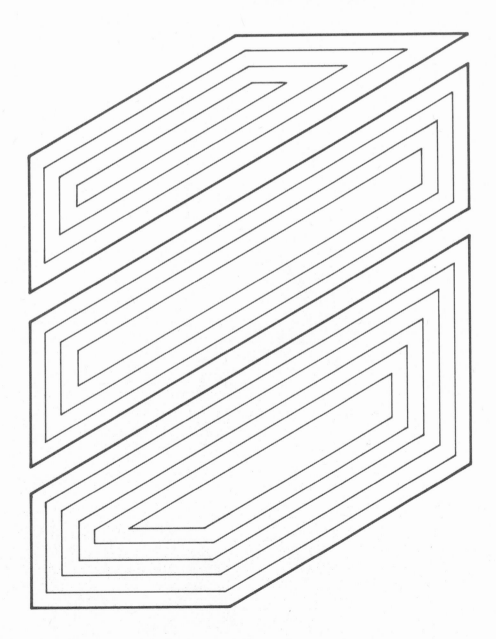

INTRODUCTION

In Part I the overall measure of success, the return-on-assets, was dis-aggregated to two basic components, the return on sales and the turn-over rate. Part II treated inventories, the major element of invest-ment which is subject to management influence in the short run. Part III covered the wage costs to a firm, a major determinant of the cost of sales, and therefore the return on sales. The general manpower planning problem was shown to include the wage level to be paid, the degree to which the available labor could be organized efficiently, and the manip-ulation of manpower levels and other controllable variables to match fluctuating demands (orders). Part IV covers the subject of workflow planning, the principal means by which an operation raises its turnover rate (the ratio of sales to assets). That is, for any given prevailing rate of return on sales and relevant asset base (cash, receivables, plant and equipment, and inventories) the greater the throughput of goods and services (sometimes referred to as volume), the greater the return-on-assets. Figure IV-1 shows the segment of the overall management job with which Part IV is concerned.

The more competitive the industry, and the more uniform the return on sales among the competitors, the more important the turn-over rate as the final determinant of operating performance. The detailed scheduling process begins after the top-level decisions are made regarding order backlog, capacity, inventory levels, and planned throughput times. The more detailed scheduling procedures must be carried out to plan and control the flow of work on a day-to-day basis within the specified overall environment. While the top-level manpower planning problem is similar in all operations, the detailed scheduling problems and techniques are different, depending upon the type of operation. Table IV-1 shows the major situations in which management must effect workflow control. Most operational situations fall into one of these categories.

DETAILED SCHEDULING PROBLEMS

Continuous Processes The problems in scheduling continuous produc-tion processes are to insure a high rate of utilization of the expensive facilities and to sequence products through the facility in such a way that changeover costs are minimized.

Job Shops The problems in scheduling a job shop are twofold. First, to set the work-in-process level in such a way that a given order-release rate (into production) provides an optimum or ideal cycle time (throughput interval). With this accomplished, the second problem is to sequence the separate tasks effectively on a minute-by-minute basis within the framework established previously.

One-Time Projects The problem in scheduling one-time projects is to insure the completion of all the tasks involved in the project in the least possible time for a given level of effort. The approach consists of making a list of all of the activities in the project, setting down the precedence relationships (in a diagram showing the order in which the

225

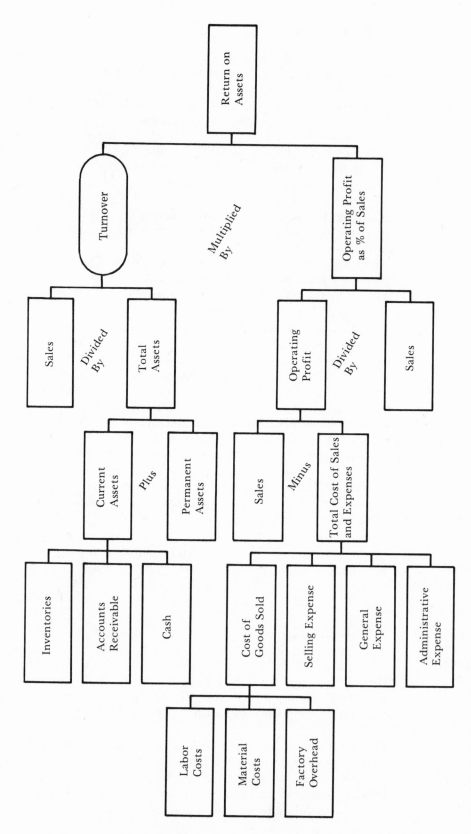

FIGURE IV-1 Relationship of Factors Affecting Return-on-Assets

TABLE IV-1 Scheduling Problems

		Process Scheduling	Job Shop Scheduling	Scheduling One-Time Projects	Assembly Line Balancing and Sequencing
Key attributes		Facility utilization	Shop load and capacity	Activities	Precedence diagram
		Throughput	Network of waiting lines	Events	Standard times
		Continuous operations	Sequencing of orders	Precedence diagram (network)	Station assignment
		Sequencing of products	Priority rules	Critical path	Balance delay
			Multiple measures of effectiveness	Slack	Open or closed stations
				PERT/CPM	
Examples		Oil refineries	Print shops	Ship building	Appliance manufacture
		Chemical plants	Machine shops	Building construction	Automobile manufacture
		Food processing	Computer center	Opening of new plant	Electrical components
		Steel mills	Hospital operating room	Installation of new computer	Furniture assembly
		Plastics plants	Job order manufacturing		

activities must be accomplished), and finding the longest path through the network. The longest path, called the critical path, determines the time which will be required to complete the project. It follows that management pressure or action will hasten the completion of the project only if it shortens the critical path.

Assembly Lines   Balancing and sequencing assembly lines is a two-level problem. First, the total workload must be determined by summing the work content for the number of units to be built in a given time period, such as a day. This provides an estimate of the number of workers which will be needed. Next, a tentative notion must be reached as to the number of work stations which will be established along the line. Finally, the total work content must be subdivided and apportioned to the work stations in such a way that the workload is balanced among the stations to the greatest extent possible. There is no direct mathematical solution to the assembly-line balancing problem. There are common-sense heuristic approaches which largely involve trying various allocations in a search for the best attainable balance. This balancing problem is complicated in the real world by the fact that there are almost no single-product assembly lines in operation. Most assembly lines are mixed-model lines, in which the work content varies from unit to unit, making the balancing problem even more difficult.

SUMMARY   In each basic situation, the impact of scheduling procedures on profitability lies in their ability to influence the turnover rate. The potential for contribution to return on investment is greatest in job shops with a labor intensive production process and extensive work in process inventories.

Job shop scheduling is covered in Chapter 9 because many production and service operations are organized as job shops, and the business graduate is likely to encounter this form of operation. Further, there are generally well-understood approaches available for increasing the throughput in job shops. The more analytical procedures for network scheduling and assembly-line scheduling are included as a supplement and a case study, respectively, to preserve the systems and management orientation of the chapters of the text. One-time projects are so widely prevalent in business (from building a new plant to installing a new computer) that every manager should understand the principles which underlie network scheduling. Critical path methodology is explained in detail in the Supplement On One-Time Projects. A case study of a system for balancing and sequencing a mixed model assembly line is included to illustrate the process of designing a daily operating system.

Job Shop Scheduling

9.1 INTRODUCTION

Scheduling workflow through job shops is perhaps the most important scheduling problem, from an economic standpoint, for managers to understand. Material in Part II, Asset Planning and Control, showed that about one-third of the assets of most manufacturing firms are invested in inventories. In durable-goods businesses, over half of the inventories are usually positioned as work-in-process inventories.

Many durable-goods manufacturers tend to be organized as job shops because they use general purpose machines, make a variety of goods to order, and serve many customers. The principles important in scheduling manufacturing job shops are equally applicable to the back-room operations in a bank, or to a computer center, or to a suite of operating rooms in a large hospital.

The fact that a major portion of the assets in a job shop operation are in work-in-process inventories makes the problem important to a profit-oriented manager. The fact that the work-in-process inventory is the major controllable portion of inventory (as described in Part II) increases the value to the manager of a better approach to workflow planning and control in job shops.

The decision to invest in seasonal or hedge inventories would normally be made at a management level higher than the plant. Raw material stock levels are usually determined by purchasing decisions, whether the purchasing function is located in the plant or at a higher level. The most important inventory decisions made at the plant level are those relating to the level of work-in-process (WIP) inventories. While the most appropriate (least-cost) levels of the cycle and buffer components can be calculated analytically, the appropriate level of WIP inventories is a function of the judgment of first-line supervisors and the effectiveness of the shop floor-scheduling system.

Vast amounts of time and effort and money have been expended in the past 20 years in the study of the scheduling of job shops. In fact, many of the factors which have made the planning problem more difficult, such as product proliferation, have influenced a shift in manufacturing from make-to-stock to make-to-order. The economic advantages of standardization and specialization of labor in assembly lines have gradually been overshadowed by the thrust of marketing efforts to customize products. Customers thus are able to choose from among a large number of options, features, attachments, styles, and colors. The greater margins on sales available from higher prices have placed a premium on the ability of the manufacturing function to deliver one-of-a-kind products. The firms which can achieve a more effective ability to schedule highly individualized products through the manufacturing facility have a competitive advantage.

BACKGROUND A number of computer simulation studies suggested the advantages to be gained from considering a job shop as a network of waiting lines with an essentially fixed short-run capacity. The aggregate behavior of job shops under the most obvious and interesting management strategies was studied by computer simulation. By 1962 results of these studies were well known, and data processing hardware and systems developments had progressed to a point where it was feasible to consider operating systems based on the results of the simulation studies. Most of the subsequent work in this area has been concentrated on implementing shop-scheduling systems.

This chapter describes the principles underlying an effective approach currently available for job shop scheduling and some details of an operating system.

DEFINITION OF THE PROBLEM Production processes are classified as job shops by any or all of several criteria. These criteria include order routing, facilities organization, variety of facilities, and whether products are produced to order or to replenish inventory. Individual orders may take any of several different routes through a job shop. Machining facilities in a job shop are general purpose, perform a variety of operations, and may be arranged functionally; that is, milling machines, drill presses, or lathes may be organized into groups of similar machines. Many shops are considered "job shops" within a particular firm if they meet one of the above criteria. A given shop might meet several or all of these criteria simultaneously.

The shop is considered to be an input-output system in which, ideally, the backlog of work is at some predetermined level, and the input of new orders equals the rate at which work is completed. The backlog would thus remain at the ideal level with a release of just enough new work each day, or any other time interval of interest, to replenish that portion of the backlog worked off.

The backlog of work, usually expressed in hours, is a set of orders waiting in lines before each of the machines. If the proper backlog is determined and maintained, and the release of work is properly controlled, the short-run control problem consists of a series of decisions that must be made regarding the job to be worked next when a man and a machine are available.

The decision about what to do next when a job is completed focuses on the jobs in the particular queue at that particular time. The method of selection of the job to be processed next is called the "queue discipline" in queuing theory. This form of scheduling is widely known as "priority scheduling."

The total problem is made more complex in the real world by the hundreds of moves that take place during a shift. A hot job (a behind-schedule job) may arrive at any instant and take its place at the head of a given queue. The decision as to the job to be assigned cannot be made until the time when the job currently being worked is completed and a man and machine are available. This scheduling problem cannot be solved mathematically, since the problem shifts minute by minute and would have changed before a mathematical solution could be reached. For instance, one medium-sized shop experienced about 1000 moves per shift, or about 2.5 moves per operator per shift, or two moves per minute. Further, the network of jobs waiting to be worked on is subject to random disturbances. That is, machines break down, orders are lost, the most effective operator doesn't report for work, and so on. These realities serve to enhance the value of a practical approach to the problem.

9.2   APPROACH TO THE PROBLEM

Scheduling and controlling such a manufacturing operation requires a data system to provide accurate status and priority information. Until the development of computers, this function was performed solely by a class of employees called expediters. Expediters physically went into the shop to find orders, hand-carried urgently needed orders from one work station to another, and exercised control over job priorities. This often required a foreman or worker to interrupt a job in process in order to work on a more critical job.

Computer simulation provides an alternative approach to this general problem. Simulation can be used to generate an expected pattern of order flow. The nature of the problem, however, causes the accuracy of a shop simulation to deteriorate as it penetrates farther and farther into the future. The proposed system is predicated on the capability to simulate adequately the very short-run period of one day or one shift. This assumes the availability of reasonably accurate time standards together with a periodically updated job-status file. While rush jobs arrive at a given machine without warning, tools break, and other emergencies occur, such events affect a small percentage of the total order flow completed per shift in most shops. The end result of the shop control system described here is a short-run simulation to assist each individual foreman in predicting order flow.[1]

The foreman is the final tactical decision point of the system. If the foreman knows the orders in his queues at the beginning of the shift, those orders that are likely to be coming into the section, and the work content and priority of the incoming orders, he can plan his work, arrange tools and materials, and have more time available for tending to emergencies.

CAPACITY LEVEL A modern job shop typically contains more machines than workers. A significant factor responsible for this relationship is that machines, though costly at acquisition, are capable of productive work long after they are fully depreciated. Short-run peak loads may be unbalanced to the extent that they require a great deal of capacity on one type of machine. The lead time for procurement and installation of machines is much greater than that required for operating personnel. It is therefore advantageous in job shops to keep extensive machine capability in order to have a reasonable assurance of meeting swings in the order mix. Short-run capacity in such a shop is thus determined by the personnel available to operate the machines.

SHOP-LOAD DETERMINATION It is assumed that the job shop facility is organized into a set of work stations and that a number of jobs are waiting in front of each station. In the company's accounting system, these stocks are carried at the financial cost of the material plus the labor and shop overhead charged to the job up to any point. At year end these values are summed to provide the dollar figure for work-in-process inventories on the balance sheet in the annual report. In the company's production control system, the jobs waiting represent requirements for man-hours of labor which will be necessary to complete the job. On the shop floor the physical material takes up floor space and provides flexibility for foremen to cope with a continuous stream of unforeseen delays and problems.

Work stations:	1	2	3	4	N

Jobs waiting:			
1	1	1	1
2	2	2	2
3	3	3	3
4	4	4	4
-	-	-	-
n	n	n	n

The total shop load at any time consists of the hours of work available for each machine, and is divisible into two categories. These

[1] Harry W. Steinhoff, Jr., *Daily System for Sequencing Orders in a Large Scale Job Shop,* presented at the Sixth Annual ORSA/TIMS Joint Western Regional Meeting, Orcas Island, Washington, April 16-17, 1964. Included as Chapter 10 in *Readings in Production and Operations Management,* edited by Elwood S. Buffa (New York: John Wiley and Sons, 1966).

are active orders in work-in-process and firm, but inactive, orders that have not been put into work-in-process as yet. The shop load is a major determinant of shop performance, since the shop's backlog of work interacts with machines and personnel available to determine the shop's capacity and the utilization of resources. Table 9-1 shows a sample of an actual weekly shop-load forecast.[2]

THE RELATION-SHIP BETWEEN WORK-IN-PROCESS INVENTORY AND LEAD TIME

There is a direct relationship between the level of work waiting in front of the work centers and the time required to get an average job through the plant. The more work on the shop floor, the longer it takes to process *each* job. This is shown in Figure 9-1. The level of WIP in a shop is similar to the level of water in a tank. If the order-release rate into the shop is equal to the production capacity, then the level will stay the same.

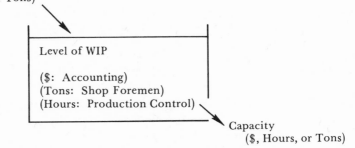

FIGURE 9-1

1) The system can be viewed in physical units, as shown in figure 9-2.

The average throughput time will be 8,000 ÷ 1,000 = 8 weeks

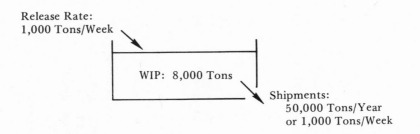

FIGURE 9-2

[2] M. H. Bulkin, J. L. Colley, Jr., and H. W. Steinhoff, "Load Forecasting Priority Sequencing and Simulation in a Job Shop Control System," *Management Science* (October 1966); included as Chapter 11 in *Readings in Production and Operations Management,* edited by Elwood S. Buffa (New York: John Wiley and Sons, 1966); adapted as a Case Study, Hughes Aircraft Company B, Harvard Business School (1966).

TABLE 9-1 Shop-Load Forecast
M-Day 605; Calendar Day 01—06—65
Machine Group Load in Standard Hours

Department MG 71—43 Mills, 6 Machines

	\multicolumn{11}{c}{Week of Performance}										Total
	1	2	3	4	5	6	7	8	9	10	Greater than 10	
Total load	208	175	227	204	126	116	42	52	28	23	53	1254
On schedule	138	122	211	186	126	114	34	52	25	14	53	1075
Behind schedule	70	53	16	18		2	8		3	9		179
Held	37	44	12	18	2							113
Total active load	123	115	102	64	46	53	21	6	15	23	53	621
On schedule	85	76	98	58	46	51	13	6	12	14	53	512
Behind schedule	38	39	4	6		2	8		3	9		109
Held	11	21	4		2							38
In machine group	96	37	26	3	8							150
Total preshop load	85	60	125	140	80	63	21	46	13			633
On schedule	53	46	113	128	80	63	21	46	13			563
Behind schedule	32	14	12	12								70
Held	26	23	8	18								75

2) Similarly, the units may be in dollars, as shown in Figure 9-3.

Throughput time = $2,400,000 ÷ $300,000/week = 8 weeks.

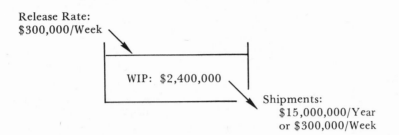

Release Rate:
$300,000/Week

WIP: $2,400,000

Shipments:
$15,000,000/Year
or $300,000/Week

FIGURE 9-3

3) The units could also be in actual man-hours. Suppose we have 500 direct workers working 40 hours/week, at a cost (wages plus overhead) of $15/man-hour (MH). Figure 9-4 depicts this situation.

Throughput time = 160,000 MH ÷ 20,000 MH/week – 8 weeks.

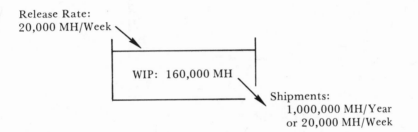

Release Rate:
20,000 MH/Week

WIP: 160,000 MH

Shipments:
1,000,000 MH/Year
or 20,000 MH/Week

FIGURE 9-4

4) Finally, the relationships could be expressed as standard man-hours (SMH), rather than as actual man-hours. Suppose we assume 90% performance (efficiency) in the case above. Then the 160,000 actual MH of load = 144,000 SMH, and the 20,000 actual MN/week of capacity = 18,000 SMN of capacity/week. This situation is diagrammed in Figure 9-5.

Throughput time = 144,000 SMH ÷ 18,000 SMH/week = 8weeks.

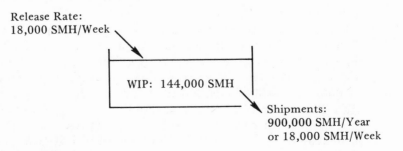

Release Rate:
18,000 SMH/Week

WIP: 144,000 SMH

Shipments:
900,000 SMH/Year
or 18,000 SMH/Week

FIGURE 9-5

The basic flows of materials, man-hours, and dollars which comprise the work-in-process inventories can be viewed as an input/output system with predictable behavior if the determining factors remain stable. For instance, all of the foregoing discussion assumed a balance between the input and output rates. Now we will consider what happens to the system when unbalances occur.

THE BEST LEVEL OF WORK-IN-PROCESS It should be clear that if the input rate is greater than the capacity, the level of WIP will build up continually. Similarly, if the capacity is greater than the release rate of new work, the WIP will rapidly run off, leading to work slowdowns and idle time of the work force. Doubtless the two rates should be balanced except when management is deliberately resetting the WIP to a new level. The obvious question is, which level is the best level? It was stated earlier that the only function served by WIP is to reduce the idle time of workers by providing a reservoir of available work in the case of production disturbances. A series of studies were made, using computer simulation, to find the best level of work-in-process. Figure 9-6 shows the result of those studies.

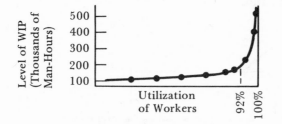

FIGURE 9-6 Level of W-I-P vs. Utilization

The shop was set up with various WIP levels (represented by the dots) and the shop was "run" for a considerable period of time at each level. A score was kept on such factors of shop performance as utilization of the work force and schedule performance. It was found that when levels of WIP were low and utilization below 90%, small increases in WIP led to large increases in utilization. Additions of relatively small increments in WIP led to large reductions in idle time. This was the case until utilizations of around 90-92% were reached. At this point the diagram shows that the situation reversed and large increases in WIP were required to attain even small increases in utilization. In fact, it was found that the WIP had to be doubled to raise utilization from 92% to 95%.

Assume a wage rate of $5/hour and a level of WIP of $2,400,000 with capacity of $300,000/week as in the earlier example. The lead time would thus be 8 weeks. With a 500-man work force working 40 hours a week, a 1% improvement in utilization would be worth $1,000/week (500 men × 40 hours = 20,000 MH; 20,000 MH × 1% = 200 hours; 200 hours × $5/hour = $1,000) or $50,000/year. If the interest cost for capital was 10%/year, then we could afford $500,000 of increased WIP (more than $500,000 of WIP @ 10% would cost more than the $50,000 saved through additional utilization). We would not invest in additional WIP inventory to the break-even point, since that would tie up scarce capital for no gain. The addition of WIP would therefore stop well short of the break-even point.

It is thus clear that unless WIP is helping attain increased efficiency, it is a waste of valuable resources. How can we then tell where the level should be? There are actually two ways. First, the problem can be studied by means of computer simulation, as in the study described. This method is expensive and time-consuming, and is complicated by the fact that each specific shop must be studied separately. The second and more appropriate method is for the management to analyze the problem as constrained by two limits. The absolute minimum throughput time is the sum of the processing times in the various work centers, assuming that jobs did not wait at all. The maximum lead time would be limited only by the resources available to finance WIP inventories. In a given shop then, the WIP inventory level should be reduced to the point at which further reduction leads to an uneconomical increase in worker idle time for lack of work. This is best done by gradually reducing the order-release rate over an extended time period. With a fixed output rate the level of WIP will gradually be reduced.

Excessive WIP levels can provide slack which helps cover for marginal shop floor-scheduling systems. If management suddenly takes away the slack in WIP, the shop's ability to meet schedules may be reduced. By gradually reducing prevailing WIP levels, management allows the shop time to sharpen its scheduling capability and shop floor controls to meet the challenge of supporting shipping promises with less slack in the system.

WORK-IN-PROCESS AND THE ABILITY TO SCHEDULE

In the study described earlier, various methods of scheduling (sequencing) work assignments were studied at different levels of WIP and utilization. The results of these studies are represented in Figure 9-7. The diagram show 3 distinct regions regarding WIP levels and scheduling sensitivity. When the shop is lightly loaded with excess capacity available, schedule dates and other criteria of shop performance can be met with almost any scheduling procedure. On the other hand, to the right of the ideal WIP zone, when the shop is more-or-less saturated, most jobs will be late, regardless of the scheduling procedures used. When the total WIP is carefully controlled to the correct level, the shop's performance is sensitive to various scheduling procedures.

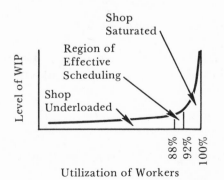

FIGURE 9-7 Level of W-I-P vs. Utilization

9.3   PRIORITY SCHEDULING OF JOB ASSIGMENTS

**INTRO-
DUCTION**

With a given shop load and capacity, a series of decisions must be made regarding the job to be worked next at each work station. The early approach to scheduling consisted of an attempt to estimate the approximate time when a given job would run. Shop orders were issued with completion due-dates that indicated to foremen when a job was needed. By contrast, the systematic study by means of simulation of the relationships between load and make-span confirms the independence of sequencing rules and aggregate schedule performance.

Sequencing rules can be devised to favor movement of orders on the basis of any desired criteria, such as schedule dates or the value of jobs or the number of orders completed. Favoring certain orders necessarily results in delays to other orders. The overall performance to schedule dates, however, is largely dependent on load ratios. For example, with an extremely heavy load, most orders will finish late; and conversely, with a very light load, most orders will be completed ahead of schedule, regardless of the detailed scheduling procedures followed.

Schedule dates may be removed from shop orders and a new approach used in which all jobs are assigned relative priorities. Provision thus has to be made to update the priorities continually. Since the relative priorities of orders shift constantly as conditions change, operating personnel require new information at frequent time intervals.

The bibliography at the end of this chapter lists a number of references which report results of priority rule studies. The most exhaustive study is reported by Conway, et. al.[3] The results of experimental simulations of the behavior of shops under various disciplines are reported, along with an extensive body of theoretical work which analytically develops the general results to be expected from various families (or classes) of rules. This book is the most comprehensive reference source available on scheduling theory.

**A STUDY OF
A LIMITED
NUMBER OF
RULES**

A simulation study of a limited number of priority rules was conducted in conjunction with the development of an actual operating system. From a large number of rules which had been studied previously, a small number which were of special interest were chosen. Arrangements were made to feed data from a file of actual shop orders to a general purpose shop simulator. The results of those studies were reported by LeGrande.[4]

The program would simulate shop operations for a period of several months and report a large number of attributes of interest in regard to the level of effectiveness of shop performance. LeGrande reported results in regard to the following 10 criteria which can be used to measure shop performance.

1) Number of orders completed.
2) Percent of orders completed late.

[3] R. W. Conway, W. L. Maxwell, and L. W. Miller, *Theory of Scheduling* (Reading, Mass.: Addison-Wesley, 1967).

[4] E. LeGrande, "The Development of a Factory Simulation Using Actual Operating Data," *Management Technology,* May 1963.

3) Mean of the distribution of completions.
4) Standard deviation of the distribution of completions.
5) Average number of orders waiting in the shop.
6) Average wait time of orders.
7) Yearly cost of carrying orders in queue.
8) Ratio of inventory carrying cost while waiting to inventory cost while on machine.
9) Percent of labor utilized.
10) Percent of machine capacity utilized.

Results were reported regarding the following priority scheduling rules:

1) Minimum processing time.
2) Minimum slack time per operation.
3) First come, first served.
4) Minimum planned operation start date.
5) Earliest due-date
6) Random selection.

Rules 1 and 2 were chosen because earlier simulation and analytical work from queuing studies indicated they were apt to be the most interesting to shop management of the new approaches proposed. If the job with the shortest operation time is always worked on first, it is intuitively obvious that the maximum number of jobs will be processed through the facility. The principal drawback to the shortest-operation rule is the fact that longer jobs might be by-passed continually.

For shops whose orders are characterized by fixed schedule dates, numerous simulation studies support the "slack time per operation" rule as the most effective. The slack time per operation index considers the following factors to determine the relative priorities of jobs:

1) The remaining calendar time to the due date (RT).
2) The remaining processing times (RPT).
3) The remaining expected queue times (RQT).
4) The number of operations remaining (NO. OPS.).

These factors are manipulated algebraically to determine priorities in the form of an urgency number for each job. The computation is indicated below:

$$\text{urgency number} = \frac{RT - (RPT + RQT)}{NO. OPS.}$$

If the remaining calendar time equals the sum of remaining processing times and expected queue times, the numerator is zero and the urgency number is zero. If the remaining time is greater, the urgency number (priority) will be positive. If it is less than the expected processing and queue times, the urgency number will be negative. This leads to a pattern in which jobs progressing according to plan have zero priorities. Positive numbers show progress ahead of planned make-span times, and negative numbers indicate the possibility of missing schedule dates unless some action is taken. All of the relevant factors are considered jointly, and the foreman gives priority to the job with the most negative urgency number.

Rules 4 and 5 were studied because they are the scheduling devices most often used in shops today. Many shop schedules display a due-date on the shop order, and expediters and shop foremen generally favor movement of orders based on the earliest due-date. Another widely used scheme in current shop practice is the calculation of a set of planned start dates for each operation which are then used by shop supervisors to move work along systematically.

Rules 3 and 6 were included as controls to aid in evaluating the simulation results. Neither would be likely to be used in a real shop situation.

Results reported by LeGrande[5] are shown in Tables 9-2 and 9-3. Table 9-2 shows the relative results of the simulation studies for each of the six priority rules. The entries shown in the table give a score of 1.00 to the rule which gave the best relative performance with regard to each criterion. For each criterion each rule was scored on the basis of its quantitative score as a decimal faction of the best score attained by any rule. For instance, with Criterion No. 1, Number of Orders Completed, the runs showed that Rule No. 1, The Minimum Processing Time, completed the most orders. Rule No. 2, The Minimum Slack Time Per Operation, completed 87% as many orders and was accordingly given a score of 0.87.

In Table 9-2 the scores for each rule on all of the criteria were summed to provide a total relative rank for each rule. It is seen that the Minimum Processing Time rule ranks slightly higher than the Minimum Slack Time Per Operation, but both scored significantly better than the other rules tested.

Table 9-3 was constructed to provide a ranking of the rules when the criteria were weighted to give more consideration to those most related to meeting schedules. Recall that according to the survey reported in Chapter 8, the most important criterion for judging manufacturing performance is the ability to meet schedules. With the weightings shown the Slack Time Per Operation rule was best, with the Minimum Processing Time rule second. Again these two rules performed significantly better than the others tested. Conway[6] discussed the possibility of a mixed strategy whereby these two rules would be used intermittently.

UPPER AND LOWER BOUNDS ON THE VALUE OF WORK-IN PROCESS INVENTORIES When released into work, the value of a typical shop order consists of the material value alone. As labor and overhead costs are subsequently added, the value increases until the order closes out of the shop. The average value of work-in-process inventory is the summation of the values of all jobs in the shop, sampled at certain times such as the beginning of each shift, and averaged for some longer period, say, a month.

[5] Op. cit.
[6] Conway, loc. cit.

TABLE 9-2 Priority Rules - Scheduling Performance

Criteria	1	2	3	4	5	6	7	8	9	10	Total Relative Rank
Relative weight:	1	1	1	1	1	1	1	1	1	1	
Rule											
MINPRT	1.00	0.83	1.00	0.20	1.00	1.00	0.76	0.91	1.00	1.00	8.70
MINSOP	0.87	1.00	0.63	1.00	0.73	0.52	0.96	0.99	0.92	0.92	8.54
FCFS	0.86	0.54	0.54	0.20	0.73	0.38	0.84	0.98	0.93	0.93	6.93
MINSD	0.84	0.48	0.46	0.22	0.68	0.36	0.91	1.00	0.91	0.91	6.77
MINDD	0.94	0.62	0.64	0.24	0.84	0.51	1.00	0.99	0.87	0.87	7.52
RANDOM	0.84	0.68	0.79	0.20	0.67	0.66	0.80	0.93	0.92	0.91	7.40

TABLE 9-3 Priority Rules - Scheduling Performance - Weighted Criteria

Criteria:	1	2	3	4	5	6	7	8	9	10	Total Relative Rank
Relative weight:	2	5	5	5	1	1	4	2	3	2	
Rule											
MINPRT	2.00	4.15	5.00	1.00	1.00	1.00	3.04	1.82	3.00	2.00	24.01
MINSOP	1.74	5.00	3.15	5.00	0.73	0.52	3.84	1.98	2.75	1.84	26.56
FCFS	1.72	2.70	2.30	1.00	0.73	0.38	3.36	1.96	2.79	1.86	19.20
MINSD	1.68	2.40	2.30	1.10	0.68	0.36	3.64	2.00	2.73	1.82	18.71
MINDD	1.88	3.10	3.20	1.20	0.84	0.51	4.00	1.98	2.61	1.74	21.06
RANDOM	1.68	3.40	3.95	1.00	0.67	0.66	3.20	1.86	2.76	1.82	21.00

Alan Rowe first explored the possibility of lowering the investment in work-in-process inventories by releasing jobs with a high-value content close to their due-dates and expediting them rapidly through the shop.[7] Since a small percentage of the orders in any shop constitutes the majority of the dollar value, it would be feasible to lower the average inventory level significantly by such a strategem. High-value orders could be assigned a planned manufacturing interval of, say, five days; medium-value orders ten days; and low-value orders 15 days. Such a concept involves a more sophisticated approach then most shop people will understand, and any approach is of little use if not fully understood and appreciated by operating people. An alternative approach, more straightforward in application, involves releasing work according to average planned span-times without regard to value. A sequencing or dispatch rule can then be used to favor consistently the assignment of jobs that are highest in value (the sum of material costs and incurred laber).

If orders are dispatched by a priority rule that depends solely on value, and if schedule dates are ignored, the completion date would be a random variable, equally likely to fall before or after the order due-date. Since orders are expedited according to value, however, high-value jobs are always given preference, and most of the high-dollar portion of the work-in-process inventory would be completed early.

Simulation studies by the author (Colley) have shown the minimum attainable investment in work-in-process inventory to be significantly different from the nominal value, depending upon the priority sequencing rule chosen. With value the sole criterion for job dispatching, the average inventory investment level in a large shop was 40% of that required for operation with a slack time rule (which fails to consider value). This means that for a given shop load, number of men and machines available, and a predetermined relationship between capacity and order release which fixes the utilization rate of personnel, the work-in-process inventory value might vary as much as 2.5 to 1, depending on the criterion used for sequencing.

The absolute difference between extremes of inventory value in a given shop is dependent upon the distribution of orders by value, and this changes over time in a given shop. Simulation provides a means for exploring the absolute minimum and nominal levels for any given shop. The maximum value might exceed the nominal value (represented by a slack time priority rule) by some such unlikely procedure as expediting the lowest-value job.

A possible compromise between these criteria would give consideration to value to supplement a basic slack time rule. For instance, ties according to slack time per operation could be broken by consideration of relative value. It is significant that through simulation, a management can know, for a given order mix, the upper and lower bounds on in-process inventory levels for as far into the future as production plans are firm.

---

[7] Alan Rowe, "Sequential Decision Rules in Production Scheduling" (University of California, Los Angeles: Dissertation presented in partial fulfillment of the requirements for the degree of Doctor of Philosophy in Production Engineering, August 31, 1958).

ADDENDUM   It is interesting to note three practical examples of the effect of specialized priority rules in certain situations. Shearon[8] studied the operation of a suite of operating rooms in a large general hospital and found that the most effective pattern of results on a day-by-day basis was achieved by sequencing the operations to be performed according to the Longest Operation First rule. Practically, this served to "get the most variable operations out of the way first," since the longest operating procedures tended to be the most variable. For instance, critical operations might take 4-5 hours, or the patient might expire soon after the procedure was started. This strategy led to the gradual attainment of stability in scheduling as the larger number of shorter and more predictable operations were tackled. Howell, Sienkiewicz, et al.,[9] found that the Shortest Operation rule achieved the greatest number of operational helicopters (on average) in the simulation of a combat maintenance depot. That is, where a number of helicopters were always awaiting the attention of the limited maintenance personnel, giving priority to the helicopter estimated to require the least repair time would maximize the fleet of available machines. Likewise, Colley, et al.,[10] found that the use of the shortest-treatment-time discipline maximized the survivors of a saturated medical facility, such as a forward aid station in a combat zone. This resulted from the phenomenon that the shorter the expected treatment time, the higher the probabiltiy of survival; thus, the rule led to getting the largest number of the most appropriate patients through the system.

9.4   SUMMARY OF SYSTEM CHARACTERISTICS

Let us restate the principles that underly a modern job shop scheduling system.

Principle 1   A shop is considered to be a network of waiting lines in which the relative urgencies of the orders are constantly shifting.

a) The problem is, therefore, not to predict the completion date of each order prior to its release to the shop.
b) The problem is rather to provide for shop foremen a more-or-less continuous stream of advisements regarding the continually shifting relative priorities of the orders.
c) The continuing application of the up-to-date priorities by the foreman each time a man and machine are available and a new job can be put into work will result in a set of sequencing decisions that constitute the best attainable set in the long run.

[8] Winston T. Shearon, Jr., "A Study of Hospital Operating Suite Scheduling Procedures (North Carolina State University: Thesis presented in partial fulfillment of the requirements for the degree of Master of Science in Industrial Engineering, 1969).

[9] M. Howell and R. Sienkiewicz, et al., "Simulation of a Maintenance System for an Assault Helicopter Company" (The Colgate Darden Graduate School of Business Administration, University of Virginia, Charlottesville, Virginia: Unpublished paper, 1975).

[10] John L. Colley, Jr., et al., "A Simulation Model of a Saturated Medical System" (Toronto, Canada: *Proceedings of the 18th Annual Institute Conference and Convention,* American Institute of Industrial Engineers, May 1967.

Principle 2   The performance of a shop with regard to schedule dates is relatively independent of the sequencing method employed.

a) The short-run capacity is fixed by the personnel available.
b) The shop load is controlled at a predetermined level through order-release strategies; it interacts with short-run capacity to give a desired average rate of worker utilization.
c) A dual penalty is paid for attempts to increase utilization by increasing work-in-process. The value invested in inventory goes up, and the average make-span is also increased proportionately to the increase in load. The increased make-span means that all orders will require, on the average, longer shop intervals.
d) The long-run performance to schedule dates is largely a function of the relationship between load and capacity. If the shop has a light load, most orders will finish on schedule. If the shop is saturated, most orders will be late.

9.5   IMPLEMENTING A JOB SHOP SCHEDULING SYSTEM

A great deal of effort has been expended in manufacturing companies during the past 15 years in attempts to implement computer-based job shop-scheduling systems. Some companies transferred a major portion of their existing (semimanual) systems onto computers while other companies employed systems specialists to develop new systems, tailored to the new capability for data processing.

Many factors influence the choice of characteristics for a specific scheduling system in a given firm. The choices among such factors as the basic approach to the scheduling problem, the breadth of the system, performance criteria, the system horizon, and the final tactical control point provide for an almost unlimited set of possible system configurations. Figure 9-8 illustrates the range of different possible systems. The choices among the several factors in any business would reflect the nature of the industry, the significant problems facing the shop, and the personal inclinations of shop management personnel and systems designers.

Each factor will be discussed briefly to illustrate the complexity of a given system.

PROBLEM APPROACHES   The first branch in the tree of Figure 9-8 shows the choices available between the manual (intuitive) methods in use for many years, contrasted with more recently proposed combinatorial and statistical approaches. Even the rapid development of computer capability has failed to make combinatorial approaches feasible. A statistical approach was adopted because of the nature of shop activities. The constantly shifting order mix in the various queues makes the choice of a statistical model a realistic one.

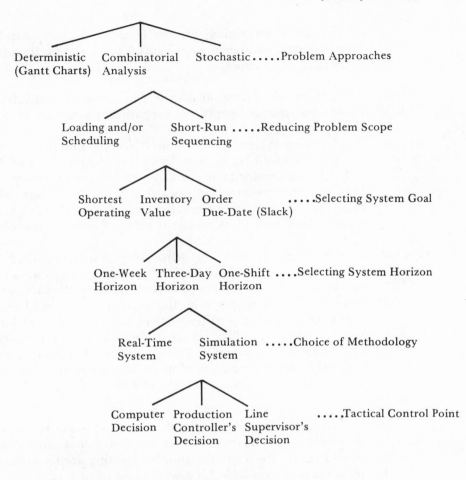

FIGURE 9-8 A Wide Range of Feasible Systems

REDUCING PROBLEM SCOPE   The relative independence of long-run planning (loading) and short-run sequencing leads to a separation of the two in the interest of practical implementation. As described earlier, the availability of a load forecast and analysis and proper attention to the relationship between work-in-process level, order-release rates, and personnel levels reduces the shop sequencing problem to one of effective short-run dispatching.

SELECTING SYSTEM GOAL   Dispatch rule studies have provided the means for maximizing shop performance relative to almost any criterion.[11] The results of these studies have been well documented, and appropriate priority schemes are available that achieve most results of interest. The Slack Time Per Operation rule is superior to any other rule under most job shop circumstances. Further, the factors in the formula (time remaining to the due-date, the number of operations remaining, and the amount of

[11] R. W. Conway, *Preliminary Report on an Experimental Comparison of Priority Dispatching Rules*, Cornell Production Control Research Committee, Discussion Paper No. 52 (April 13, 1962).

machine time remaining) are the factors generally considered by fore-men in making sequencing decisions. The method is therefore intuitively acceptable to foremen.

SYSTEM HORIZON The proper scheduling horizon is a function of a specific shop's order-cycle time, average operation time, order-release rate, etc.

CHOICE OF METHODOL-OGY A scheduling system could be built around a number of techniques, in-cluding, for instance, as near a real-time response as possible or simula-tion. It is necessary to make a choice between working toward a real-time systems response or toward a simulation approach. In a given situation the value of information regarding probable future order-flow patterns must be compared to the value of inquiry capability.

TACTICAL CONTROL POINT The implementation of a scheduling system requires choosing the agency that will make the final tactical choice regarding work sequences. The nature of most job shops renders unlikely the successful implemen-tation of a system wherein the system makes rigid machine assign-ments. Data regarding differences in the capabilities of individual oper-ators or the desirability of job splits would be very difficult to build into a system, for instance. The system should therefore be constructed to provide relevant information to the foremen, who then make the final decisions regarding job assignments.

An operating shop-control system is seen to depend on many decisions regarding system characteristics that should be made with consideration for a specific shop's operating peculiarities. The tools and techniques are available for a wide range of systems.

THE SHOP OPERATING SYSTEM The operating system should utilize a short-run simulation to provide foremen with information about expected patterns of order flow. [12] The simulation scheduler can be devised to run each night with up-to-date status information as input. Shop foremen should receive the simulation results at the beginning of each shift and use the expected order flow to derive work plans which integrate orders in-station with other orders that are likely to arrive during the shift.

Inputs to the simulation scheduler include the basic order-routing and time-standard files, together with data on open orders, current order status (location), prevailing performance factors (relating actual performance to standard times for each machine group), and data describing shop capacity (men and machines anticipated to be avail-able). The logic of one such simulator scheduler has been well docu-mented elsewhere, and will not be described in detail here. [13]

It should be recognized that the actual pattern of order flow will not correspond to the simulated pattern for a variety of reasons. These

[12] J. L. Colley, Jr., *Computer Oriented Business Systems*, (University of Southern Califor-nia, Los Angeles: Unpublished doctoral dissertation, August 1964).

[13] Steinhoff, loc. cit.

reasons include inaccuracies in time estimates and the disparity between foreman assignments of jobs and the computer's simulated assignments, among others.

The utility of a simulation scheduler is related to its close connection with a major shop problem: the provision of work-in-process inventory to prevent excessive idle time as a result of operators "waiting for work." If the level of work in queues before the various machines constitutes 15 days of load relative to capacity, it is implicit that only a small portion of the orders will receive attention during the next shift. A major goal of a properly constructed scheduling system is to provide a method of focusing the attention of foremen on the most critical of the jobs.

A simulation scheduler can call attention to the most critical jobs and trace their probable movement through successive machines. When one operation is completed, for instance, the order might enter the next machine group at the head of the line of jobs awaiting assignment, preempting the jobs already waiting. Some orders might, in fact, move through as many as four or five operations in a single shift. The simulation scheduler can record these patterns of order flow and provide the foreman a summary of orders in his section at the beginning of the shift, together with their relative priorities for assignment.

Additionally, the foremen can be informed regarding jobs that could be expected to arrive during the course of the work day. These data include (for each order) the estimated arrival time, the work center from which it will arrive, the work content (in hours), and the slack priority it will have upon its arrival.

To achieve simulation accuracy sufficient to maintain confidence in the system's output, allowance has to be made for deviations from plan that are inherent in job shops. The success of the simulation approach doubtless depends heavily on its abiltiy to cope with these realistic problems. These exceptions to plan include unplanned orders, out-of-sequence orders, and write-in operations. If shop data identify an order which is unknown to the computer, simulation should proceed, based on the average time per piece in the given work center.

In certain instances location data from the shop indicate that an order is in a station not called for in the order's planned routing. In such cases the scheduler might assume shop personnel will complete an extra operation, called a "write-in operation." The scheduler should assign an estimated time to the order and proceed with job assignments.

Operation 7 for a given order might be reported as complete while the computer's file indicates that Operations 5 and 6 remain to be completed. Operation 7 may have been worked "out-of-sequence," and the scheduler would assign Operation 5 next. On the other hand, Operations 5 and 6 may have actually been completed, but not reported. The scheduler could operate in either mode, as directed by shop management.

9.6   SUMMARY

This chapter has presented an approach to computer-based scheduling systems for job shops that blends together modern data processing capability and findings from simulation studies. The approach outlined begins with the total scheduling problem being divided into two parts: 1) the balance, over time, of shop capacity with load to provide a desired level of operator utilization; and 2) given the fixed short-run capacity determined by (1), a proper sequencing of orders according to desired completion patterns.

This subdivision of the total problem provides several important advantages.

1) Proper consideration is given to the basic difference between, and the independence of, the two subproblems.
2) The proper adjustment of manpower levels and shop load provides a consistent pattern of queue lengths before the various machines. Such consistency is desirable for personnel reasons, if for no other.
3) Operating personnel and shop supervisors are comfortable with system objectives that orient their short-term actions to following prescribed sequencing rules.

It was pointed out that a scheduling system for a particular job shop is specified by decisions regarding numerous facets of the system. A large number of different systems can be defined by sets of decisions regarding sequencing rules, response time, or other system elements. It should be stressed that the system for a given shop should be custom-tailored to that shop's order characteristics, data accuracy, operating discipline, and computer/data processing maturity.

9.7   BIBLIOGRAPHY

Baker, C. T., and Dzielinski, B. P. "Simulation of a Simplified Job Shop." *IBM Business Systems Research Memorandum*, August 1, 1958; also *Management Science*, April 1960.

Baker, C. T., Dzielinski, B. P., and Manne, A. S. "Simulation Tests of Lot Size Programming. *Management Science*, January 1963.

Baker, Kenneth R. "Priority Dispatching in the Single Channel Queue with Sequence-Dependent Setups." *The Journal of Industrial Engineering*, April 1968, pp. 203-205.

Carroll, D. C. "Heuristic Sequencing of Single and Multiple Component Jobs." Ph.D. thesis, MIT, June 1965.

Cobham, A. "Priority Assignment in Waiting Line Problems." *Operations Research*, February 1954.

Conway, R. W. "Priority Dispatching and Work-in-Process Inventory in a Job Shop." *Journal of Industrial Engineering*, March 1965.

_____. "Priority Dispatching and Job Lateness in a Job Shop." *Journal of Industrial Engineering*, March 1965.

_____. "An Experimental Investigation of Priority Assignment in a Job Shop." RAND Corporation Memorandum RM-3789-PR, February 1964.

Conway, R. W., and Maxwell, W. L. "Network Dispatching by the Shortest Operation Discipline." *Operations Research* February 1962, pp. 51-73. Also Muth, J. F. and Thompson, G. L., eds. Industrial Scheduling. Englewood Cliffs, N. J.: Prentice-Hall, 1963.

Conway, R. W., Johnson, B. M. and Maxwell, W. L. "An Experimental Investigation of Priority Dispatching." *Journal of Industrial Engineering,* May 1960.

Elmaghraby, S. E., and Cole, R. T. "On the Control of Production in Small Job Shops." *Journal of Industrial Engineering,* July 1963.

Gere, W. "A Heuristic Approach to Job-Shop Scheduling." Ph.D. thesis, Carnegie Institute of Technology, 1962.

Heathcote, C. R. "A Simple Queue with Several Preemptive Priority Classes." *Operations Research,* September 1960.

Holstein, William K., and Berry, William L. "The Labor Assignment Decision: An Application of Work Flow Structure Information." *Management Science,* March 1972, pp. 390-400.

_____ . "Work Flow Structure: An Analysis for Planning and Control." *Management Science,* February 1970, pp. B-324 — B-336.

Jackson, J. R. "Networks of Waiting Lines." *Operations Research,* August 1957.

_____ . "Simulation Research on Job-Shop Production." *Nav. Res. Log. Quart.,* December 1957.

_____ . "Some Problems in Queueing with Dynamic Properties." *Nav. Res. Log. Quart.,* September 1960.

_____ . "Sample Distribution of Mean Waiting Time in Queues." Research Report 67, *Management Sciences Research Project,* UCLA, September 20, 1960.

_____ . "Simulation of Queues with Dynamic Priorities." Research Report 71, *Management Sciences Research Project,* UCLA, March 20, 1961.

_____ . "Queues with Dynamic Priority Discipline." *Management Science,* October 1961.

_____ . "Waiting-Time Distributions for Queues with Dynamic Priorities." *Nav. Res. Log. Quart.,* March 1962.

LeGrande, E. "The Development of a Factory Simulation Using Actual Operating Data." *Management Technology,* May 1963.

Moodie, C. L., and Novotny, D. J. "Computer Scheduling and Control Systems for Discrete Part Production." *The Journal of Industrial Engineering,* July 1968, pp. 336-341.

Rowe, A. J. "Sequential Decision Rules in Production Scheduling." Ph.D. thesis, UCLA, August 1958. . .

_____ . "Toward a Theory of Scheduling." *Journal of Industrial Engineering,* March 1960.

Trilling, D. R. "Job-Shop Simulation of Orders That Are Networks," *Journal of Industrial Engineering,* February 1966.

Wilbrecht, Jon K., and Prescott, William B. "The Influence of Setup Time on Job Shop Performance." *Management Science,* December 1969, pp. B-274 — B-280.

SUPPLEMENT ON SCHEDULING ONE-TIME PROJECTS

INTRODUCTION

This supplement covers network scheduling methods which are particularly useful in the management of research and development projects, building or bridge construction, ship building, or other one-time projects. These network scheduling methods are identified by a number of titles, including the Critical Path Method (CPM) and Program Evaluation and Review Technique (PERT) as the most widely used. The bibliography at the end of this supplement lists references which cover the variations of network scheduling methods which are most widely used.

Two factors combine to make the problem of scheduling one-time projects essentially different from process sequencing, assembly-line balancing, or job shop scheduling.

1) Careful organization of the work so that a high level of utilization of both manpower and facilities is attained is a critical factor in the other scheduling situations.
2) Since the same general type of work is performed in similar, repetitive patterns, the facilities are organized for an efficient flow of work in the other scheduling situations.

While the same facilities may be used in constructing two different buildings, and similar work elements must be completed by various work crews, the important distinctions from the factory setting are the inability to organize the facilities for efficient use and the lack of enough scheduling options to insure a high rate of utilization of the skilled personnel employed.

Many one-time projects involve sequential activities which include administrative, engineering, or research activities, interspersed with activities requiring facilities. Since the project is unlikely to be repeated exactly, management requires a flexible planning tool which emphasizes the uniqueness of the job at hand. Also, since each new project presents a new set of operational and coordinative problems, the flow of work must constantly be replanned and the project plans revised as various problems arise and are dealt with.

A project network provides the required degree of flexibility. The network is a pictorial representation of the various activities which must be completed to finish the project. The network also shows the various sequential constraints which determine how the work must be performed. The network is completed by adding time estimates for each element of work.

Planning and controlling the completion of a project by CPM thus involves the following steps:

1) All of the activities required to complete the project must be listed.
2) A network must be prepared in which the activities (represented by arrows) are arrayed to show the precedence relationships.
3) The longest path through the network (the critical path) must be found by computation.
4) Management attention can be focused on planning with the understanding that the lapsed time to complete the project can be reduced only by reducing the time required for activities along the critical path.
5) The network must be constantly revised and updated as work progresses.

A number of detailed aspects of critical path methodologies are not covered in this supplement. Specialized texts and papers listed in the bibliography treat such details as the distinction between activity- and event-oriented networks, definitions of various types of "float" or "slack" time, and activity-numbering methods for including cost accumulation and control in network systems. Readers interested in more detailed treatment of the methodologies should consult Moder and Phillips or Flagle.

The remainder of this supplement describes the basic approaches to developing and analyzing project networks. The details of network construction are presented, along with the computational procedures for finding the critical path. Since many projects involve activities with highly variable time requirements, the standard PERT methods for the statistical analysis of optimistic, most likely, and pessimistic time estimates are presented. These include the calculation of activity expected times and variances, the location of the critical path, and the determination of the probability of meeting a given schedule date.

NETWORK PREPARATION

THE ACTIVITY ARROW   The "activity" as used in CPM scheduling is one item of work in a total project. Each activity or increment of work is represented by an arrow, as shown in Figure 1. It should be noted that this is not a vector

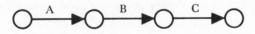

FIGURE 1

technique. That is, the length and direction of the arrow are meaning-
less and do not affect the calculations or interpretation of the network.
The circles at each end of the arrow represent the events (points in
time) at which the activity begins and ends. For purposes of identification, each arrow has a task description, as shown in Figure 2.

FIGURE 2

Sequential events are represented by various linkings of arrows. One
should start at the beginning of the project and arrange the arrows to
show the logical flow of the work. As each task is added to the diagram,
it should be examined in relation to the other tasks, and the following
questions should be asked:

a) What other activities must be completed before this task can start?
b) What can be done concurrently?
c) What activities cannot start until after this task is completed?

When one activity precedes another, they are represented as shown in
Figure 3. When activities may be worked on concurrently, they may be
represented as shown in Figure 4. Some other typical examples of
situations encountered in the development of the arrow diagram are
shown in Figures 5, 6, and 7.

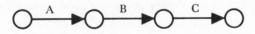

FIGURE 3

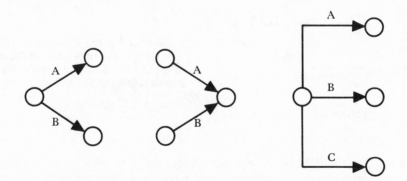

FIGURE 4

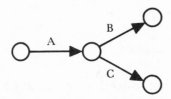

A must be completed before either B or C can start.

FIGURE 5

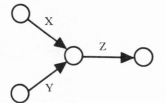

Z cannot begin until both X and Y are completed.

FIGURE 6

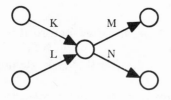

Both K and L must be finished before either M or N can start.

FIGURE 7

THE DUMMY ARROW   Another technique used in CPM diagramming is the dashed arrow or "dummy task". The dummy task is not, in itself, an activity, but it is used to show a relationship between activities. The dummy arrow has no time duration but acts as a restraint in order to keep the flow of work in a logical sequence. Astute use of dummy activities in arrow diagramming can lend substantial accuracy to the overall project network. Figure 8 illustrates the use of a dummy arrow.

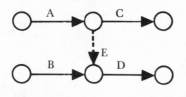

Both A and B must be completed before D can start. C depends only on the completion of A, not on B. E is a dummy to insure the logical sequence of events.

FIGURE 8

EVENTS   The identifiable reference points in time which mark the starting and completion of each activity arrow are defined as events. To facilitate reference to individual activities, the events of a project network diagram are numbered serially, usually from left to right, as shown in Figure 4. Activities can then be identified by their starting and finishing event numbers rather than by lengthy job titles or task descriptions.

Where heads or tails of several arrows come together, there is a common event number. Origin and terminal event numbers are not necessarily in sequence, but events should be numbered so that the head of each arrow always carries a number larger than its tail. Activity A in Figure 9 has an origin event (1) and a terminal event (2) and may be called "Activity 1-2." Activity B has an origin event (2) and a terminal event (3) and may be called "Activity 2-3." Activity C has an origin event (1) and a terminal event (3) and may be called "Activity 1-3." All network or arrow diagrams have origin and terminal events, such as (0) and (6) in Figure 10.

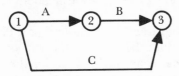

FIGURE 9

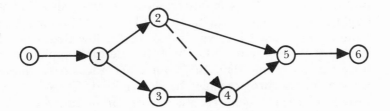

FIGURE 10

In order to provide unique identifications for activities with the same origins and terminals, dummy arrows are used. In Figure 11 Activities A, B, and C would all be referred to as Activity 1-2. With dummies added, however, a clearer representation of the relationships can be made. This is essential for quick reference when discussing activities and in the use of computers for network analysis. Figure 12 is an example. Activity A is now Activity 1-2, Activity B is now Activity 1-4, and Activity C is now Activity 1-3. The dummy activities are numbered 2-4 and 3-4.

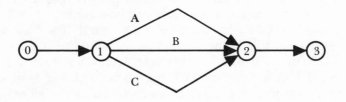

FIGURE 11

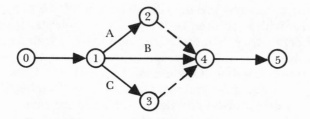

FIGURE 12

FUNDA-
MENTALS OF
SCHEDULING Up to this point we have been primarily concerned with the preparation of the plan. The next step in the utilization of CPM techniques is to estimate the time required for performance of each activity, and, using these times, to determine the length of time needed to complete the entire project.

To estimate the time required to complete a CPM activity, an available set of resources must be either known or assumed. By common practice, time estimates are defined to be the least-cost time durations for the activities. This estimate is defined as the shortest time in which an activity can be completed at lowest direct cost (e.g., out-of-pocket costs). For example, assume a job could be performed by one man in two days at lowest cost. Assume also that the same job could be completed at the same cost by using two men for one day, but would cost more by using three men for less than one day. Then the least-cost time required (the shortest time for completing the activity at lowest cost) is one day. In this manner a least-cost duration for each activity in the project must be determined. These estimates must be provided by the person responsible for completing the task.

The time durations for each activity are marked on the arrow diagram underneath the job description. Time may be expressed in minutes, hours, days, weeks, etc., but all task estimates should be in the same time units.

EARLIEST
EVENT TIME The Earliest Event Time (EET) is the earliest time a given event can occur, or the earliest completion of the longest chain of activities leading up to that event. The calculation of the earliest event time always proceeds from the beginning of a project arrow diagram to the end, and is frequently called the "forward pass" calculation. Figure 13 will be used for illustrative purposes. The earliest time (EET) that event (1) can occur is 3 days after the operation starts since it will take 3 days to complete Activity A. The earliest time that event (2) can occur is 5 days after the project starts (Activity A + Activity C = 3 + 2 = 5 days). Event (3) has 2 activity chains leading into it. The EET for event (3) is 10 days, since this is the longest path leading to it (A + B). Similarly, the EET for each of the remaining events has been calculated and is shown in Figure 13. The EET for event (7) is the least time in which the entire project or operation can be completed if all activities proceed at the estimated rate.

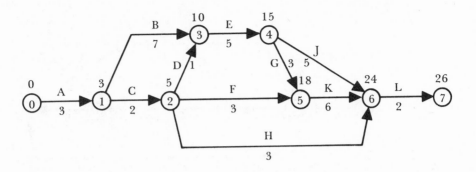

FIGURE 13

In general, the rules for calculating the EET are:

a) Start at the project origin event and use zero for the EET. Proceed toward the project terminal event.
b) The EET for an event cannot be calculated until the EET is calculated at the origins of all arrows terminating at that event.
c) If only one arrow terminates at an event, the EET of the terminal event equals the EET at that arrow's origin plus the activity's expected duration.
d) If two or more arrows terminate at an event, calculate the EET + activity duration for each activity and use the greatest figure calculated as the EET for the terminal event.

LATEST EVENT TIME The Latest Event Time (LET) for any event is the latest time the event can be completed without delaying the completion of the project. The latest completion time for a project (e.g., the final event) is the same as the earliest completion time, since there is no reason for extending the job beyond its earliest completion time.

The LET is calculated by subtracting from the total project duration (EET) the sum of all the activities in the longest activity chain connecting an event with the project terminal event. Calculations are performed in reverse order to those for EET since we start at the end of the project and work back to the beginning. This series of calculations is called the "backward pass."

Figure 14 shows the results of the "backward pass" calculations in the network previously described. The LET is written above the EET on the arrow diagram. The LET for event (6) is 26 - 2 = 24. The LET for event (4) is 15, since we must take the longest path back from the completion of the project, event (7). Latest event times for the remaining events have been calculated similarly in Figure 14. In general, the rules for making the "backward pass" calculations are:

a) Start at the project's terminal event and make the LET the same as the EET. Proceed in reverse order toward the project's origin event.
b) Do not calculate the LET for one event until all arrows originating at that event have had the LET calculated at their terminals.

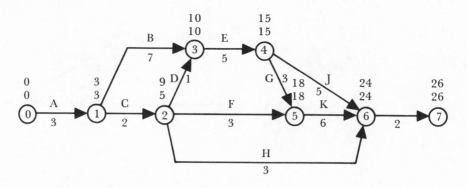

FIGURE 14

c) If only one arrow originates at an event, the LET equals the LET at that arrow's terminal minus its job duration.
d) If 2 or more arrows originate at an event, calculate (LET - duration) for each activity and use the smallest figure obtained.
e) LET for the project's first event should work out to be zero.

THE
CRITICAL
PATH

All activities in a project are important. Certain activities, however, control the time required for the completion of the entire project. These are the critical tasks — critical because a delay in any one of them will affect the schedule for the completion of the project. These critical jobs have no spare time available — the time required to perform the activities is equal to the time available.

The critical path is the longest path in time through the network diagram for the project. The remaining activities are less critical because they have some spare time or "float." There will always be one or more continuous paths of critical jobs running from start to finish. This is the "critical path" from which the method derives its name.

Determining the critical chain of events by traditional methods — i.e., Gantt charts — is very difficult. With the arrow diagram the critical path can be seen at a glance — study the diagram in Figure 15. Take, for example, activity 3-4. Note that the earliest and latest event times for

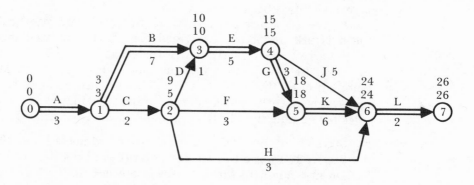

FIGURE 15

this job's start and finish are the same in each case. There is no leeway or float in either the start time or the finish time for this activity. The time available for the job (15 – 10 = 5) equals the job's duration. Activity 3-4 is therefore critical. The same situation exists for activities 0-1, 1-3, 4-5, 5-6, and 6-7. These activities, in sequence, comprise the critical path. The following are the rules for identifying the critical path:

a) The earliest and latest event times for the start event are identical (EET start = LET start).
b) The earliest and latest event times for the finish event are identical (EET finish =LET finish).
c) The time available for the activity is equal to its activity duration (LET – EET = duration).

All these criteria must be met. Note activity 4-6, which meets the first two criteria. The time available (24 – 15 = 9 days), however, is greater than the job duration of 5 days. Activity 4-6 is therefore noncritical. The critical path is usually identified on the arrow diagram with heavier arrows, colored lines, hash marks, etc.

FLOAT   On jobs which are not on the critical path, slack time known as "float" is available. Float may be used to schedule noncritical tasks in the most convenient way from a management standpoint. Note that if all of the float available for a task is utilized or has elapsed, the task then becomes critical and a new critical path is formed.

The total float associated with a given activity is the total time available to do the job minus the job's duration. It is calculated as follows: Latest finish event time minus earliest start event time minus duration equals total float (LET finish – EET start – duration = TF).

COST
CONTROL
CONSIDERA-
TIONS
A critical path network provides a useful means for the control of costs during the course of a project. Expenditures may be coded to apply to the activities within a project, thus utilizing the project network as a basis for project accounting. This enables management to monitor the costs incurred as well as the scheduled progress of the work.

While the theory of network cost control is relatively simple, progress in its practical application has been sporadic. The successful utilization of the concept necessarily involves overhauling existing and standardized costing systems, and the computer programs developed for one company are unlikely to be applicable to other companies.

NETWORKS FOR HIGHLY VARIABLE ACTIVITY TIMES

Some projects are comprised of activities for which the times required are highly variable, either because they are of very long duration or because the activities themselves are new and different, such as the development of a new device for a space mission. The development might take three months, or it might take a year. When highly variable activities must be accomplished along sequential paths in a network, a method must be available to compound the variability statistically in order to provide an estimate of the total variability inherent in the expected completion time (i.e., the expected length in time of the critical path).

A method for handling highly variable activity times was devised for use on the development of the Polaris submarine in the late 1950's. The technique was called the Program Evaluation and Review Technique (PERT) and combined a statistical approach to activity variability with the network principles described earlier. The PERT technique uses three time estimates for each activity to provide a measure of the expected time and the possible time variation for each activity.

Consider the activity shown in Figure 16. Three time estimates have been provided instead of the single estimate provided earlier. These time estimates are referred to as the Most Optimistic (2), the Most Likely (4) and the Most Pessimistic (8).

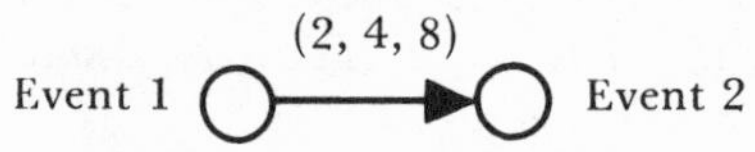

Event 1   (2, 4, 8)   Event 2

FIGURE 16

The three estimates are combined into a weighted average to provide an estimate of the expected time for the activity. The Optimistic time (a), the Most Likely time (m) and the Pessimistic time (b) are entered into the following formula to provide an estimate of the expected time (t_e) for this activity.

$$t_e = \frac{a + 4m + b}{6}$$

The expected time for the activity above would thus be

$$t_e = \frac{2 + 4(4) + 8}{6} = \frac{26}{6} = 4.3$$

The variation inherent in the expected time is expressed as the statistical variance, whose properties are well known to those who have had a first course in statistics. The variance and its square root, called the standard deviation, are the most widely used measures of the dispersion in statistical data. The variance of the expected time of an activity is calculated as

$$V_{t_e} = \left(\frac{b - a}{6}\right)^2$$

The standard deviation (SD) is the square root of the variance (V) and thus:

$$SD_{t_e} = \frac{b - a}{6}, \text{ or } 1/6 \text{ of the range of the estimates}$$

When the three time estimates are used, the t_e and V_{t_e} are calculated for each activity. These are then used to make all of the calculations described previously, with the values of t_e for each activity used instead of the single time estimates employed before. In addition, the activity variances are summed along with the Earliest Event Times (EET's) to provide the V_{EET}'s for each activity. These are written below the event designation. The network shown in Figure 15 has been recast with three time estimates for each activity, as pictured in Figure 17.

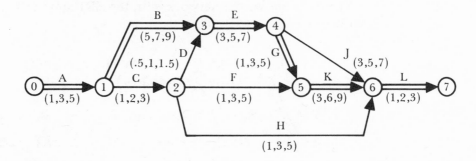

FIGURE 17

Table 1 shows the calculation of t_e and V_{t_e} for each activity in the network in Figure 17.

TABLE 1

Activity	$t_e = \dfrac{a + 4m + b}{6}$	$b - a$	$\dfrac{b - a}{6}$	$\left(\dfrac{b - a}{6}\right)^2$	$V_{t_e} = \left(\dfrac{b - a}{6}\right)^2$
A	3	4	2/3	4/9	16/36
B	7	4	2/3	4/9	16/36
C	2	2	1/3	1/9	4/36
D	1	1	1/6	1/36	1/36
E	5	4	2/3	4/9	16/36
F	3	4	2/3	4/9	16/36
G	3	4	2/3	4/9	16/36
H	3	4	2/3	4/9	16/36
J	5	4	2/3	4/9	16/36
K	6	6	1	1	36/36
L	2	2	1/3	1/9	4/36

The network in Figure 18 shows the t_e and the V_{t_e} for each activity.

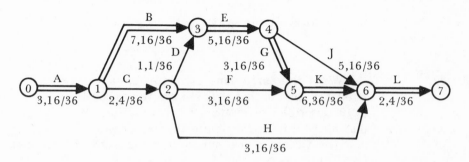

FIGURE 18

Figure 19 shows the network with the EET and the V_{EET} for each event.

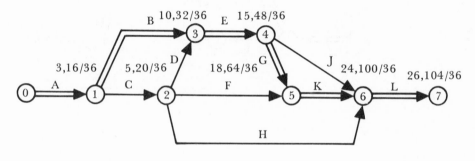

FIGURE 19

The EET for the final event is called T_E. In addition to the latest times for the activities and for the network and the slack in the various paths through the network (described previously), the estimate of the variance in T_E for the network provides a means of estimating the probability of meeting a given schedule date (T_S).

It is seen that

T_E = 26 for the terminal event (7)

V_{T_E} = 104/36 = 2.89

SD_{T_E} = 1.7

Based on the central limit theorem from statistics, summing the distributions of the individual activities will provide a distribution of the total network time, which will be a normal distribution with mean equal to T_E and variance equal to V_{T_E}.

When arrayed on a time scale, the distribution pattern appears as shown in Figure 20.

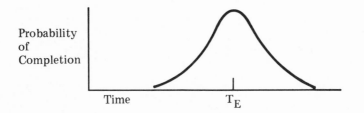

FIGURE 20

Thus, the likely pattern of probable outcomes is assumed to be a bell-shaped curve with the mean equal to T_E (the most probable time) and receding probabilities as we move away from T_E, either earlier or later.

Suppose we were asked the likelihood of completing the project by a scheduled date, T_{S1} or T_{S2}, shown in Figure 21. We would be very skeptical of meeting a schedule date of T_{S1} and quite optimistic about a schedule date of T_{S2}. The problem is more complicated, on the other hand, if the scheduled completion date is within the distribution of possible completion times, as shown in Figure 22.

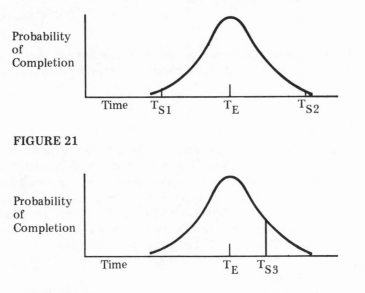

FIGURE 21

FIGURE 22

The shaded area in Figure 23 represents the proportion of the possible completion times which are on or after the schedule date.

Since T_E and V_{T_E} are assumed to be the mean and variance of a normal distribution, the shaded area in Figure 23 can be found by referring to tables of the normal distribution. The standard normal deviate (Z) is found by calculating

$$Z = \frac{T_S - T_E}{SD_{T_E}}$$

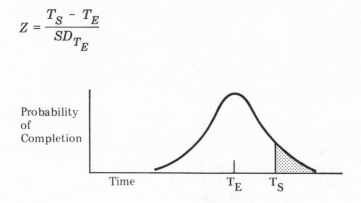

Probability
of
Completion

Time T_E T_S

FIGURE 23

For the network shown in Figure 19, with a schedule date of 28, the Z value is calculated as

$$Z = \frac{T_S - T_E}{SD_{T_E}} = \frac{28 - 26}{1.7} = \frac{2}{1.7} = 1.18$$

Reference to tables of variates of the normal distribution gives the probability of meeting the scheduled completion date as 0.88.

CONCLUSION

The output of a CPM analysis is not better than the input. The implementation of these techniques is often difficult because using CPM requires extra effort to prepare the network and to keep it up to date. Network methods also lead to more exposure of management performance than would otherwise be the case. The process of preparing the arrow diagram forces project personnel to go into more detail than usual. The overall network plan is open to view by all. The potential benefits to be gained are numerous, once the initial resistance to change can be overcome.

It should be borne in mind that critical path scheduling is not a panacea for curing the ills of a disorganized project. It will help to do a job more effectively than would otherwise be the case. It will help a project manager organize his work initially, will head off many potentially serious problems before they can occur, and provides a means for continually adapting to the problems which arise as the project goes forward.

BIBLIOGRAPHY

Abernathy, William J. "Subjective Estimates and Scheduling Decisions." *Management Science*, October 1971, pp. B-80 — B-87.

Block, Ellery B. "Accomplishment/Cost: Better Project Control" *Harvard Business Review*, May-June 1971, pp. 110-124.

DOD and NASA Guide, PERT Cost Systems Design. Office of the Secretary of Defense and the National Aeronautics and Space Administration, U.S. Government Printing Office, Washington, D.C., June 1962.

Duesenbury, Warren. "CPM for New Product Introductions." *Harvard Business Review*, July-August 1967, pp. 124-139.

Flagle, C. E. "Probability Based Tolerances in Forecasting and Planning." *The Journal of Industrial Engineering*, March-April 1961, pp. 97-101.

GE 225 Application, Critical Path Method Program. Bulletin CPB 198B, General Electric Computer Department, Phoenix, 1962.

Howell, Robert A. "Multiproject Control." *Harvard Business Review*, March-April 1968, pp. 63-70.

IBM 7090 PERT Cost Program. IBM Program Applications Bulletin H20-6297, International Business Machines Corporation, Data Processing Division, 112 East Post Road, White Plains, New York, 1962.

Miller, Robert. "How to Plan and Control with PERT." *Harvard Business Review*, March-April 1962, pp. 93-104.

Moder, J. J., and Phillips, C. R. *Project Management with CPM and PERT.* New York: Reinhold Publishing Corp., 1964.

Saitow, Arnold R. "CSPC: Reporting Project Progress to the Top." *Harvard Business Review*, January-February 1969, pp. 88-97.

Siemens, Nicolai. "A Simple CPM Time-Cost Tradeoff Algorithm." *Management Science*, February 1971, pp. B-354 — B-363.

Thomas, Warren. "Four Float Measures for Critical Path Scheduling." *Journal of Industrial Engineering*, October 1969, pp. 19-23.

Vasonyi, Andrew. "L'Histoire de Grandeur et de la Décadence de la Méthode PERT." *Management Science*, April 1970, pp. B-449 — B-455.

Williamson, J. D. *Critical Path Planning Handbook.* Plant Design and Construction, Western Electric Company, 1964.

ASSEMBLY-LINE BALANCING
A Case Study

INTRODUCTION

This case study describes a daily operating system developed to support a mixed-model truck-trailer assembly line. Each individual assembly line presents a unique problem for the operations manager. A large number of interrelated variables must be planned and controlled, including the total number of personnel, their assignment to work stations, and the timing and sequence of launching products down the line. These controllable variables tend to be influenced in each assembly-line situation by the size and nature of the product, the throughput cycle, and the degree of mechanization (automation) of the line.

Many of the factors that create a need for planning have contributed to a trend away from highly regularized assembly lines. Product proliferation, customization, and other marketing trends have tended to diminish the number of single-product lines in use. The rapid pace of new product development has placed sufficient risk on the heavy capital investment involved in assembly lines to limit somewhat their engineering and construction.

No mathematical solution is available for balancing assembly lines. Logical procedures must be combined with efficient search techniques to provide a suitable solution to a given line-balancing situation. Past theoretical work on assembly-line balancing has largely been concentrated on single-product, long-running assembly operations characterized by automotive or home appliance manufacture. The objective of that work has been to arrive at an assignment of work elements to assembly stations in such a way that idle time of the workers and congestion along the line of the products being assembled are minimized.

The notion of similar products being assembled over relatively long periods of time is implicit in the methods reported by Kilbridge and

Wester[1] and Tonge.[2] Kilbridge and Wester employed a precedence diagram and heuristic[3] (logical) procedures for adjusting work-station load to arrive at an acceptable line balance. The details of the procedures for balancing single-product lines are not reported here since they are available in numerous, more specialized, texts. Also, for the reasons cited above, they are of less interest to the business student seeking to understand workflow-planning methods as they relate to turnover rate and return on investment.

Further work by Wester and Kilbridge[4] treated the situation of mixed-model assembly in which cycles of several standard models of the same basic product must be assembled on a common assembly line. Thomopoulos[5] evaluated the sequencing procedure of Kilbridge and Wester by means of a computer simulation of a truck assembly line in which a number of different models of trucks were assembled on the same line in more-or-less fixed ratios of one model to another. It was therefore necessary to cycle the several models to be assembled in a fixed order, such as A, D, C, B. The technique was evaluated by its comparison with the performance of randomly generated sequences. The criteria for evaluation of the approach assumed a cost for idle time twice the cost of congestion. Thomopoulos reported that the procedures of Kilbridge and Wester would be superior to all but about 0.6% of the population of feasible sequences (with regard to the stated criteria). No theoretical methods are available, short of enumeration, for finding the optimal sequence for a cyclic, mixed-model assembly line.

STATUS OF ASSEMBLY LINE BALANCING METHODOLOGY

The current status of theoretical work and related applications on assembly-line balancing and sequencing may be summarized as follows.

1) Prior theoretical work has dealt largely with continuously moving conveyor belts and one operator per station. Such work is repetitive

[1] M. D. Kilbridge and Leon Wester, "A Heuristic Method of Assembly Line Balancing," *The Journal of Industrial Engineering* 12, no. 4 (1961): 292-298; idem, "The Balance Delay Problem," *Management Science* 8, no. 1 (1962): 69-84; idem, "A Review of Analytical Systems of Line Balancing," *Operations Research* 10, no. 5 (1962): 626-638; idem, "Heuristic Line Balancing: A Case," *Journal of Industrial Engineering* 13, no. 3 (1962): 139-149.

[2] F. M. Tonge, *A Heuristic Program for Assembly Line Balancing* (Englewood Cliffs, N.J.: Prentice-Hall, 1961); idem, "Summary of a Heuristic Line Balancing Procedure," *Management Science* 7, no. 1 (1960): 21-42.

[3] Defined by Webster as "valuable for stimulating or conducting empirical research but unproved or incapable of proof."

[4] L. Wester and M. D. Kilbridge, "The Assembly Line Model-Mix Sequencing Problem," *Proceedings of the Third International Conference on Operations Research, 1963* (Paris: Dunot), pp. 247-260.

[5] N. T. Thomopoulos, "A Sequencing Procedure for Multi-Model Assembly Lines" (Doctoral thesis, Industrial Engineering Department, Illinois Institute of Technology, 1966); idem, "Line Balancing — Sequencing for Mixed-Model Assembly," *Management Science* 14, no. 2 (1967): B-59 — B-75.

for a period of months in a 'model year' or some longer time period.

2) Most published work deals with assembly lines on which one standard item is assembled. Because of extensive production runs, work elements are estimated with (an assumed) high degree of accuracy. The assembly work may be divided into hundreds or thousands of work elements. These elements must then be arranged in a so-called precedence diagram (similar to a CPM network) which indicates the order in which the elements must be performed. Elaborate methods must then be used to assign the elements to the several stations of the line to 'balance' the work load among individual operators.

3) Less attention has been given to the problem of the so-called mixed-model assembly line. A mixed-model line is one on which different models of the same general product are assembled.

4) The reported procedures (even restricted as described above) are approximate or heuristic (logical or common sense) in nature. No explicit mathematical optimizing procedure exists for balancing or sequencing assembly lines, even for one man per station, one product, and continuous movement.

Wild[6] provides the most comprehensive summary of tools and techniques available for balancing and sequencing assembly lines of which the authors are aware.

GENERAL DESCRIPTION OF A BALANCING AND SEQUENCING SYSTEM

The remainder of this case study describes an application of heuristic line-balancing procedures to the development of a system to support the operation of a truck-trailer assembly line in which 70% of the orders were for unique, custom-made trailers.[7] Most of the orders were for 1 or 2 trailers, although a few orders were for as many as 5 or 10 units.

The system was developed to balance and sequence a moderately large (300-400 workers) assembly line. Customer requirements led to large differences in the characteristics of individual trailers. Each order therefore required a planning and engineering cycle in which the order was analyzed, a list of parts to be fabricated and purchased was prepared, and the expected production labor content was estimated.

Commitments for delivery to customers specified either a week during which shipment was to be effected or a latest date to which the sales organization had made a commitment. The assembly line was capable of producing 70 trailers per week (based on 14 per day) with a one-shift operation. Final decisions regarding assembly schedules were

---

[6] Ray Wild, *Mass-production Management* (London: John Wiley & Sons, 1972).
[7] J. L. Colley, Jr., "A Daily System for Balancing and Sequencing a Mixed-Model Assembly Line," *Proceedings of the Fifth International Conference of Operational Research, Venice, Italy, 1969* (London: Tavistock).

the subject of weekly meetings between sales, purchasing, and production management. An integral feature here was the prerogative of management to "freeze" the time of assembly of a given trailer. That is, the week or day during which a specific trailer would be assembled could be specified. The system was devised to operate on a small computer which was used for accounting, purchasing, and inventory control in the plant.

The backlog of orders in hand was input to the computer, along with the associated assembly times for each trailer on each station on the line and restrictions as to the stipulated launch times. The system considered units frozen for assembly during either of two consecutive weeks and selected additional units from an order file to provide a balanced load between the two weeks. The system next assigned the two-weeks' load (140 trailers) into subsets of 14 each which provided the best balance from day to day. Finally, the system determined a sequence for launching the 14 trailers during a given day in such a way that idle time and congestion were minimized.

If the units to be put on the line during a given shift were determined *for the system* (via agreement between sales, purchasing, and production management), then the balance (or lack of it) from day to day was uncontrollable. The scheduling system's job in that case was to find the best sequence(s) for the given grouping(s). The system was also capable of accepting a set (or up to 10 sets) of 14 trailers expected to be released during a given shift(s). The within-shift sequencing procedure could thus be run independently. Figure 1 gives a general system flow chart.

DETAILED PRODUCTION PLAN

The system described here was developed from a consideration of the following production plan:

1) The main assembly line was a ten-station line, followed by a number of finishing stations.
2) Subassembly work had to be completed for each trailer prior to the main line.
3) The work performed at the first four stations was more-or-less similar from trailer to trailer, leading to an inherent semblance of balance at these stations. The work content was much more variable in stations 5-10.

The system was designed with due consideration for the accuracy of available time standards. There would be no advantage in having an elaborate procedure for use with time standards which were rough estimates for large blocks of assembly time. Standard times based on historical data, together with prevailing performance factors (efficiency factors), were available to support the system. The system required efficiency factors for each station to convert standard times to estimated actual times.

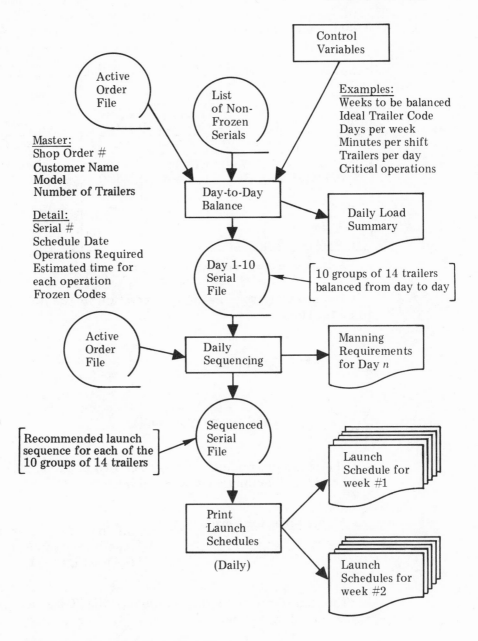

FIGURE 1 General System Flow Chart

THE BALANCING AND SEQUENCING PROCEDURES

The input to the balancing and sequencing subroutine consisted of the status of the work in progress with regard to balance (over or under the ideal cumulative balance position at the end of the previous period) as well as the data shown in Table 1 for each trailer.

The following calculations develop the figures required for the balancing and sequencing procedures.

TABLE 1 System Input Data

(1)		(2)	(3)	(4)	. . .	(11)	(m)
Trailer Identification							Total Work Content for a Given Trailer
Shop Order Number	Serial Number	Assembly Time (Minutes)					
		Sta. #1	Sta. #2	Sta. #3	. . .	Sta. #10	
8876	35754	32.4	33.6	32.2			—
—	—	—	—	—			—
—	—	—	—	—			—
Total work content							

The assembly time in the ith operation of the jth trailer is defined to be t_{ij}. Then

$$\sum_{j=1}^{14} t_{ij} = \text{Minutes/station}$$

$$\sum_{i=1}^{10} \sum_{j=1}^{14} t_{ij} = \text{Total assembly minutes}$$

The minimum number of operators (n_i) to accomplish the work in station i in a 450-minute day is found by

$$\frac{\sum \text{Model times for a given station}}{450} = \text{number of operators required to man the station } N_i \text{ (rounded to the next integer).}$$

The sum of the operators required for the 10 stations gives the total men needed for the line.

$$n = \sum_{i=1}^{10} n_i$$

The actual load per operator for the ith station is

$$\frac{\sum_{j=1}^{14} t_{ij}}{n_i} = \text{Actual load per operator (in minutes) for the } i\text{th station}$$

The natural model cycle time (c_j) is computed in the following way:

$$\text{Natural model cycle time} = c_j = \frac{\sum\limits_{i=1}^{10} t_{ij}}{n} = \frac{\sum \text{Model's operations times}}{\text{Total number of operators}}$$

The optimal launch rate would be the average of the natural model cycle times:

$$\text{Average of the model cycle times} = \frac{\sum\limits_{j=1}^{14} c_j}{14}$$

The optimal launch rate (the weighted average cycle time) was not used in the system described here. For a variety of management reasons a fixed launch rate was used instead (assumed to be one trailer every 30 minutes for the examples in this chapter).

To minimize idle time, the models were assigned (to a week, a day, or launch sequence) so that

$$\sum_{j=1}^{k} c_j - kL \geqslant 0$$

The cumulative sum of the unit cycle times (to the kth trailer) should be $\geqslant k$ times L (the 30-minute launch interval).

In order to also control congestion, the units were assigned so that the difference between $\sum\limits_{j=1}^{k} c_j$ and kL (at each launch) was as small as possible.

The foregoing results in the balancing and sequencing format are shown in Table 2.

Figure 2 illustrates graphically the effect of the assignment procedure.

RUN DESCRIPTIONS

The major subsystems of the balancing and sequencing system were the Day-to-Day Balance Run and the Daily Sequencing Run. The same basic assignment procedure was used for both. The difference was in

TABLE 2 Balancing and Sequencing Format

| (1) Trailers | (2) Multiples of Launch Rate kL | (3) Trailer Identification | | (4) Natural Model Cycle Time c_j | (5) $\sum_{j=1}^{k} c_j - kL$ |
		Shop Order Number	Serial Number		
	min				
1	30	8976	35754	35	5
2	60	8981	35766	26	1
3	90	8992	35784	33	4
4	120	8978	35759	28	2
5	150	.	.	.	.
6	180	.	.	.	.
7	210	.	.	.	.
8	240	.	.	.	.
.	.	.	.	.	.
.	.	.	.	.	.
.	.	.	.	.	.
.	.	.	.	.	.
14	420	.	.	.	.

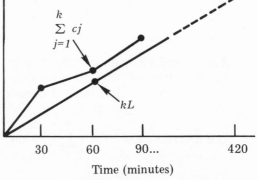
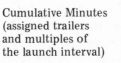

Cumulative Minutes (assigned trailers and multiples of the launch interval)

Time (minutes)

FIGURE 2 Cumulative Actual Times vs. kL

the degree of aggregation of the assembly times. The day-to-day balance run was based on the total work content of the main line operations which were designated critical in the system inputs. The within-day sequencing run was based on the highly variable main line operations 5-10 together with a constant 30-minute launch rate. The balancing and sequencing runs functioned jointly to provide rational work plans. Efficient within-shift sequences would be of little use with wide variations in day-to-day load. Similarly, a well-devised day-to-day balance in workload would be of little use if ill-conceived launch sequences led to disruption up and down the assembly line.

The following control variables were input to the system.

1) Minutes per shift.
2) Trailers per day.
3) Number of critical main-line operations and their operation numbers.
4) Number of trailers on order in the file.
5) Future date limit (horizon limit).
6) Option code for calculation of the ideal average trailer.

The primary input for the balancing run was the active order file. This file consisted of all existing shop orders (perhaps as many as 500 orders). There was one master record for each shop order. Each master record contained the shop order number, the customer name, the model, and the number of trailers on the order. There was one detail record for every trailer on a shop order. Detail records contained the serial number, pertinent dates, frozen schedule codes, manufacturing operations required, estimated time for each operation, and a code to indicate whether the operation had been completed. Detail records were variable in length because the number of operations varied with each trailer. The master record file was in sequence by shop order number. The detail records which followed each master record were in sequence by serial number. Master and detail records were deleted from the file when all trailers for a shop order had been shipped.

Balance (from week to week and day to day) was based on the critical mainline operations specified in the control card. This allowed the emphasis of the system to be adjusted if the nature of the workload shifted from operation to operation. Each day was described as a "time-bucket" and was identified by a week-day code,— 11, 12, 13, 14, and 15 for the five days of the first week, and 21, 22, 23, 24, and 25 for the second week. The active order file was read and the launch interval (the ideal average time) was calculated as determined by the code in the control card. The launch interval could be based on the critical operations, or it could be stipulated (input). Further, it could be based on the trailers frozen for the two weeks or on all trailers in the file available to the system. The fixed 30-minute launch interval was normally stipulated.

Data for each serial were moved to one of three areas based on the serial's frozen code. A trailer's assembly could be stipulated for a given week, or a given day, or it could be available for assembly as most convenient. If a trailer was not frozen to a day but was frozen for either of the two-week periods, the required data were moved to one of the weekly serial files. During this processing, counters were incremented to keep track of the number of serials frozen in each of the ten-day intervals and the numbers frozen in each of the two weeks. When the entire active order file had been read or 70 frozen serials had been processed for each week, the balancing routine was used to assign the serials frozen for Week 1 to the Week 1 daily intervals by the procedures outlined in the section on Balancing and Sequencing Procedures, using the operations designated critical. When each of the

10 daily files contained 14 trailers, the total time for each serial at all stations and the total time for each station were accumulated for each daily file. The following calculations were also made and printed:

1. Number of men required for each station.
2. Actual load per man at each station.
3. Ideal launch rate for the day.

The 10 lists were written on an output tape, and the daily load summary was then printed. The output tape was called the Day 1-10 Serial File and was input to the Shift Sequencing Run, which determined the best launch sequence for each day's serials.

Each daily set of 14 serials was arranged in a recommended launch sequence by the method described previously. The basic difference from the day-to-day balance run was use of the total times for each trailer in the highly variable main-line operations, 5-10.

SYSTEM OUTPUT

When all 10 sets had been arranged in the recommended launch sequence, the system provided the following as outputs:

The Daily Load Summary (Figure 3) presents the load in hours at each main-line station for each of the 10 days.

FIGURE 3 Output of day-to-day balance run

		Daily Load Summary (hours)									Date xx/xx/xx Week 36, Rev. = n
		Day Number									
		1	*2*	*3*	*4*	*5*	*6*	*7*	*8*	*9*	*10*	*Total*
Main-line stations	1	xx.x										xxx.x
	2											
	3											
	4											
	5											
	6											
	7											
	8											
	9											
	10											
	Total	xxx.x										xxxx.x

The Daily Manning Requirements (Figure 4) lists the number of men required at each of the 10 main-line stations and the number of actual hours of load per man for each day.

The Launch Schedule (Figure 5) shows the individual trailers which

FIGURE 4 Output of day-to-day balance run
(one report for each time bucket)

Date xx/xx/xx
Week 36, Day 1
Revision #0

Manning Requirements for Day *n*

Station	Men Required	Actual Hours of Load per Man
1	x	xx.x
2	x	xx.x
3	x	xx.x
4	x	xx.x
5	x	xx.x
6	x	xx.x
7	x	xx.x
8	x	xx.x
9	x	xx.x
10	x	xx.x

Optimal launch rate: xx minutes

FIGURE 5 Output of print launch schedules run

Launch Schedule   Date xx/xx/xx
Week #36, Day #1
Revision #0

Launch Number	Shop Order Number	Model	Serial Number	Natural Model Cycle Time (minutes)
1	C-8902	295	35448	xx.x
2	C-8931	295T	35656	xx.x
3	C-8903	295T	35639	xx.x
4	C-8963	295T	35719	xx.x
5	C-8965	285T	35722	xx.x
6	C-8944	295TD	35682	xx.x
7	C-8964	295TD	35721	xx.x
8	C-8954	288TF	35704	xx.x
9	C-8929	285TG	35655	xx.x
10	C-8958	295DD	35711	xx.x
11	C-8929	295TDRS	35654	xx.x
12	C-8906	225TZ-1	35424	xx.x
13	C-8942	225TZ	35679	xx.x
14	C-8952	225TZR-1	35702	xx.x

should be assembled during each day of each week for best attainable balance within the constraint of the frozen units. The recommended (best attainable) sequence for launching (starting) the units scheduled for each day down the line is based on the assumption that the stipulated constant launch rate will prevail.

SUMMARY

This case study has described a system developed to support a moderately large mixed-model assembly line. Because of the make-to-order nature of this trailer manufacturing facility, it was necessary for the system to be rerun regularly since the work content of the orders received was highly variable.

The system functioned in two stages to provide a rational launch plan. The first stage provided sets of trailers for daily assembly for which the load was balanced from day to day. This balance was based on the assembly-line operations designated critical by a control card. The second stage of the system accepted from one to ten sets of 14 trailers and determined the most desirable launch sequence(s).

Outputs of the system included manning requirements for the assembly stations; the ideal launch rate; a summary of the daily load, by station; and the most effective launch sequence for each day.

BIBLIOGRAPHY

Bowman, E. H. "Assembly Line Balancing by Linear Programming." *Operations Research* 8, no. 3 (1960): 385-389.

Helgeson, W. G., and Birnie, D. P. "Assembly Line Balancing Using Ranked Positional Weight Technique." *Journal of Industrial Engineering* 12, no. 4 (1961): 394-398.

Hoffman, T., R. "Assembly Line Balancing With a Precedence Matrix." *Management Science* 9, no. 4 (1963): 551-563.

Ignal, E. J. "A Review of Assembly Line Balancing." *Journal of Industrial Engineering* 16, no. 4 (1965): 244-254.

Mastor, A. A. "An Experimental Investigation and Comparative Evaluation of Production Line Balancing Technique." *Journal of Industrial Engineering* 12, no. 2 (1970): 73-77.

Thomopoulos, N. T. "Some Analytical Approaches to Assembly Line Problems." *Production Engineering*, July 1968, pp. 345-351.

_____. "Mixed Model Line Balancing With Smoothed Station Assignments." *Management Science* 16, no. 9 (1970): 593-603.

V

SUMMARY

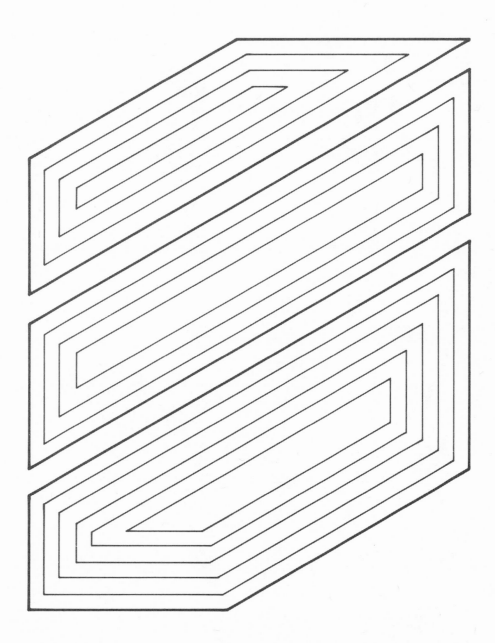

INTRODUCTION

The first four parts of this text developed a systematic approach to the problem of operating a business unit at a satisfactory level of profitability. A business unit might be a manufacturing or service company, a decentralized division or profit center of a large corporation, or a bank or other financial institution. This part reviews briefly the most important points of each of the topics covered and closes with a look at computer-based operations planning models.

Based on the premise that operating problems can be avoided if anticipated, more easily than they can be solved if they occur unexpectedly, many organizations employ computer programs to continually evaluate the effects on desired results of a myriad of possible shifts or movements in the numerous factors covered in the text and cases. Since the actual movements of man-hours, efficiency, absenteeism, strikes, inventories, shop orders, machine breakdowns, order arrivals, or shipment delays cannot be forecast, it is essential that a wide range of likely or potential opportunities or problems be explored and contingency plans developed. The general format of such planning models is described, and some examples of model outputs are provided.

Summary

10.1 PART I – PLANNING

Chapter 1 introduced the planning problem faced by every profit-making business enterprise. The root of the problem was seen to lie with the financial community, including the professional financial analysts and bankers who control the firm's access to the funds needed to finance growth. In good times or bad, regardless of general economic conditions or foreign competition, members of the financial community have a very simplistic notion of satisfactory business performance: a smooth pattern of gradually improving returns on the investment in the business. Firms are evaluated by comparison with industry in general and the companies with which the firm competes most directly. *Forbes* magazine's annual report on American industry for 1975 ranked the management performance of 929 companies on the basis of the five-year levels of profitability and growth.[1] The industry and the companies within each industry grouping were ranked on each measure. A firm's ability to raise capital by issuing stock and the interest rate at which it may borrow money are influenced by its level of profitability. Beyond the level of profitability, the outside evaluators seek stability in earnings and a degree of credibility in forecasting future performance. These are considered reflective of the degree of control the management exercises over operations. Figure 10-1 presents (in flow-chart form) the numerous factors which must be planned and controlled in order to achieve the desired pattern of results. Those factors circled in the ROA chart in Figure 10-1 were

[1] *Forbes*, January 1, 1976, p. 42.

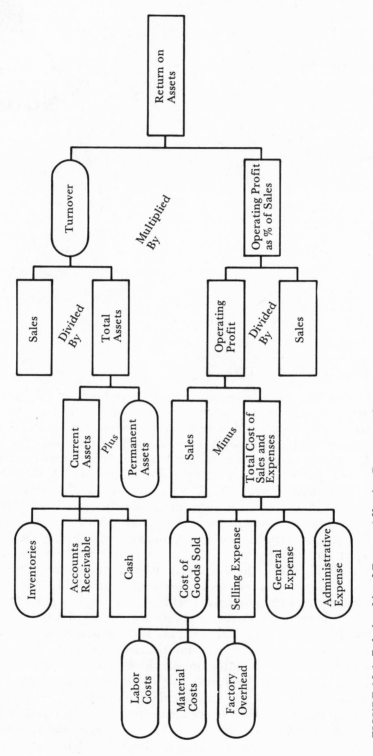

FIGURE 10-1 Relationship of Factors Affecting Return-on-Assets

covered in the text. The various physical flows through the enterprise are directly reflected in the financial statements. It is therefore imperative that the control process be focused on the movements of orders, man-hours, inventories, and shipments which are the heart of the enterprise.

Chapter 1 also covered the planning process which is typical in well-managed firms. The thrust of the planning process was seen to be toward a forcing of controllable expense levels to accommodate a desired level of profit, as shown in Figure 10-2. In order to accomplish the desired result, a manager must carefully control each of the major business functions; finance, marketing, and production or operations. The collective result is dependent upon the ability of the marketing function to deliver the forecast level of revenues, through a complex scenario of constantly changing product mix, prices, and advertising and distribution expenses. The finance function must provide the accounting system, the analytical vehicle for control, and must manage the debt and equity portions of the asset base to provide the funds to support the basic business strategy. The operations function manages most of the people, most of the expenses, and most of the assets. It is therefore essential that systems are available to plan and control all of the remaining factors in the return-on-assets (ROA) puzzle. Because of the dispersion of the decision-making authority through several levels of organization and into various departments, an orderly planning process must be in place.

It was pointed out that because of the large number of individuals whose activities must be coordinated, attempts to implement detailed planning systems have met with mixed success. The requirements for profit performance are so clear and the coordinative problems so great that an effective planning process must be developed.

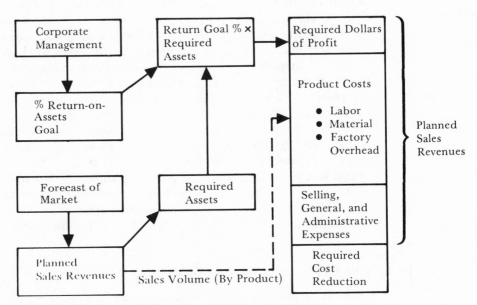

FIGURE 10-2 Planning for a Required Return-on-Assets

10.2   PART II – ASSET MANAGEMENT

The initial step in the planning process is the setting of ROA targets for each business unit. With an ROA target in hand, an estimate of the asset base leads to the target level of dollars of profit. As can be seen from the ROA chart, the assets are invested in cash, receivables, plant and equipment, or inventories. The levels of cash and receivables, required tend to be controlled by external factors and are difficult to manipulate in the short run. It is conventional to plan or forecast them in terms of "days of sales." Likewise, it is difficult in the short run to alter the level of investment in fixed plant and equipment (P&E). The level of investment in P&E at the beginning of a time period, less the depreciation, plus the new acquisitions yields the end-of-period investment level. With this in mind, most firms begin their planning process with a determination of the new capital investments to be made. This effectively sets the level of three of the four uses of the firm's asset base. Chapter 2 presented the various types of capital projects and introduced the procedures typically used for screening capital projects.

The remaining portion of the investment base, inventories, was covered in Chapters 3 and 4. Chapter 3 explained the four basic uses of inventories as pipeline stocks, cycle stocks, buffer (or safety) stocks, and anticipation (or seasonal) stocks. Chapter 4 covered typical inventory ordering systems for either forecast demand or scheduled requirement demand situations. The material presented to this point provided for determining the asset level and the dollars of profit required.

10.3   PART III – MANPOWER PLANNING AND CONTROL

With a knowledge of the profit required, the manager's next task is to derive an overall manpower/inventory plan to provide the level of output of goods and services required within acceptable cost levels and with timely schedule performance. Chapter 5 covered methods of work measurement and wage payment schemes in highly structured workplace settings. Chapter 6 covered unstructured work environments. Chapter 7 introduced the general aggregate planning or master scheduling problem by means of an illustrative example. Chapter 8 presented the results of a survey aimed at surfacing current real-world approaches to this key problem. The survey results were incorporated into a manpower/inventory planning model based on a demand/capacity matrix with 9 cells, and validation results were presented. A research study presented the results of a series of tests of the behavior of the model in a systematic study of planning horizons, demand patterns, and planning rules. The results were very close to the optimal solution of the HMMS paint factory example in terms of costs and provided smoother manpower adjustments, a more palatable result for managers.

10.4   PART IV – WORKFLOW PLANNING AND CONTROL

With the level of capital investment set and with wages – the major controllable costs – properly planned, the final determinant of ROA is the level of turnover of the asset base achievable. For a given level of assets, the greater the level of sales or throughput attained, the higher the ROA. The principal means by which a firm outdistances its competitors in turnover is its ability to schedule the flow of work through its facilities. The introduction to Part IV segmented the scheduling problem into broad, operational types. Chapter 9 treated the most widely encountered scheduling situations, make-to-order job shops. A key facet of the job shop scheduling problem is the need to properly control the level of work-in-process (WIP) inventory, the major controllable element of inventory investment. In fact, the interface between manpower and inventory levels is the point at which most can be done to reduce investment, shorten lead times, reduce costs, and improve schedule performance.

10.5   THE REMAINING PROBLEM AREAS

The most important issues raised in the book and not covered in detail are the levels of material costs and overhead expenses. Since material costs are roughly 50% of total costs in many businesses and overhead expenses another 15-20%, these are major problems to the manager of a business unit.

Paradoxically, few firms have placed enough emphasis on the purchasing function, in terms of staffing or setting explicit targets for procurement performance improvement. The major thrust of cost-reduction efforts in many firms is toward reducing the material cost in products, because of the large percentage of total costs vested in materials. Continuous cost reductions over time take the form of lowering the physical content of material or altering the type of material by substitution of a functionally suitable type of material.

The planning process outlined in Chapter 1 and shown in Figure 10-2 makes clear the role expense control plays in the final determination of profitability levels. For a given asset base, revenues, and material and direct labor costs, the dollar level of gross margin is either profit or expense, depending on the tenacity and cleverness of the management. The ability to organize and staff the expense activities to provide the essential services at lower costs than competitors is the ultimate task of the manager. This is probably why demanding managements correlate so well with high levels of probability.

10.6   COMPUTER-BASED PLANNING MODELS

How then are the numerous plans outlined above to be integrated rapidly to provide a profile of the course the firm is likely to pursue? How also are the effects of the continuing stream of deviations from all of the plans to be integrated to guide or control the business through each operating cycle? Numerous companies have turned to computer-based planning programs for assistance in this process.

**BUSINESS
PLANNING**

Formal planning assists the process of reaching decisions affecting an organization's future. Formal planning is not a new managerial function. Rather, it usually involves most aspects of operations. Substantial amounts of effort go into the formulation of various functional plans such as sales and marketing plans, research and development plans, manufacturing plans, capital requirements plans, manpower plans, and financial plans.[2] These efforts can then be summarized into a comprehensive business plan which presents top management with a detailed picture of the expected operational and financial performance statistics during a specified planning period. Such a procedure may be looked upon as a logical extension of the budgeting process where profit and expense goals are established for the subsequent year's activities. Planning procedures should also encompass and emphasize the development of action programs to deal with anticipated business conditions and opportunities.

The planning process can provide a logical and consistent approach for the manager to follow in judging the long-term implications of various commitments. The process can also outline the effects of each action program which supports any commitment and the financial results that can be expected to accrue from such a commitment.

Effective planning and the making of intelligent decisions about the composition of future programs are time-consuming activities. Management must analyze a wide spectrum of possible products or contracts, and the alternative courses of action that are available to fulfill them. There is empirical evidence to suggest that effective planning correlates positively with successful performance. In studying the effect of planning on the success of acquisitions, Igor Ansoff and others[3] reached the following conclusions:

1) On virtually all relevant financial criteria, . . . planners . . . significantly outperformed . . . nonplanners.
2) Not only did the planners do better on the average, they performed more predictably than nonplanners. Thus, planners appear to have narrowed the uncertainties in the outcomes of . . behavior.

**COMPUTER-
IZED MODELS**

Nearly all manual planning processes suffer from the following inherent weaknesses:[4]

1) Forecasting methodology and logic are usually inconsistent and ill-defined between different planning periods and between different iterations of the same plan.

[2] See Robert J. Mockler, *Business Planning and Policy Formulation* (New York: Appleton-Century-Crofts, 1972).

[3] H. Igor Ansoff, Jay Avner, Richard G. Brandenburg, Fred E. Portner, and Raymond Radosevich, "Does Planning Pay? The Effect of Planning on Success of Acquisitions in American Firms," *Long Range Planning*, December 1970, p. 7.

[4] Ronald A. Seaberg and Charlotte Seaberg, "Computer Based Decision Systems in Xerox Corporate Planning," *Management Science*, December, Part II, 1973, pp. 579-580.

2) Control of changes to forecasts of important variables and the relationships between such variables are usually inadequate.

3) Insufficient time and resources exist for analyzing contingency plans and "what if" situations.

To help negate the above weaknesses, many firms have begun to use computer-based modeling. A recent study conducted by Thomas Naylor and Horst Schauland of Social Systems, Inc., identified over 2,000 corporations "either using, developing, or planning to develop some form of corporate model."[5] In fact, a considerable amount of space in the literature has been devoted to discussions of the corporate planning models at Xerox, Sun Oil, First National City Bank, Pillsbury, General Electric, Inland Steel, and other large firms.[6]

In general, computer-based planning models have the following distinct advantages over most manual planning processes:[7,8]

1) A computer-based model supplies speed, accuracy of calculation, and consistency of logic between plan iterations.

2) The number of options or potential what-if conditions available for analysis is increased by a computer-based model.

3) A computer-based model "provides documentation and precise definition of the assumptions and rules upon which a plan is developed."

4) A computer-based model provides economical analysis of complex planning considerations.

5) Operating results can be explicitly incorporated into the planning process with a computer-based model.

The decision to develop and implement a computer-based planning model must be weighed carefully. Naylor and Schauland found that computer-based models required an average of approximately $83,000 and eighteen man-months of effort to develop.[9] Several large corporate models are, however, known to have required expenditures substantially higher than this average. The Sun Oil financial model, for example, required thirteen man-years of effort to develop and required an additional ten man-years to familiarize management with the model and to alter the model in accordance with management suggestions.

Complicating the decision of whether or not to develop a computer-

[5] Thomas H. Naylor and Horst Schauland, "A Survey of Users of Corporate Simulation Models," *Management Science*, May 1976.

[6] For further discussion see Albert N. Schrieber, ed. *Corporate Simulation Models* (Seattle, Wash.: Graduate School of Business Administration, 1970); Thomas H. Naylor, "Corporate Simulation Models," *Simulation Today*; James B. Boulden and Elwood S. Buffa, "Corporate Models: On-Line, Real-Time Systems," *Harvard Business Review*, July-August, 1970.

[7] P. L. Kingston, "Concepts of Financial Models," *IBM Systems Journal*, No. 2, 1973, p. 116.

[8] Seaberg and Seaberg, op. cit.

[9] Naylor and Schauland, op. cit., p. 8.

based planning model is the selection of the "type" of model desired. Many options are available which will affect the development time, cost, and ease of implementation of such a model. Figure 10-3 shows a schematic diagram of the major decisions facing those who wish to formulate a computer-based planning model.

It is beyond the scope of this discussion to treat, in detail, each modeling option shown in Figure 10-3. In fact, such treatment is not necessary at this point since an overwhelming majority of computer-based models implemented to date conform to the following specifications:[10]

1) *Financial models* are "representations of business problems in terms of accounting considerations."[11] Stated another way, a financial model is "nothing more than a mathematical statement of a firm's accounting and financial identities."[12] Well-known examples of financial models are the Dow Chemical model, the Sun Oil model, and the First National City Bank model.

2) *Simulation models* test the effects of different variables, policies, and assumptions about the firm's external environment. These are the so-called what-if models and are in contrast to optimization models, which maximize or minimize single or multiple functions such as profits or costs.

3) *Deterministic models* do not include random or probabilistic variables. Thus, these models avoid a multitude of statistical and computational complexities introduced by various probability distributions.

A few firms have been able to integrate financial, production, and marketing operations into corporate simulation planning models, and some firms are reported to be experimenting with models of the external environment, in addition to their internal planning models.

10.7   A PLANNING MODEL FOR A HYPOTHETICAL FIRM

We next present a planning model which is typical of those currently in use in business. The hypothetical firm manufactures large, nonstandard industrial products in five separate plants. The products are highly engineered and must be manufactured in accordance with demanding quality requirements. On the average, the products require a span of time greater than one year for design and fabrication. Each major contract won by the firm through a competitive bidding process has a sales value of several millions of dollars.

The company uses a percentage-of-completion accounting system, wherein the shipments and cost of shipments for each contract are recorded on the basis of the percentage of the total estimated fabrication man-hours completed to date. Organizationally, the firm controls the contracts by means of a project management system.

[10] Ibid, p. 10.

[11] Kingston, op. cit.

[12] Naylor, op. cit., p. 61.

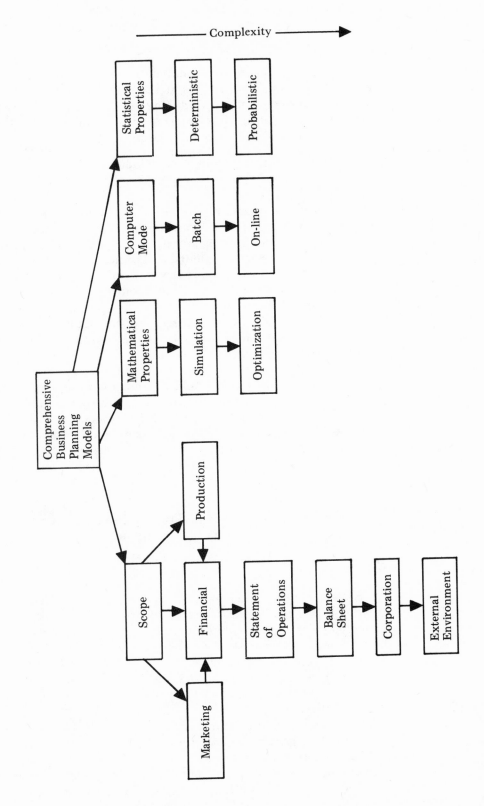

FIGURE 10-3

THE MODEL   The planning model utilizes a modular approach so that each major set of calculations is performed in a separate subroutine. The model operates on a five-year forecast interval, with the first year segregated into quarters and with each of the following four years treated as a yearly total. The model is contract-oriented, performing all cost-escalation and workload-spreading calculations at the contract level for both firm and forecast contracts, before producing consolidated output statements. Contracts with fabrication spans that extend beyond the forecast interval of the model are provided for in the model logic.

Input   Input to the planning model consists of three general categories:

1) Contract data are entered by individual contract or by a grouping of similar contracts. These data include all relevant information regarding selling price, cost elements, escalation terms, fabrication span dates, man-hour requirements, and projected shipping schedules.
2) Cost-escalation indexes are entered and stored by month in the computer and can be changed during any run. Selling price-escalation indexes are specific indexes published monthly by the U.S. Bureau of Labor Statistics. Cost escalation indexes are the firm's internal indexes segregated by material, labor, overhead, labor performance, and engineering.
3) Operating data are entered by a number of variables and ratios which relate to current policies and operating experiences in the areas of direct labor, engineering, overhead, and general and administrative (G&A) expenses. Examples of the data required include man-hour loads for each plant, direct labor wages for each worker, average overhead expenses for each plant, average salaries for indirect and G&A employees, and various supplemental inflation rates.

The effects of variations in any of these input items can be studied independently or jointly by using the model.

Logic

General   The model logic is divided into two distinct parts. The first logic section is the contract section, which is used to calculate expected sales prices and the cost of sales at the time of fabrication performance. These costs and revenues are then spread according to the projected shipping schedules into the appropriate time pockets of the model. From this point the sales and costs of sales can be summed to yield gross profit summaries for project managers, product lines, and the total company.

The second logic section of the model deals with the calculation of overhead and general and administrative expenses. This section of the model generates the manpower schedules, overhead schedules, and the expense portion of the statement of operations. Expenses are calculated in total, by period, and are then prorated to individual product lines in proportion to their percentage of the cost of sales (or labor hours, or investment).

Detail   The model contains thirteen (13) modules or subroutines. The following brief statements describe the thirteen modules.

Module 1 the main program, controls the flow of the model by calling the different subroutines in the proper sequence.

Module 2 reads all the contract and product line data, escalation indexes, and project manager names, and then stores them for future usage. This module also prints a table of escalation index revisions and a table of contract input assumptions, shown in Table 10-1.

Module 3 is used to build, from the abbreviated data input for anticipated or forecast contracts, detailed contract data similar to that supplied for firm or backlog contracts.

Module 4 escalates the costs and selling prices on all specified contracts and prints the contract financial analysis shown in Table 10-2.

Module 5 spreads the selling price, overhead cost, and total cost remaining to be recorded on each contract over the time frames of the model according to the projected percentage completion schedules supplied for that contract. This subroutine then sums the selling prices and costs by period over all contracts to produce product line, project manager, and company totals. The sum of the selling prices yields the total sales for the period, the sum of the costs yields the total cost of sales, and the sum of the overhead expenses produces the total overhead absorbed for the period.

Module 6 reads all the direct labor, overhead, and G&A data inputs and then stores them for future use.

Module 7 prints the input assumptions read in Module 6, the period data input assumptions, and the works and general data input assumptions.

Module 8 computes the direct hourly, indirect hourly, and indirect salaried manpower schedules for all plants or works. This module also computes the G&A manpower schedules. Manpower costs during each period are also computed by Module 8. The plant manpower schedules and the total manpower schedules are presented as shown in Tables 10-3 and 10-4.

Module 9 computes the overhead expenses (by major accounting series) by period for each plant. The schedule for Plant A is shown in Table 10-5. A derived overhead rate for each period is then calculated which would produce a burden variance of zero for that period. The overhead expenses for each works are then totaled to generate the total overhead expenses.

Module 10 calculates the depreciation expense for projected new building and equipment, using either straight-line depreciation or the sum-of-the-years'-digits calculations. The module then adds this calculated depreciation to the base depreciation, which is supplied as input data, to produce the total depreciation expense.

Module 11 calculates G&A expenses. These expenses are computed as a total only and are then prorated to each product line on a basis proportional to the product line's percentage of the total cost of sales.

TABLE 10-1 Contract Input Assumptions

Contract Number	Fabrication Span	Selling Price	Labor & Overhead Cost	Material Cost	Engineering Cost	Total Cost	Recorded to Date Price	Recorded to Date Cost
892–5123	3/74–5/77	2,024,000	835,000	785,000	58,000	1,678,000	0	0
892–6134	4/72–1/75	7,123,000	2,000,000	2,648,000	318,000	4,966,000	7,051,000	4,916,000
892–7238	2/73–3/75	2,078,000	740,000	800,000	216,000	1,756,000	2,072,000	1,756,000
892–7962	12/77–8/79	16,312,000	5,560,000	7,732,000	474,000	13,766,000	0	0
892–8011	5/76–3/79	10,557,000	4,329,000	6,322,000	662,000	11,313,000	0	0
899–1023	6/76–6/78	4,963,000	999,000	2,664,000	37,000	3,700,000	0	0

TABLE 10-2 Contract Financial Analysis (Time-of-Performance Dollars)

Contract Number	Labor Cost	Material Cost	Overhead Cost	Engineering Cost	Total Cost	Selling Price	Estimated to Complete	Remaining Sales Value
892–6133	1,980,000	5,981,000	3,682,000	624,000	12,267,000	13,772,000	12,267,000	13,772,000
892–6784	816,000	3,072,000	1,623,000	341,000	5,852,000	7,123,000	5,852,000	7,123,000
892–7638	283,000	891,000	543,000	231,000	1,948,000	2,078,000	0	0
892–7963	3,146,000	16,166,000	7,613,000	543,000	27,468,000	27,989,000	13,714,000	13,974,000
892–8077	1,646,000	8,236,000	3,571,000	679,000	14,132,000	10,877,000	14,132,000	10,877,000
892–8412	2,042,000	11,499,000	4,840,000	152,000	18,533,000	19,632,000	9,261,000	9,810,000
892–8501	682,000	2,618,000	1,479,000	151,000	4,930,000	4,721,000	4,930,000	4,721,000

TABLE 10-3 Plant Manpower Schedules

	1st Quarter 1975	2nd Quarter 1975	3rd Quarter 1975	4th Quarter 1975	1976	1977	1978	1979
Plant A								
Direct labor	411	400	330	367	329	330	332	332
Indirect hourly	62	60	49	55	49	49	50	50
Indirect salary	41	41	39	42	39	40	40	40
Plant B								
Direct labor	449	449	441	438	575	612	581	581
Indirect hourly	94	94	93	92	121	129	122	122
Indirect salary	52	52	53	54	59	60	58	58
Plant C								
Direct labor	501	501	465	482	553	659	654	614
Indirect hourly	180	180	167	174	199	237	235	221
Indirect salary	116	119	117	120	121	125	123	122
Plant D								
Direct labor	484	451	455	452	459	521	485	478
Indirect hourly	106	99	100	99	101	115	107	105
Indirect salary	59	59	61	61	61	63	60	60
Plant E								
Direct labor	901	967	856	866	900	966	931	909
Indirect hourly	135	145	128	130	135	145	140	136
Indirect salary	107	112	107	111	110	112	109	109

TABLE 10-4 Total Manpower Schedule

	1st Quarter	2nd Quarter	3rd Quarter	4th Quarter	1976	1977	1978	1979
Total — All Plants								
Direct labor	2746	2768	2547	2605	2816	3088	2983	2914
Indirect hourly	577	578	537	550	605	675	654	634
Indirect salary	375	383	377	388	390	400	390	389
G&A	407	407	407	407	407	407	407	407

TABLE 10-5 Overhead Schedule — Plant "A"

Overhead Series	1st Quarter 1975	2nd Quarter 1975	3rd Quarter 1975	4th Quarter 1975	1975 Total	1976 Total	1977 Total	1978 Total	1979 Total
200—Payroll taxes	359,225	382,086	336,520	434,273	1,512,102	1,385,437	1,596,471	1,730,752	1,849,517
300—Salaries & wages	520,692	541,413	486,387	657,747	2,206,238	2,048,197	2,514,642	2,742,796	2,951,853
400—Building repair & maintenance	25,350	25,450	25,550	25,650	102,000	111,540	127,534	141,951	156,146
500—Machine repair & maintenance	89,417	92,641	86,833	98,813	367,703	385,315	453,907	519,658	591,178
600—Small equipment purchases	250	250	250	250	1,000	1,100	1,210	1,331	1,464
700—Supplies, lube & tools	93,616	99,152	89,180	109,750	391,698	397,973	489,384	573,281	664,184
800—Utilities	54,450	54,650	54,850	55,050	219,000	261,360	325,152	394,502	473,402
900—Sundry	154,000	154,000	154,000	154,000	616,000	677,600	745,359	819,894	901,883
Depreciation	59,012	59,012	59,012	59,012	236,048	265,635	260,789	254,800	244,366
Abnormal expense	53,750	53,750	53,750	53,750	215,000	236,500	260,150	286,164	314,780
Associated expense	3,400	3,400	3,400	3,400	13,600	13,200	5,200	1,320	0
Totals	1,413,160	1,465,802	1,349,730	1,651,690	5,880,382	5,783,850	6,779,791	7,466,445	8,148,769
Total direct labor dollars	814,465	875,299	765,710	991,755	3,447,227	3,118,611	3,587,365	3,876,000	4,128,000
Derived overhead rate	173.5	167.5	176.3	166.5	170.6	185.5	189.0	192.6	197.4

Module 12 computes the firm's total asset base and the return on assets (ROA). Several elements of the investment base are derived from user input. Examples of these data are the initial beginning balances for accounts receivable, inventories, and permanent investment. Other elements of the investment base (such as amounts invoiced and actual costs entered into work-in-process inventory) are derived from calculated statement-of-operations line items and specified inputs. Additional data, such as shipments and estimated cost input, are taken directly from the previously computed statement of operations. The return-on-asset calculation is based upon the following standard formula:

$$\text{ROA} = \frac{\text{Operating profit}}{\text{Shipments}} \times \frac{\text{Shipments}}{\text{Total assets}}$$

Module 13 prints the project manager gross profit summary, shown in Table 10-6 the product line statement of operations, and the statement of operations shown in Table 10-7. This module also calculates and prints the asset base (Table 10-8), the return on assets (Table 10-9), and the financial statement ratios (Table 10-10).

CONCLUSIONS AND MODELING GUIDELINES

Computer-based planning models have been used to study the following business problems, among others:

1) Evaluating the profitability of new and existing business.
2) Testing the financial effects of changes in the operational capabilities of the firm.
3) Experimenting with proposed operational policies.
4) Measuring the impact of changing business conditions (including inflation and economic trends).

Consideration of the following guidelines should help smooth the way through the development and implementation of a model project.

1) A commitment to the model must exist at the top level of management, since this level will derive the major benefit from the model.
2) A planning model, if it is to be successful and useful, must be user-oriented. Users invariably prefer minimum requirements for input data. The model outputs must be readily understood by all users. In addition, it is important to maintain a degree of complexity in the modeling techniques selected that is consistent with the original level of management understanding.
3) Extensive and explicit documentation is a must for a successful computerized planning model. A model with inadequate documentation can become worthless if the people most familiar with its design and logic leave the organization. Proper documentation also

TABLE 10-6 Project Manager Gross Profit Summary[1]
John R. Doe, Project Manager

	1st Quarter 1975	2nd Quarter 1975	3rd Quarter 1975	4th Quarter 1975	1975 Total	1976 Total	1977 Total	1978 Total	1979 Total
Shipments									
Firm	6,953	15,721	8,191	4,466	35,331	40,742	10,714	34,494	5,544
Forecast	0	0	0	0	0	0	0	0	0
Total	6,953	15,721	8,191	4,466	35,331	40,742	10,714	34,494	5,544
Cost of shipments									
Firm	5,544	12,941	7,560	4,422	30,467	43,171	12,781	43,790	6,893
Forecast	0	0	0	0	0	0	0	0	0
Total	5,544	12,941	7,560	4,422	30,467	43,171	12,781	43,790	6,893
Total gross profit	1,409	2,780	631	44	4,864	(2,429)	(2,067)	(9,296)	(1,349)

[1] Figures are in thousands of dollars.

TABLE 10-7 Statement of Operations — Total of All Contracts[1]

	1st Quarter 1975	2nd Quarter 1975	3rd Quarter 1975	4th Quarter 1975	1975 Total	1976 Total	1977 Total	1978 Total	1979 Total
Shipments									
Firm	34,011	45,394	59,498	25,294	164,197	183,288	158,074	153,898	59,182
Forecast	6,706	9,015	6,271	7,779	29,771	59,514	179,444	252,134	381,944
Total	40,717	54,409	65,769	33,073	193,968	242,801	337,518	406,032	441,127
Cost of shipments									
Firm	30,913	38,947	61,689	26,819	158,368	192,861	157,044	171,627	60,427
Forecast	3,715	4,930	3,473	4,573	16,691	37,809	135,135	199,477	312,368
Total	34,628	43,877	65,162	31,392	175,059	230,670	292,179	371,104	372,794
Gross profit	6,089	10,532	607	1,681	18,909	12,132	45,339	34,928	68,332
Over (under) absorbed overhead expenses	(160)	347	92	613	892	3,126	8,845	6,943	5,015
Expenses									
G&A	3,304	3,833	4,565	3,271	14,973	17,307	22,499	27,255	30,276
R&D	298	306	300	354	1,258	1,383	1,522	1,674	1,840
Other income	(12)	(54)	(55)	43	(78)	500	800	1,000	1,000
Operating profit	2,315	6,686	(4,221)	(1,288)	3,492	(2,932)	30,963	13,942	42,231

[1] Figures are in thousands of dollars.

TABLE 10-8 The Asset Base[1]

	1975 Total	1976 Total	1977 Total	1978 Total	1979 Total
Cash					
Total	7,294	9,611	12,174	15,462	15,533
Accounts receivable					
Beginning balance	13,393	8,866	14,720	12,100	11,750
Add: Shipments	193,968	242,801	337,518	406,032	443,417
Less: Invoicing	198,495	236,947	340,138	406,382	443,417
Total	8,866	14,720	12,100	11,750	9,460
Average	9,983	11,793	13,410	11,925	10,605
Inventories					
Beginning balance	35,421	57,343	103,000	113,375	123,412
Add: Cost input	197,071	276,327	302,554	381,141	399,494
Less: Est. cost sales	175,059	230,670	292,179	371,104	372,794
Total	57,433	103,000	113,375	123,412	150,112
Average	53,281	80,217	108,188	118,394	136,762
Total working capital	70,558	101,621	133,772	145,781	162,900
Permanent investment					
Beginning balance	72,190	76,242	81,546	87,926	94,086
Additions	7,006	4,292	6,750	6,400	7,006
Total	79,196	80,534	88,296	94,326	101,092
Average	78,212	79,865	84,415	91,311	97,709
Total assets	148,770	181,486	218,187	237,092	260,609

[1] Figures are in thousands of dollars.

TABLE 10-9 Return-on-Assets

	1975 Total	1976 Total	1977 Total	1978 Total	1979 Total
(1) Shipments (thousands of $)	193,968	242,801	337,518	406,032	441,127
(2) Operating profit (thousands of $)	3,492	(2,932)[1]	30,963	13,942	42,231
(3) Margin (%)	1.8	(1.2)	9.2	3.4	9.6
(4) Assets (thousands of $)	148,770	181,486	218,187	237,092	260,609
(5) Turnover rate (ratio) (1) ÷ (4)	1.30	1.34	1.55	1.71	1.69
(6) Return on assets (%) (2) ÷ (4) or (3) × (5)	2.4	1.6[1]	14.2	5.9	16.2

[1] Negative ROAs are not normally shown.

TABLE 10-10 Financial Statement Ratios

	1st Quarter 1975	2nd Quarter 1975	3rd Quarter 1975	4th Quarter 1975	1975 Total	1976 Total	1977 Total	1978 Total	1979 Total
Gross profit/shipments	15.0	19.4	0.9	5.1	9.8	5.0	13.4	8.6	15.5
Gross profit/C.O.S.	17.6	24.0	0.9	5.4	10.8	5.3	15.5	9.4	18.3
Op. profit/Shipments	5.7	12.3	(6.4)	(3.9)	1.8	(1.2)	9.2	3.4	9.6
Op. profit/C.O.S.	6.6	15.2	(6.5)	(4.1)	2.0	(1.3)	10.6	3.8	11.3
G&A/Shipments	5.0	3.7	3.1	6.2	4.2	3.7	2.9	2.7	2.7
G&A/C.O.S.	5.9	4.6	3.1	6.5	4.6	3.9	3.4	2.9	3.2

prevents the model from becoming inextricably tied to any single individual or department. It should be recognized that the requirement for thorough documentation is complicated by the fact that most successful models continually change through the interaction between users and model builders.

4) Models should be constructed in a manner such that future changes are facilitated. Eventually, most successful planning models encompass aspects of the organization not understood at the time the original model design was formulated. A modular programming approach is ideal in this regard.

In summary, computer-based comprehensive planning models are powerful tools which can provide insight into the likely future performance of a firm. Models are costly, however, and involve a great deal of effort for development and implementation. They provide the most effective means for management to study the combined effects of a range of possible results in each of the numerous variables affecting a business. Planning models are thus indispensable tools of the performance-oriented manager.

BIBLIOGRAPHY

Bergstrom, Gary L., and Smith, Barnard E. "Multi-Item Production Planning — An Extension of the HMMS Rules." *Management Science,* June 1970.

Boulden, James B., and Buffa, Elwood S. "Corporate Models: On-Line, Real-Time Systems." *Harvard Business Review,* July-August 1970.

Dooley, Arch R., and Stout, Thomas M. "Rise of the Blue-Collar Computer." *Harvard Business Review,* July-August 1971.

Levitt, Theodore. "Production-Line Approach to Service." *Harvard Business Review,* September-October 1972.

Russell, John R.; Stobaugh, Robert B., Jr.; and Whitmeyer, Frederick W. "Simulation for Production." *Harvard Business Review,* September-October 1967.

Subject Index